D1231970

Our Man in the Crimea

Studies in Maritime History

William N. Still, Jr., Series Editor

*Stoddert's War: Naval Operations
During the Quasi-War with France, 1798 1801*
by Michael A. Palmer

The British Navy and the American Revolution
by John A. Tilley

Iron Afloat: The Story of the Confederate Armorclads
by William N. Still, Jr.

*A Maritime History of the United States:
The Role of America's Seas and Waterways*
by K. Jack Bauer

Confederate Shipbuilding
by William N. Still, Jr.

Raid on America: The Dutch Naval Campaign of 1672–1674
by Donald G. Shomette and Robert D. Haslach

*Lifeline of the Confederacy:
Blockade Running During the Civil War*
by Stephen R. Wise

Admiral Harold R. Stark: Architect of Victory, 1939–1945
by B. Mitchell Simpson, III

History and the Sea: Essays on Maritime Strategies
by Clark G. Reynolds

*Predators and Prizes: American Privateering
and Imperial Warfare, 1739–1748*
by Carl E. Swanson

*"We Will Stand by You":
Serving in the Pawnee, 1942–1945*
by Theodore C. Mason

OUR MAN
IN THE CRIMEA

*Commander Hugo Koehler
and the Russian Civil War*

edited by **P. J. Capelotti**

University of South Carolina Press

Copyright © 1991 University of South Carolina
Published in Columbia, South Carolina, by the
University of South Carolina Press

Manufactured in the United States of America

Library of Congress Cataloging-in-Publication Data

Koehler, Hugo William, 1886–1941.
  Our man in the Crimea: Commander Hugo Koehler and the Russian Civil
War / edited by P.J. Capelotti.
      p.   cm.—(Studies in maritime history)
  Includes bibliographical references and index.
  ISBN 0-87249-734-8 (acid-free)
  1. Koehler, Hugo William, 1886–1941. 2. Soviet Union—History—
Revolution, 1917–1921—Personal narratives, American. 3. Soviet
Union—History—Revolution, 1917–1921—Secret service. 4. United
States Navy—Biography. 5. Seamen—United States—Biography
I. Capelotti, P.J. (Peter Joseph), 1960–   II. Title.
III. Series.
DK265.7.K56A3   1990
947.084'1'092—dc20   90-20310
[B]

For my mother
and for C. L., with love

Contents

Illustrations

Photographs

Maps

Foreword

From time to time—not often—there appears on the world's screen an individual of extremely sharp insight, broad powers of observation and analysis, and an unusually lively curiosity. Such an individual was Hugo William Koehler—bold, adventurous, urbane, generous, and with a savoir faire that gained him ready entrance to the highest circles of international society.

Something of a prophet, he foresaw the rise of Hitler's Germany, the ensurance at Versailles of a new world war, and bolshevism's inevitable collapse. In that cataclysmic time of world war and civil war, I know of no other American who so intimately associated with Russians of all levels, White and Red. Koehler slept, ate, and galloped over the steppes like a cossack with them, week in and week out, at ease with their personal quirks and characteristics.

What those Russians are like and what they might do was revealed with stunning clarity by Commander Hugo Koehler.

Rear Admiral Kemp Tolley, U.S. Navy (ret.)

I looked at him as if I pitied a man so ignorant as not to know the famous Koehler.

The young Hugo Koehler

Preface

Commander Hugo William Koehler (1886?–1941), a career officer in the U.S. Navy, was witness to and participant in many of the twentieth century's most sublime events. The brilliance of his observations of these great events lay in his singular combination of wit and wile that could be as sympathetic as it could be ruthless, finding expression in extraordinary places amid extraordinary times. On the Yangtze during the Chinese Revolution, commander of a subchaser squadron out of Queenstown, Ireland, during the First World War, first U.S. officer in Berlin at the end of hostilities, behind Bolshevik lines during the Russian Civil War; he was a spy of magnificent dimensions, and his writings, whether letters to his mother or dispatches sent to the State Department or the Office of Naval Intelligence, equaled his grand adventures. Those letters and dispatches—"rambling conversational," as one reader described them—had to be unrambled and made slightly less conversational to bring their keenest observations to the surface.

Koehler apparently wrote in much the same way as he spoke. In his view, dirty conditions were "unspeakably filthy," and a grubby ship was "going to rack and ruin." He often composed his dispatches through the night, and they imitated his own conversational habits. Wherever possible, the navigation of Koehler's thoughts has been smoothed by correcting spelling and punctuation errors. Because of variant spellings of Russian names in French and English, some inconsistencies remain in transliterations. Repetitive passages were omitted, and personal chitchat was kept to a minimum.

I have given the most exact location that could be traced for all documents cited. In many cases, simple abbreviations (NA for the National Archives, LC for the Library of Congress, and DF for the State Department's decimal file) were used. Where a precise source could be located, it is given. Historians wishing to consult the original research notebooks on Commander Koehler written and collected by Margaretta Potter may do so in the Special Collections Department, University

Library, University of Rhode Island, Kingston, Rhode Island. Admiral McCully's family apparently allowed Potter access to the admiral's diaries currently archived at the Library of Congress. Quotations from McCully's diary used herein are taken from Potter's notes. These important diaries are now closed to researchers; hence the author was unable to verify the veracity of the quotes.

Footnotes have been used to identify personages and clarify Koehler's letters. Historical detail was added to give perspective on Koehler's times and render them accessible to modern readers, but the work does not pretend to biography or historiography; it is simply an edited collection of those letters and dispatches of a remarkable officer that survived the oblivion of time and overprotective relations.

Koehler's writings shine a stunningly bright light onto a murky era in U.S. foreign policy and give Western readers a fresh and unique perspective on the horrible sufferings of the Russian people during the Russian Civil War. Koehler's observations also contribute to a fuller understanding of the Bolshevik consolidation of power. They help to explain how a minuscule but well-organized group of Communists managed to overpower and still hold (if now only tenuously) an immense number of people.

Acknowledgments

This collection of letters and dispatches was pieced together, at the request of Senator Claiborne Pell, from sources within the National Archives in Washington, especially the State Department decimal file in the Diplomatic Branch (NNFD), and from letters in the possession of Hugh Gladstone Koehler, only son of Hugo William Koehler. Much of the collection was prepared in 1983–1985 by Margaretta Potter, the last surviving intimate of Koehler. Margaretta died in 1985.

In June 1986, the Senator asked me to finish the work Margaretta had started. It took more than two years to sort through more dispatches and documents and track down letters mentioned by Margaretta whose source she had failed to note. For me, the letters and dispatches contained so much material of historic—not to mention cinematic—value that they cried out for publication.

I would like to thank especially Rear Admiral Kemp Tolley, U.S. Navy (ret.), who offered suggestions and criticisms and assisted with historical notes and all matters Navy from his own long experience in the Soviet field. The admiral and his Russian-born wife, Vlada, also were gracious hosts during my visits to their home in the Maryland countryside. Admiral Tolley was unflagging in his support and encouragement through three years and six drafts of the manuscript.

Timely support and encouragement were offered also by Dr. Richard A. von Doenhoff of the Military Reference Branch of the National Archives, by Dr. William N. Still, Jr., codirector of the Program in Maritime History and Underwater Research at East Carolina University, and by Ken Scott of the University of South Carolina Press. Without them Hugo Koehler would have been lost to history.

Professor Winifred Caldwell in Kingston, Rhode Island, helped through several drafts of the manuscript to salvage some drama out of the murky waters of my prose; no person in my experience has a finer sense of the English language. University of Rhode Island archivist David Maslyn was indispensable in locating Koehler materials at the Rhode Island archives.

Faculty of the history department at the University of Rhode Island deserve many thanks. Professors Gino Silvestri and Mort Briggs were helpful with suggestions and patient with my oft-extended deadlines. Professor Gary Thurston was especially incisive in his comments and suggestions, and he extended the immeasurable kindness of carefully checking the contents of *Sbornik Statey,* the 1934 work on Hugo W. Koehler's "sworn brother," General A. P. Kutepov, to see if it contained any references to Koehler. It did not.

The publisher Clarkson N. Potter went out of his way to help locate Koehler photographs, as did Ed Finney at the Naval Historical Center in Washington. Pat and Rags Barclay gave me the run of their cottage on Cape Cod, where the first draft of the book was composed. Hugh Gladstone Koehler, only son of "the Commander," contributed unflinchingly his at times painful memories of his singular father, memories lightened by a carefree August 1988 afternoon at Bailey's Beach in Newport and over a lunch in snowy December 1989 at the Riverside Yacht Club in Riverside, Connecticut. On 14 August 1990, Hugh Koehler died quietly in his sleep at his home and so did not live to see the book about his father whose publication he had come to anticipate. Fitzhugh Green, the biographer of George Bush whose writer-father knew Hugo Koehler from their Annapolis days and who helped further my understanding of both Newport and the Navy, himself passed away on 5 September 1990, just days after he and Senator Pell and I had met in Newport to mourn the loss of Hugh Koehler. Fitzhugh was a kindred spirit, and his loss will be keenly felt.

Senator Pell introduced me to Koehler, his remarkable stepfather, and even with the constant pressures placed on a senior U.S. senator, he still found the time to warmly and personally encourage my progress. A finer gentleman never lived.

Finally, I want to thank Donna Webb, Dick Boudreau, Mike Lennon, Norman Mailer, Barbara Wasserman, and Mark, Jim, and Edna Sykes, who helped through the years to keep body and spirit on the path to the sunlit uplands.

Any strengths in the book are theirs; all errors are my own.

P. J. Capelotti
Narragansett, Rhode Island

Our Man in the Crimea

Prologue

An Officer and a Spy ⎯⎯⎯⎯⎯⎯⎯⎯

The whole trick for the officer is to seem what you would be, and the formula for dealing with fear is ultimately rhetorical and theatrical: regardless of your actual feelings, you must simulate a carriage that will affect your audience as fearless, in the hope that you will be imitated.

Paul Fussell

⎯⎯⎯⎯⎯⎯⎯⎯⎯⎯⎯⎯⎯⎯⎯⎯⎯⎯⎯⎯⎯⎯

June 1920. Three burly Cossacks made quick work of padlocks on the abruptly abandoned Bolshevik headquarters in Melitopol. Thirty-three-year-old U.S. Navy Lieutenant Commander Hugo W. Koehler rushed the stairs and quickly realized the office of the chief Bolshevik commissar. There he found haphazardly strewn around the room hundreds of documents of the dread *Tchresvichaika*,[1] the Bolshevik counterterrorist organization, all hastily stuffed into sacks, like letters in a mailbag, evidence of an interrupted and disorderly departure.

It was a valuable trove Koehler had discovered, thanks to his keen instincts: those intangible reflexes of a man engaged for a great deal of his life in clandestine intelligence and amateur espionage had not betrayed him. Only that morning Koehler had joined as an observer a group of White Russians who had captured the Crimean city just north of the Isthmus of Perekop, causing a greater force of Bolsheviks to flee in haste, leaving their locked and barred headquarters to be ransacked by Koehler's Cossack bodyguards.

While Koehler merrily gathered the scattered intelligence material, a tremendous clatter arose outside. From the window he saw a troop of White Cossack cavalry dash by in a panic. "For God's sake," one of the retreating Cossacks yelled at him, "get out!" The Red Army, learning from a spy how small the attacking party was, had launched a full-scale counterattack. Red troops in strength had already reentered the town from the north, and Koehler and his Cossacks were about to be cut off and trapped. Koehler's thought? "This was rather a mess for me. . . . "[2]

According to records of the U.S. Navy Department, Hugo William Koehler (he pronounced it "Kay-ler") was born in St. Louis, Missouri, on 19 July 1886. This information may or may not be true, and during his short life Koehler himself would never be sure of it, though he would be given bizarre accounts of his beginnings. Vital Statistics in the St. Louis Health Division contain no certificate of his birth, but this proves nothing, as such records were not compulsory before 1910. He was to be haunted throughout his entire existence by the savage irony that he had access to a plethora of information about his supposed parents yet was to be denied any certain knowledge of himself.[3]

Koehler came to believe that he had been taken from his real parents as an infant and that he was the adopted child of Oscar Carl and Mathilda (Lange) Koehler, who were married in St. Louis on 15 August 1885. Oscar Carl was eldest son of Henry Koehler. Henry, born in Austria in 1828, emigrated to America in 1849. He is listed as head of the Koehler Brewing Company in the St. Louis City directory of 1851 and again in 1881.[4]

Possibly one of the reasons Hugo Koehler would later question his place as a natural child of Oscar and Mathilda was that as a youngster his parents excessively deferred to him. He was treated quite differently from his brothers and sisters: he had the finest pony and pony cart and the most delightful toys, and, perhaps most vital in his memory of childhood, he was not disciplined as they were.[5]

Little survives of his boyhood beyond a few vague personal vignettes. He recalled a humiliating experience when on a misbegotten boat outing he attempted to assume his future role vis-à-vis the ladies. There was a girl in the party he wished to impress, so he paraded along the railing in front of her, though his mother warned him he could fall overboard. He persisted in showing off and promptly fell in. After he was fished out—no dry clothes available—his mother borrowed a petticoat from his recent inamorata, and Koehler cringed through the rest of the trip with the girl's petticoat draped around his neck.[6]

Hugo journeyed with his grandfather to England, where he made the acquaintance of philosopher-chemist John Scott Haldane and statesman-naturalist Lord Grey of Falloden; then on to Austria, where he was introduced to the court of Franz Joseph, emperor of Austria. "After all that," he commented, "water pistols were not very interesting."[7]

Already precocious, Koehler did his best to infuriate his grandfather, but the old man handled the boy with impeccable grace. As a wine collector, Henry Koehler was in the habit of organizing wine-tasting dinners for his friends, whose task it was first to taste and admire and then to identify the wines as to their vintage and origin. To young Hugo this seemed just so much Old World cant and affectation: he decided one evening to substitute for each wine a bottle of humbler ancestry, certain that his grandfather's friends would never notice the difference. He slid quietly behind the window curtains, convinced that it would be amusing to observe their defeat. Instead, he was startled by the extent of his grandfather's distress. The old man sprang to his feet, exclaiming, "Gentlemen, I cannot understand how this has happened. The man from whom I bought this is an honest fellow and invariably sells good wine—there must have been some mistake, some error. I apologize." Later, after Hugo confessed, his grandfather was more grieved than angry—for a well-bred man from Vienna, there were certain lines no gentleman ever crossed.[8] For young Koehler, already part of a new twentieth century that would delight in watching old traditions crumble, there were few lines he would ever feel that way about.

When Hugo Koehler was fifteen, in 1901, Oscar Koehler died, and thereafter his grandfather Henry took charge of his education. He sent the boy to Phillips Exeter Academy in New Hampshire for his senior year of school, where he could study Latin, Greek, German, French, English, and the sciences. Upon his graduation in 1903, Koehler was voted "cheekiest" member of the senior class, an honor even at that age he undoubtedly cherished.[9]

As he grew, Koehler developed an almost abnormally cool and seemingly detached view of whatever situations he found himself in, almost as if he were watching his own life unfold on a movie screen. This almost cruel remoteness translated into impressive literary powers of description: at times Koehler seemed to be writing of himself and his experiences in the third person. Later, in his travels abroad, his writing contained decidedly unmilitary echoes of the great foreign correspondents, particularly Hemingway. His naval dispatches lacked the clipped syntax of most military reports; instead they flowed from overarching strategic views down to minute and sympathetic descriptions of people and places and to ruthless portraits of nationalities and governments. It was a skill discovered and honed early.

He wrote his mother from Exeter (in his words "a quaint and quiet old New England town, with streets lined with huge, old elm trees and also apple trees, but the apples, although they are easily in reach of the smallest child, are never disturbed") of his first journey to Boston.

The people in Boston seem to me to be greatly more refined than many Western people . . . the first thing one notices on arriving. . . is the way the people talk. I haven't heard anybody pronounce an "r" since I am here . . . they never pronounce "a" as we do in "bat" but always as "a" in "far." This way, although incorrect according to the dictionaries, is . . . more musical than the correct way of speaking, but perhaps it is only pleasant because I have never heard it before this.

Invited to Thanksgiving dinner at the Union Club ("Boston's most aristocratic and fashionable club") Koehler's minute recollection of what was served is as notable as the meal itself.

"I write as much of the menu as I remember," he informed his mother, "but a good many things I had never seen before . . . but suffice to say we had some of the queerest-looking vegetables and meats (I really don't know which) that you could imagine. . . .

Blue points (half shell)
Green turtle soup (real)
Smelts with mushrooms (funny little animals,
think it was fish)
Scallops (look like real small, round doughnuts)
Turkey with chestnut stuffing (awfully good,
recommend it to you)
Artichokes (like a dwarf black cabbage, eaten by
picking off leaves and biting off the ends)
Etc. etc. vegetables of which I do not know the
names
Various kinds of cranberries
Ices (in shape of a turkey)
Grapes (big as a plum and black as ink)
Cob and beech nuts (couldn't find out
how to eat them)
Candies, cake, coffee, etc. etc. (didn't have
enough room left)
Frozen crème de menthe

Now about the drinkables:
1. Chateau Ecam (spelled correctly?)
2. Pommery, Moet & Chandon Brut, imperial special vintage
3. Burgundy
4. Sauterne, etc., etc.

Don't be afraid of this wine list. Thank God I knew what wine was at home and so . . . knew that a very *little* was a *great* sufficiency. Don't you think that this was a pretty good dinner interspersed as it was by good stories and wit?[10]

These early letters are redolent with promise: they anticipate what would be heard again twenty years later in Koehler's naval intelligence dispatches from Europe and Russia. It would take those reports, however, to also reveal his encompassing grasp of European military and political strategy.

A revealing story survives from his senior year at Phillips Exeter. Koehler and a few of his friends advertised that they had a cure for what appeared to be a common malady. In describing the incident in later years, Koehler would alternate between two versions, so it is not certain whether their cure was for rheumatism or hernia. Their remedy was a harmless pink liquid they concocted, and they did a brisk business with it until school authorities, learning of their scam, quickly ended it. The school itself was thereupon sharply divided between those who considered the experiment "unprincipled" and others who considered it valuable proof of public gullibility.[11]

During a summer trip to Europe, grandfather Koehler asked Hugo what he thought he might like to do with his life: the boy responded, prophetic by two-thirds, that he would like to be philosopher, or a Jesuit, or a naval officer. His grandfather's incisive rejoinder was that Hugo was "a bit of a philosopher already" and that being a Jesuit involved "more disadvantages than advantages." And he made clear that "if you want to be a naval officer, you will have to get some education first, for the Naval Academy gives you only a training."[12]

It's possible that Koehler indeed absorbed some of this advice, for he did permit Harvard University to shape him, but only for one year. A fellow Harvard student who met Hugo then recalled that "in his almost fierce keenness he reminded me of a young eagle . . . [indeed] he seemed a very Odysseus."[13] After the year in Cambridge a laconic notation on his record card states: "Gone to Annapolis."[14]

During the summer that separated Harvard and Annapolis, Koehler motored from Cambridge to New York City accompanied by three friends. They arrived without cash after blowing three old tires and paying for three new ones. Ravenously hungry and with no prospects of cashing a check, Koehler suggested, of all things, that they go to the theater. In 1920, as a naval agent in a much more lethal situation, he would employ similarly brazen strategies to bluff his way through war-torn Russia. "'Come,' said I," he wrote later:

We marched down to the theater and with the most blasé air I had, I went up to the ticket office. . . . "I say," lisped I, "gimmi mi tickets." "What name?" politely asked the man at the window. "Why, Koehler," said I, looking at him as if I pitied a man so ignorant as not to know the famous Koehler. "Oh yes, pardon me, sir," answered the smiling ticket man, as he started looking for my tickets. Of course he couldn't find them and he said: "I'm sorry but they don't seem to be here." "What," yelled I, "has that blooming idiot Tyson (the ticket broker . . .) again forgotten to send them in time! Call him up and see about it." "His office is closed," answered the agent, as I very well know. . . . "But I can give you some that I have here." "All right," I answered with great condescension: "front row, right aisle." Whereupon we went to the theater. . . . we paid for the tickets the next day, for we thought we might want to work the same game again.

After the theater, hungrier than ever—but with Koehler insisting that "something would turn up"—they walked up Fifth Avenue, where by a lucky chance they bumped into one of Hugo's best friends, who bailed them out. Such coincidence would be repeated many times throughout his life; Koehler seemed to possess a beneficent parachute that popped open precisely when he needed it.[15]

The winter of 1904 was spent cramming for entrance exams in Annapolis. However, the cold months were not all work, as a letter in which Koehler describes two elaborate balls, one for midshipmen and one for officers, reveals. The letter also points to the fine and ongoing development of an eighteen-year-old's calculating and cataloguing eye.

> [The officers were] in special full dress uniform . . . covered from head to foot with gold braid, brass, and epaulets. Of course most of the officers belonged to the Navy, but the other branches . . . were also represented, the cavalry officers in blue and yellow, the artillery in light blue and red, the infantry in light blue and white, the Marine Corps in dark blue and red.
>
> Besides this, several foreign warships were in port and the officers of these attended, Germans in green, Englishmen in red, Italians in black and yellow.
>
> If I ever cared a snap of my fingers to get into the Navy before I came here, I certainly am ten times as anxious to get in now that I have seen more of the Navy life. And this, in spite of the fact . . . I have realized more than ever what hard work it will be.[16]

1. Hugo Koehler, entering the Naval Academy after a year at Harvard, 1906. (Photo courtesy of Clarkson N. Potter.)

Soon afterward, his dream accomplished, Koehler was able to write on stationery headed "United States Naval Academy, Annapolis, Md.": "I have just passed my first night as midshipman, United States Navy. . . .

> Everybody in town, officers, professors, and "cits," thinks it most extraordinary that I should go into the Academy . . . they say that for a man who has tasted life at Harvard, it is a mighty hard thing to buckle down to the exact routine [and] discipline . . . in practice here . . . [but] I am going to do my very best here, to make up for my past, and to do something for my future and for the future of the ones I love.[17]

What secret it was from Koehler's past that, at the age of eighteen, he felt he had to make up for has never been made clear.

No arrival of Koehler's ever went unnoticed, and accounts of his arrival at the Naval Academy vary only in the degree of their outrageousness. One version has it that he arrived with a horse and valet, while another reports it was with horse and cook. It was unusual in either case. While in Annapolis, Hugo maintained a pied-à-terre, staffed by a steward or cook, where hot food was always available to all comers. This, and the fact that he never overlooked the ladies, to whom he regularly sent American Beauty roses, was duly noted in the academy classbook, *Lucky Bag*, of 1909.[18]

His graciousness as host was more impressive than his grades, which fluctuated wildly. In May 1908 his standing in his class was: for seamanship, 12th; ordnance, 16th; math and mechanics, 16th; efficiency, 93rd; and in marine engines, 161st. At the end of a 28 August 1908 practice cruise, he stood 4th in his class. By his final year, 1908–1909, he stood 68th scholastically, saved only by a 4.00 in languages. The latter accomplishment was the result of previous training, for as a boy Koehler had been taught to speak and write German and French as well as English. As an adult he spoke British, not American, English, with a slight Germanic accent underlying a trace of the Midwest.[19]

Discipline was never his strong suit. His standing in "conduct" was 174 in a class of 175, attained, no doubt gleefully, by virtue of his having accrued 215 demerits. On one occasion he fought with his roommate so savagely that they both landed in the hospital. Even so, if the *Lucky Bag* report is accurate, Koehler's roommate, Ernest Gunther, "managed to room with Hugo for four years and still maintains his equilibrium of mind."[20] Eventually Koehler graduated in the exact middle of his class.

As to his circumstances, they were always something of a mystery: and one it seems that even Hugo himself was unable to entirely dispel. He was forever borrowing money, loans always paid back by a nebula one classmate called "the executors."[21] Koehler may have suspected the fountain from which this money flowed, but it wasn't until his senior year that he learned of its extraordinary source.

During the winter before Koehler's graduation from the Academy, his grandfather, Henry Koehler, Sr., passed away. At some moment before his death, according to Hugo, the old man, now past eighty, revealed the secret of his grandson's birth.[22] He confessed to the midshipman that his father was not Oscar Koehler, the kindly man who had died in 1901. His father was instead Archduke Rudolph, crown prince of Austria and once the heir to the throne of the decaying Austro-Hungarian Empire. It was the liberal Rudolph who, along with his young lover Mary Vetsera, died suddenly and violently, either the result of murder or a double suicide, at the hunting lodge at Mayerling on 30 January 1889.

There is no record extant of how Koehler responded to this, though it is not difficult to imagine the swirling thoughts of a man suddenly ripped forever from familiar moorings. Neither is it difficult to imagine that he must have been both stunned and yet somehow unsurprised; unsurprised, possibly, because he recalled the extreme deferential treatment his supposed parents had extended to him as a child. Further, there were the strange visitors from Austria and the trip to Vienna, where his grandfather had introduced him to the emperor, and the trip to England, where he met Empress Elizabeth. Why, Koehler must have wondered, why was I the only one to accompany him on these travels? Why did he never take either my brother or my sisters on these important journeys? Only now must the turbid waters have cleared.

For many years after this supposed extraordinary revelation, Koehler searched for proof, any proof, of his origins. But it was a search that yielded only conflicting opinions and speculation as to the nature of Rudolph's demise. According to the best account Koehler could find, Rudolph had written the pope asking that his unhappy marriage to Stephanie be annulled, for she had not produced a son and was incapable of bearing more children. It also revealed that Rudolph's request (which was denied) together with a full account of the Mayerling tragedy, was locked in the archives of the Vatican. It would never have been possible for Koehler to verify this information in his own lifetime. Vatican archives are sealed for ninety-eight years, making 1987—years after his own demise—the earliest date the alleged report about the 1889 deaths at Mayerling could be released.[23]

Was Hugo a natural son of Rudolph? And who was his mother? If his portrait is compared with those of the famous Hapsburgs (especially with photographs of Rudolph), his chin seems a modified version of that marked Hapsburg facial conformation that no other family possessed. To add a measure of plausibility to the hypothesis, there was also a trust fund. Koehler once told his friend Margaretta Potter that "all the money" (meaning all *his* money) had come from Franz Joseph, the Austrian emperor.[24] Koehler's stepson, Senator Claiborne Pell (D–R.I.), believes that there was indeed a trust fund, a benefice, which paid moneys to Koehler until 1927. He bases this belief on otherwise unexplained income Koehler possessed and on the fact that Koehler had to go to Vienna at the time of his marriage to Matilda Bigelow (Pell's mother) to seek termination of the trust because Hugo, a Roman Catholic, in marrying a divorced Protestant, was no longer eligible to receive it.[25]

Senator Pell at one point asked Mrs. Oscar Koehler—the only woman Hugo ever knew as his mother—point-blank, was the story that Hugo was Rudolph's son true? The woman only laughed and, while certainly not confirming the story, did not directly deny it then, and her later demise preserved this silence.[26]

There is a further element in the Koehler puzzle. In the spring of 1941, aware that he was dying, and perhaps to serve as a reminder of what he would tell his doctor, Koehler wrote a poignant memorandum in which he listed his symptoms. To this list he added:

> Father [Oscar Koehler] and maternal grandfather [Lange] died of Bright's disease, father at 45, mat. grandfather at 50. Two of my father's brothers died of heart trouble, one at 45, other at 65. Other brother died at 46 of stomach trouble, probably ulcers. Mother's brother and sister still living.[27]

It is possible that his doctor did question him about he heredity, and, of course, lacking any concrete evidence to the contrary, Hugo could only write of the Koehlers. On the other hand, if Oscar and Mathilda Koehler were not, as rumor would have it, his real parents, why would he have deceived his doctor? Further, since Hugo had told the story of the crown prince only to a handful of his closest friends, there seems little motive for making it up.

Here, as in so many other parts of Commander Koehler's unrecorded past, a melancholy silence closes over him like the depths of the sea.

In the spring of 1909, Koehler graduated from the Academy. His feeling toward Annapolis was, "Whatever the Naval Academy did or failed to do, it taught a young man to stand on his own feet, think for himself, and not ask for help from anyone."[28]

Undoubtedly transformed in some profound and eerie way by his grandfather's deathbed confession, Koehler entered the oceanic world with a new eye. Congenitally, by temperament, by intellect, and in ability, he was different from those around him: but now his grandfather's revelation must have assumed the aspects of a command, increased his awareness of these distinctions, to the point of his seeing

2. Hugo Koehler, near the time of his graduation from the Academy, 1909. (Photo courtesy of Clarkson N. Potter.)

them as necessary, for, as he once told Margaretta, "I have to be different."[29] And this he was.

Koehler's naval career, a bellicose chronicle of the early years of our twisted century, was extraordinary no matter what the truth of his lineage. He breathed thinner air than most lieutenant commanders of his or any day. His connections with the upper classes came in part because the socialite Spencer Fayette Eddy and then Assistant Secretary of the Navy Franklin Roosevelt had largely transformed the Office of Naval Intelligence into a club for "college boys, rich young men, [and] well-to-do yachtsmen." Some of these young men were recruited to spy on naval officers vacationing in Newport, and Hugo met many of them there, including Herbert Pell, husband at the time to the woman Hugo was destined to marry.[30]

Moving in the even more rarified atmosphere of British aristocracy, Koehler was a close friend of Herbert Gladstone, son of the former Prime Minister, and Gladstone's wife, Dolly. Hugo and Lady Gladstone kept up a less-than-secret affair that lasted more than twenty years. When Koehler died, Dolly in her sadness wrote that "it is impossible to realize that I shall never see him again. It is as if the sun had ceased to shine."[31]

Muscular and attractive to women, Koehler also had a capacity for ruthlessness with those he considered inferior, be they women, children, or nations. "I have never been fair to an ugly woman," he admitted.[32] His only son, a boy of eleven when his father died, knew him only as "the Commander," remote, feared, and hated.[33]

In Germany in 1919, when the Germans were beaten and the German Empire disintegrated, and long before *Anschluss* and Sudetenland, Koehler observed the behavior of the German women in their fields and predicted World War II. Who but the Commander would have asked young German mothers if they were raising their babies simply to be cannon fodder in the next war?

Koehler was sent to south Russia as a special agent for the State Department in 1920, just as the White resistance to Bolshevik rule was crumbling. There he became the first American intelligence operative to witness and to calculate the Soviet threat. His job in south Russia (a "situation so complex that it is very doubtful whether the people in the very midst of it all have the slightest idea of what is really happening all about them") was to "find out what is really happening, what is at the bottom of it all, what it will lead to, what it means, whether Bolshevism is a real force, a workable idea, one that will endure, or whether it is the false doctrine it appears to be."[34] Koehler would be fascinated to know that nearly seventy years after the end of the Russian civil war, many of these questions remain largely unsolved.

But the Commander labored mightily to answer them. His methodology combined aspects of journalism, history, sociology, military tactics, propaganda, international strategy, even anthropology. "In a question such as this," he wrote,

> which concerns not only a nation or a race, but includes dozens of races and a hundred million people, and affects as many more, it is as necessary as it is difficult to get at the real source of the movement; and the question is not made less difficult by the fact that all

along the line one comes upon answers that seem sound enough, at first, but are really only superficial. So for the real answer one must go to the people themselves—to people by the hundreds and thousands—and from them one must learn what they probably do not know, or realize, themselves. For the people who are in the midst of these conditions are too close to be able to get a perspective—their ideas are already distorted by the very conditions they would analyze—just as in the case of a doctor who himself is ill and knows that he dare not prescribe for himself since his illness has already disturbed his sense of proportion.[35]

The hatred of the Bolsheviks on the part of many of the Russians Koehler met partly explains why his initial estimate of the staying power of communism was considerably off the mark. Yet he never allowed himself to be gulled by propaganda from the Left or the Right. And while in Poland in 1921–1922 he predicted with uncanny accuracy the future of Russia.

He seldom believed what he did not see with his own eyes. As he once wrote to his mother: "as long as I am not in direct contact with Russia and Russians, and breathing Russian air, and living in the Russian dirt, and feeling the currents and countercurrents that move the great masses of Russians, my opinion about things Russian is simply not worth a damn," and "you must remember that when I say the villages are burned or pianos requisitioned . . . it means that I have seen villages burned . . . and pianos seized . . . for so much inaccurate information about all this has been given out, that I have found that I can no longer credit anything unless I have seen . . . it myself."[36]

It was an extraordinary situation for a young American naval officer to be in—dodging the wrath of the Cheka at the dawn of a Communist nation: "chasing around about all over this end of the world, horseback, afoot, motorcycle, motorcar converted to run on railroad tracks, sailing, climbing, crawling—sometimes as a smart young naval officer, more often a very dirty, bedraggled one; often as a Cossack, once as a very greasy, oily rug merchant."[37]

Koehler's strategic vision went beyond the seemingly endless chaos he observed in 1920 south Russia to a day, not long in coming, when Russia would rise again and bid for world supremacy. An innate master of military tactics and strategy, Koehler could anticipate the imminent rise of another national power. His love of and for America was not a patriotism that blinded him.

In south Russia in 1920, he observed with equal clarity the ruthless brutality of both the Whites and the Reds. His own streak of objective brutality was a coldly honest reflection of his times and of the Europe in a state of becoming. The Commander struggled manfully to record a world of Total War, one in which—even as late as 1920—cavalry charges were still used to murderous effect, a world that despised the heavy hand of an imperious British Empire, a long-ago world that had yet to feel the weight of the American arm. The honesty in his observations, at times scathing to the brink of cruelty, could also startle to the point of being, in our time, remarkable, as when Russian Cossacks arranged themselves in a line in front of him and offered a lusty cheer to "America! America!"[38] Given the Cossack's love for their American naval officer friend, the cheer could as easily have been "Koehler! Koehler!"

Bolsheviks could easily have slit his throat while he was in their custody in Odessa in 1920. Instead, General Uborevich—who would have his own throat cut by Stalin in 1937—deferred to him. Koehler's own American revolutionary dialectic was forcible, his courage at once calculating and reckless. Who but "the famous Koehler" would have divined the demise of the White Russians in General Anton Denikin's mustache?

1

The Right Spy
1909–1918

*The battlefields are still hardly touched—the ground is still covered with shells, bullets, bits of arms, and you can see the whole battle almost as clearly as the day—or months—it was fought.
(August 1911)*

Hugo Koehler's voluminous observations of the world after Annapolis parallel America's arrival as a world power. His caustic pessimism and reckless bravery were closely matched to the revolutionary shattering of the calm and order of the world before August 1914. But these were not the only traits that gained his entry into palaces and staterooms around the globe: whether or not he was Rudolph's illegitimate son, he certainly *considered* himself every bit the equal if not the superior of the many dignitaries, functionaries, autocrats, plutocrats, and theocrats he met. In a society stratified for a thousand years, he never doubted that he himself belonged at the top.

Yet, if his instincts were aristocratic, his impulses were proletarian. Koehler cultivated just as many friends in low places. He could run on both tracks, at times simultaneously. In a rigid system of naval discipline, he followed his own star. He seemed, to one young reserve ensign, later a rear admiral, "very much of a specialist . . . rather than . . . regular Navy."[1] His exploits were well known to fellow officers, and his legend grew even as in later years his naval career waned and died. Another rear admiral recalled a story from the mission to south Russia. "[Admiral Newton A.] McCully [Koehler's commanding officer] had notified one of the destroyers in his command (in the Black Sea) that he would be aboard shortly. So the OOD [officer of the day] was of course alerted to watch out for any approaching boat. Naturally he was much astonished to hear shouts in the water some time later— from McCully and Koehler. They had swum out in the buff."[2]

Koehler filed an official protest in 1917 when his battleship division commander told the captain of Koehler's ship that Hugo's mustache had to go. "I have worn this mustache almost continuously since my graduation from the Naval Academy, some eight years ago," he wrote to superiors, "and men of my family have worn similar mustaches for some generations."[3] His argument carried; he kept his mustache.

Koehler's Kaiser Wilhelm mustache was one of the main reasons many thought him perpetually in disguise. Sneaking around south Russia in 1920 he wrote that "it was fortunate the strenuous time dashing about the last few months—sleeping in haystacks or a soft place on the ground—had added a sufficient touch of bolshevism to my unkempt and too-long beard to make a sadly disreputable peasant out of me when I got into my greasy sheepskin and the remnants of a pair of bad boots."[4]

The Navy prepared Koehler well for his work in Russia: his first job was in China with the Yangtze Patrol—as translator for a revolution.

During the early decades of this century of total war, gunboats under innumerable flags shielded foreign concessions and foreign traders along the rich coastal and riverine waters of China. "Legal principles," such as the British decree of extraterritoriality in 1842, had exempted Victoria's subjects from local laws and law enforcement agencies while in China. Other countries followed suit. Chinese resentment of foreigners smoldered as she was carved into spheres of alien influence. Attempts to rid China of foreigners led to the Boxer Rebellion in 1900, and a republican revolution led by the redoubtable Sun Yat Sen was in full storm in 1911, just as Hugo Koehler arrived for duty with the Yangtze Patrol.

Two years from Annapolis found Passed Midshipman Koehler with the Asiatic Squadron: a twenty-three-year-old linguist, he patrolled Chinese waters in the gunboat *Villalobos*, "on the broad principle of extending American protection to wherever this country's nationals resided for Gold, Glory, or Gospel."[5] By an odd chance, Koehler also entered China at the confluence of history and Hollywood: his *Villalobos* was the model for the *San Pablo* in the movie version of Richard McKenna's *The Sand Pebbles*, and Koehler shipped with the Yangtze Patrol bare weeks before Pu-yi, known to us today as "The Last Emperor," was booted from his throne. Koehler was at Wuchang when the impassioned confrontation took place that deposed the boy emperor. The corrupt old regime was then at its worst, because, as Koehler put it, "they all realize that the crash is coming, and they want to make their pile before it comes."[6]

Before reporting to the *Villalobos* in August 1911, however, Koehler detoured to the battlefields of Port Arthur, site of Russia's disastrous exchanges with Japan during the Russo-Japan War of 1905. For Hugo, these were to be the first of many footsteps on Russian soil. He wrote:

> The battlefields are still hardly touched—the ground is still covered with shells, bullets, bits of arms, and you can see the whole battle almost as clearly as the day—or months—it was fought.[7]

— ❧ —

The expedition was also a valuable opportunity to sharpen his eyes and ears. He found some easy marks, especially among the Japanese.

> I met an Englishman in Peking, formerly exchange cashier of the Yokohama Specie Bank—the government bank of Japan. . . . He himself was concerned in the negotiation when the Yokohama Specie Bank paid General Stoessel £80,000 gold, sterling, just before the surrender of Port Arthur, the money being deposited in Paris. He did not know why the money was paid, only that it was paid by a Japanese and kept secret. The fact illuminates the situation a bit, for it is well known that Port Arthur could have held out for months more. At the time of the surrender there were over six months' full supplies on hand and an immense amount of ammunition. I have been over every inch of Port Arthur, talked with many eyewitnesses, and the only conclusion I can arrive at is that the Japanese were not victorius, but the Russians simply presented them with a victory. . . . As for our having a war with Japan—I cannot help smiling. There is no doubt that every man, woman, and child in Japan wants war with us, but the powers that be are too wise—they know they are bankrupt already and even victory would ruin them absolutely.[8]

— ❧ —

His Germanic appearance and facility with languages both helped and hindered access to sources, but even this Koehler turned to his advantage. Returning home via Japan at the outbreak of World War I, Koehler used his Kaiser Willie to bait the Japanese into arresting him as a suspected German spy. ID cards not then being the custom, Koehler spent some uncomfortable days in a Japanese hoosegow until the U.S. naval attaché in Japan, who didn't know Koehler personally, received a cabled description of him from Washington. Koehler bid farewell to his captors, whom he hated ("with Japan and things Japanese . . . I detest them more each day") happy to have learned what interested the Japanese.[9]

3. Hugo Koehler, en route to Kuling, China, 500 miles up the Yangtze River, 1912. Rear Admiral R. F. Nicholson, Asiatic Fleet, left, in sun helmet and white uniform; Hugo Koehler, center, in British sun helmet and white suit. (U.S. Naval Historical Center Photograph neg. no. NH 84456.)

Aboard the *Villalobos* in October 1911, four hundred miles up the Yangtze from Shanghai, Koehler watched a revolution smolder in Wuchang. The discontent of the Chinese masses was palpable: both foreigners and the impotent imperial government that grew fat on foreign capital were despised. During the summer of 1911, revolution was seen to be inevitable.

By 15 September 1911 the roadstead at Hankow was crowded with the *Villalobos, Samar, Elcano,* and the *New Orleans,* flagship of Rear Admiral J. B. Murdoch, commander, Asiatic Squadron. The admiral departed for Hong Kong soon after, and the revolution proceeded without him.

On 9 October 1911 antigovernment plotters were secretly making bombs at the Russian concession at Hankow when there was an explosion. A police investigation produced a list of confederates amongst officers of the local garrison; to protect them, the planned uprising had to be immediately carried out.

"Fires ashore," Koehler reported in the log of *Villalobos* on 11 October, two days later. He described further:

Wednesday, 11 October 1911

> Commences and until midnight.
> Cloudy to partly cloudy and pleasant. Light air backing from NE to SSW. Barometer steady. At 4:01 A.M. the [imperial] viceroy's yacht at Wuchang was burned. At 5:40 A.M. a boarding officer from HMS *Thistle* came on board to confer with the captain regarding the situation at Wuchang. At 6:00 A.M. a Chinese gunboat stood in from downriver and anchored, and sent a landing party of about 10 men ashore at Hankow. . . .
> At 8:00 A.M. Mids. H. W. Koehler, U.S. Navy, boarded the Chinese gunboat to obtain further information regarding the situation at Wuchang. . . . Wuchang . . . was entirely in the hands of rebels and there was no possibility of communication with the American residents.[10]

The following day, as Kemp Tolley has written:

> *Helena* had returned to Hankow from upriver to find the roadstead looking like the rendezvous for an international naval review. Present were USS *Villalobos* and *Elcano*, six British ships, four German, three Japanese, one Austro-Hungarian, and one French. Two Russians arrived soon after. . . . Nine assorted Chinese cruisers and gunboats were there, but none could safely say on whose side they would be five minutes later.[11]

As Koehler recorded in the *Villalobos* log, pleasant weather continued on the twelfth—and so did fires in Wuchang:

> all evidently incendiary in origin, accompanied by rifle firing. Chinese men-of-war continued patrolling the river throughout the night and forenoon. . . .
> The USS *Helena* sent ashore an armed patrol of marines and bluejackets. SMS *Vaterland* and HMS *Thistle*, *Woodcock*, and *Nightingale* sent ashore armed patrols with three automatic guns.[12]

— ❧ —

These men, sent ashore under orders from the senior officer present, Vice Admiral Kawashima of the Japanese navy, suppressed looters and put out the fires in the German concession.

On Friday, 13 October 1911, the log continues:

> Midshipman Koehler attended a conference of the consular body at which the Japanese rear admiral [Kawashima] presided, the meeting

having been called to consider communications of the rebel commander in chief, in which he stated the aims of the rebel party, and offered to send troops to protect the foreign concessions. The offer was not accepted. . . . At 6:15 P.M. sent ashore two Colt automatic guns to American consulate in order to facilitate landing of armed party. . . . Incendiary fires in Wuchang throughout the night.[13]

— ❦ —

During the nights that followed, American sailors patrolled near the French concession until relieved by men from a French gunboat; U.S. sailors guarded the Russian municipal building until relieved by Italians; and the Americans sent three landing forces to guard the Japanese municipal building. "It is doubtful," wrote Tolley, "whether such a game of international military musical chairs has ever been played before or since."[14] By the middle of November, the Yangtze and all China was in the hands of the rebels, by which time "the gunboaters could get back to the normal routine of golf, billiards, tennis, and light conversation."[15] Pu-yi, the boy emperor, abdicated in January 1912.

As for Koehler, the Navy soon realized that they had more than a midshipman on their hands: on 28 March 1912, Koehler was commissioned an ensign to date from 5 June 1911.

Koehler's international wanderings continued, in even more bizarre surroundings, during ten days of postrevolution leave in November. To his mother he wrote of his "wonderful tiger-hunting expedition in Mongolia." Since tigers were all but extinct there, this was a way for a son to relate interesting experiences to his beloved mother while avoiding any mention of the real nature of the hunt.[16]

The expedition was comprised of Koehler as well as Prince Pappenheim, a first cousin to King Edward and the Kaiser; Baron Cottu, who "put through and financed the Canton-Hankow-Peking railroad line"; and "Count Fabricotti, of the great Florentine family of that name—the best-looking man in Europe, the wildest and greatest rake." Koehler did not need to consult the *Almanach de Gotha*—he already knew all the interrelationships. He described Fabricotti's wife as "perfectly lovely, adores him and understands him not at all," a description that years later would well fit his own wife, Matilda.

Fabricotti finds three kindred spirits, Pappenheim, Cottu, and myself, and off we are for tigers in Mongolia. Can you think of four people more different—a Frenchman, a German, an Italian, and an American—all ages, life, and training as different as it is possible to be different. . . . But it was a famous party—we had luck; we had the best of spirits and fun without end—what more can one ask of the world? Everyone laughed at the idea of four such characters going off together, but, strange as it may seem, since we've been back, we've been together ever since, whenever it has been possible.[17]

— ❦ —

Koehler was a twenty-six-year-old ensign, attached to a small U.S. Navy gunboat; yet he was already accepted as a tiger-hunting peer by a member of European royalty, a French international financier, and a well-born Italian rake.

You are doubtless wondering how it happens a naval officer can get away from his ship so often and spend his time tiger hunting. Officers in general most certainly could not do so, but in this particular part of the world Navy regulations and laws don't count except that the admiral's word is law, regulation, and judgment all in itself. Then, if one happens to be the admiral's "little white-haired boy" and if young and charming Mrs. Admiral happens to want a tigerskin shot for her by one of her youthful admirers, why then, it may so happen that the admiral decides it is time for you to have a rest, and so, off you are.[18]

— ❦ —

But this reasoning is incomplete; it doesn't explain why Hugo was held as an equal by his sterling companions. It is evident that they must have seen something extraordinary in him as well. One answer can be found in a letter by then Secretary of the Navy Josephus Daniels of 16 September 1914. Daniels quoted Koehler's commanding officer when he stated: "This [Koehler] is very adaptable and possesses a military spirit unusual in one of his rank. At the same time he has produced a smart ship, a contented crew, and the ship in general and the engine room are the cleanest I have ever seen."[19]

On 2 January 1913, Koehler was detached from the *Villalobos* "with tears in my eyes" and ordered to the *Saratoga*, Commander H. A. Wiley. Koehler was to become translator for an extended tour of Asian ports. For Hugo, it was an opportunity to boost his chances for the naval attaché billet in Moscow, which, since his meetings with the Russians, had become his obsession. As he wrote: "The admiral is shortly going to make a tour of all the various ports, to Saigon, the French port, Tsing Tao, the German, Macao, the Portugese, and Vladivostok, and he wants someone with him who speaks the languages. . . . I have been studying hard, for I intend to learn Russian. So many of my friends are Russian, and I like the Russians, so . . . you see I am still thinking of my billet as attaché."[20]

After the many port calls, Koehler assumed command of the tug

4. Hugo Koehler with two U.S. Navy members, at Kuling, China, 1912. (U.S. Naval Historical Center Photograph neg. no. NH84449.)

Piscataqua in the Philippines on 26 January 1914. Serving under him were three other ensigns and forty enlisted men. He was twenty-seven. Part of Koehler's legend in the Navy rests upon an incident that took place while he was in command of the *Piscataqua*, when he paid his crew and men from several other ships out of his own pocket when Congress failed to pass the naval appropriation in time that year.[21]

To add to his eccentricity, Koehler kept a small zoo on board his ship. There was a minor tragedy, however, when Koehler's pet boa constrictor swallowed his little spotted deer: her sharp hoofs pierced the constrictor's side, and they both died. Loose with rules, Koehler was precise with language. The quartermaster's "stood out" became in his vernacular "cast out," and "shoved off" became "cast off."

During the week of 1–6 June 1914, *Piscataqua* was ordered to tow a barge from Cavite to Olongapo. Koehler cast out, found the barge "unseaworthy" (she leaked), and returned to Cavite, where his superior there insisted on the seaworthiness of the barge and ordered Koehler to carry out his orders. With no choice, Koehler towed the barge, which, true to his prediction, promptly capsized and sank, with "consequent loss of stores." The superior officer was court-martialed; Koehler was cleared.[22]

By this time his superiors knew that Koehler could and would penetrate foreign intelligence sources and secrets. As a result of this prowess and zeal, as Koehler bluntly wrote his mother, the Navy, after receiving a particularly incisive report on German gunnery tactics, ordered him "to France and Germany to get more such secret information."

Mind you, I'll not be a spy—they will all know who I am, but they also know that France and America are not going to have a war for many, many years to come, so they will let me find out a lot that would be valuable to us though at the same time not dangerous to them. I've had experience in this and I've found that all the information about armaments, treaties, and fortifications is not obtained in dark corners and underground caves as one reads in novels, but simply and quietly in after-dinner conversation or a chat over a cup of tea. . . .

I have acquired more or less of a reputation for handling foreigners, and as my admiral has always forwarded letters of commendation about me from foreign admirals to the Navy Department, where they have been filed with my record, the powers that be in Washington also know the circumstances.[23]

— ❧ —

Throughout his career—at some not inconsiderable risk to his career—he enjoined his mother to the utmost secrecy. And, in turn, his mother—need it be said?—never betrayed her son's confidences.

War canceled the European journey. Instead of sipping tea with French admirals, Koehler shipped on the USS *South Carolina* in late 1915. The battleship then steamed off toward decidedly unromantic winter maneuvers. During the summers of 1916 and 1917, while the dead were piled in the mud of the western front, there were leisurely drills and maneuvers and target practice off Block Island. By then, the United States was in the war: President Wilson had signed the proclamation on 6 April 1917.

Koehler was finally detached from the Atlantic Fleet in February 1918. Meanwhile, he had passed his examinations for lieutenant, senior grade, and was sent to the subchaser base in New London, Connecticut.[24]

As they would do twenty-five years later, German submariners in 1918 harassed shipping from the North Sea to Long Island Sound. While on the *South Carolina* Koehler had worked on a tracking machine the Navy thought could be adapted for plotting submerged submarines. That is how he landed at New London. Once there, he rented a house with Harold S. "Mike" Vanderbilt, who sent Hugo the following memorandum.

To: Lieutenant Koehler, U.S.N.

1. You are hereby appointed official furniture mover in the house we are about to lease.

H. S. Vanderbilt

To which Koehler responded:

From: Lieutenant H. W. Koehler, U.S.N.
To: H. S. Vanderbilt, U.S.N.R.F.

1. Returned: appointment accepted.
The enemies of Cicero, wishing to bring discredit upon him, had him appointed Garbage Remover of Rome. When the enemies gathered to see Cicero's discomfiture, Cicero remarked—"If the office will not bring me honor, I will bring honor to the office." Rome was very badly in need of a garbage collector. Cicero became the most efficient garbage collector that Rome had ever known, and as a result Cicero was made consul and his fame has descended down through the generations.

Hugo W. Koehler[25]

Koehler's stay on the banks of the American Thames was brief: in July 1918 he was ordered to Queenstown, Ireland, to assume command of a detachment of submarine chasers. Mike Vanderbilt, who would arrange for Koehler's entry into upper-class society in Britain, went with him. On the trans-Atlantic voyage, Koehler described Vanderbilt as the

"boy navigator," for he showed them all how to take a sight. We had some days in New York before we left, and he carried a sextant around with him everywhere, and even slept with it, I have no doubt. (Somehow or other, Mike has always been rather platonic!) I almost began to suspect him of carrying around that sextant more to impress the waiters at Sherry's and the old gaa-gaas at the Union Club, than for the purposes of navigation. However, he really did take a sight on the way over, and I am creditably informed (by no less person than himself)

that the sight actually showed our position as somewhere in the North
Atlantic, and not on the top of a mountain, as is sometimes the case
with boy navigators. But at any rate the captain of the ship did not take
his advice too seriously and so we arrived safely.[26]

— ❧ —

By the time Koehler arrived in Queenstown, on 17 August 1918, to
take command of a group of U-boat chasers, all along the western front
the German army was retreating. With the Second Battle of the Marne
in July a last forward gasp, the Germans in mid-August fell back under
heavy blows from British tanks and increasing numbers of Allied
troops. From the Marne, the Great War began a three-month death
grind to the November armistice.

The war might be drawing to a close, but in Queenstown, near Cork,
the endless struggle for Ireland dragged on. With the exception of loyal
Protestant Ulster in the northeast, Catholic Ireland wanted an end to
British rule. The split showed dramatically on the western front. Ulster
had quickly organized a division of its fearless men for the trenches of
France; other Irish soldiers deserted as soon as they were conscripted.
Separatists were actively helpful to German sub crews who sneaked
ashore for supplies. (In 1916, a repressed Easter separatist uprising was
aided by German agents.) Early in 1918, British authorities arrested
leaders of the separatist Sinn Fein ("Ourselves Alone") party on
charges of subversion. Frustrated by the British action, republicans
followed Sinn Fein to victory at the ballot boxes in the 1918 parliamen-
tary elections. Yet, instead of taking their seats in the House of Commons in London, the Sinn Feiners formed their own "Irish Assembly,"
which was promptly suppressed by the British.

Unlike 1914 Japan, republic-minded, anti-British Ireland welcomed
Koehler's Germanic appearance, if not his pro-British attitude. Never
one to avoid political controversy, Koehler at once gave Irish politics
the same precise attention as his naval duties.

To those who saw him as he arrived in Queenstown, Koehler made a
vivid impression. One, Lieutenant Thomas Robins, remembered
Koehler as "a very Teutonic-looking man and we knew that he went to
Sinn Fein meetings, but just who he pretended to be we never knew."[27]
After dinner one night at the mansion Mike Vanderbilt and Hugo
rented in Queenstown, Robins watched as Koehler "left the table and a
few moments later I saw him sneaking out the front door in civilian
clothes, made up to be even more Germanic than usual."[28] Of course,
Koehler had to pretend to be somebody other than who he was—Sinn
Fein meetings were strictly off limits to U.S. personnel.

To his mother Koehler wrote:

> We were most strenuously forbidden to attend any Sinn Fein activities or gatherings of any sort to prevent any construction on the part of Sinn Feiners that such attendance meant sympathy with their cause. So I finally decided that the spirit of these orders would not be violated if I attended Sinn Fein meetings without my identity being known. Accordingly I worked up a rather effective disguise, and as I had an excellent cicerone, I was able to gather a good deal of information. I acquired a brogue thick enough to be cut with a knife; fortunately the various brogues are so different that imperfections are not readily noticed, and it is comparatively simple, if one is properly introduced, to pass as a particularly wild Irishman from County Clare.[29]

— ❧ —

Lieutenant Robins could "never forget Hugo's appearance, for one thing, the 'handlebar' mustache—very German. Then he wore boots with soft tops, very non-reg, but for some reason he was allowed this deviation. I recall a story of his arrival for duty in the Pacific with several trunks—a cargo net was lowered to pick up his personal baggage—then a rumor got around that the trunks were full of disguises!"[30]

If the accommodations and their location suited Koehler's taste, the people—at least their politics—did not. "Queenstown has a beautiful harbor," he wrote,

> but in every other aspect it is the end of the earth. (Still that only makes it a fit place for the Irish who live here.) There isn't much more enthusiasm for the Irish among our people here than there is among the English, and I am far from sure the Irish deserve more. For surely a more shiftless race never littered the earth. I was much in sympathy with President Wilson's statement to the English that the Irish situation was their problem and their job to settle—and soon. But my sympathies are wavering and are now all for the British. The British would like nothing better than to settle the Irish question at almost any price. But how satisfy a people split into factions, each faction demanding something different, and each wanting that same thing only as long as they know they cannot have it. The moment they get what they've asked for, it no longer has any value for them. . . . The Home Rule has its stronghold in the south and is solidly Catholic. The Ulsterites, or North Irish party, almost as solidly Protestant, are opposed to Home Rule for the simple reason they realize the minute the South Irish party takes charge, all industries of Ireland—about 95 percent of which are in the north—will shortly be taxed out of existence. Then there are the

Sinn Feiners. I have never yet been able to discover just what the Sinn Feiners want, nor has anybody else been able to put a finger on anything definite, although they have stirred a tremendous agitation about this indefinite something. The fiery orator I heard two days ago expressed it best. Speaking for the Sinn Feiners, he said he wanted no government by an English king, no government by any parliament, British or Irish, no democracy or anything like it; what he wanted was no government at all; all he wanted was liberty and freedom, just that, nothing more nor less. It is hard to understand how a grown man could utter such rot, to say nothing of how other grown men could listen to it. But as a matter of fact these are not grown men, they are simply children. Taxes here are much less than in England. Irish per capita representation in Parliament is greater than that of any county in England. Food is plentiful. There are no food restrictions, and the English supply them with more food than they give their own people. And yet they have a hymn of hate for the British no less venomous than the German hymn. . . .

This morning while walking into town with a lot of youngsters, I noticed a tall spire in the distance and asked what it was. One of the youngsters replied that it belonged to the Catholic church. I remarked that it looked like a fine big church. "Aye, and it's bigger inside, it is," he answered in a brogue thick as pea soup; nor had he any idea he had said anything droll. This drollness is the most attractive part of the Irish. If one doesn't see too much of them one forgives them half their sins on account of it. But Freud was right when he said of Ireland that it was a land blessed of God but cursed of the people.[31]

— ❦ —

Koehler, who as this passage demonstrates could at times sound like a retired brigadier/plantation master, mellowed somewhat after an extended visit to London. There he had the opportunity to befriend rapscallions on both sides of the Irish question. "I went to special pains to get a clear conception of the Irish situation," he wrote to his mother from London,

and not allow my judgment to be influenced by any preconceived ideas or expressions of opinions heard on all sides. The statements contained in the English papers are as accurate as the wild accounts that appear in the Sinn Fein papers. The so-called Sinn Fein Oath has been published in almost every English paper, yet I have talked to many of the most rabid Sinn Feiners, and though they have spoken to me in entire confidence I have never yet come across one who has really taken this so-called oath or heard of anyone who had. It is simply a poisonous collection of absurdities and extravagances, and though there are doubtless many Irishmen who could conceive of such absurdities, this oath has been far more effective as English propaganda than as an oath to bind Sinn Feiners. Although the Irish hate the English, and right cordially, their hatred has apparently not taken this form except perhaps in the case of those who are ignorant to the point of being defective. . . .

English papers insist the Home Rule majority is comparatively small, but that this is not accurate has just been demonstrated by the clean sweep for Sinn Feiners at the recent election. Even Ulster counties elected Sinn Feiners. As some 78 Sinn Feiners were elected to Parliament, and the majority of these are in prison, an anomalous situation has been brought about. This idea of electing as members of Parliament men who have announced they will accept a nomination, but will not sit in Parliament if elected, results not merely from the Irish sense of humor, which laughs at the ridiculous side of electing men to sit in Parliament who will not sit, but more from the conviction deep rooted in the minds of Irishmen in Ireland that Irishmen in Parliament, due to the pernicious climate of England and the subtle bribery of English politics, soon lose their real Irish nationality. This question has two sides, for it is possible to point to case after case of Irish representatives who have slackened on their convictions as soon as they were seated pleasantly in Parliament, and before long became quite innocuous. The English claim is, of course, that when these Irish delegates come to England and talk to enlightened and rational men they see the error of their ways and change accordingly. The Irishmen claim these men lose their virility as soon as they get to England and that bribery in the English system finishes the job and they become English minded. Be that as it may, it is a fact the so-called Irish Party in Parliament has entirely lost the confidence of Irish at home and is without any influence whatever in Ireland. . . .

Everywhere in Ireland men are drilling, drilling, drilling, although drilling is forbidden by the mighty Defense of the Realm Act and is punishable by imprisonment. In view of the fact that the country is overrun with British soldiers (mostly Scots), it is obvious the country is solidly behind the Sinn Feiners as they otherwise would not be able to get away with all this drilling. They drill not only in bands of tens and twenties but by companies and even battalions. Whenever a drill is held, half of the company is detailed as scouts and pickets while the others drill. It would appear that where so large a number of men are concerned, information would surely leak to the local police and constabulary. I have mentioned this to the British in Ireland and they say the Irish constabulary is loyal to the British and not in league with Sinn Feiners. Irish constabulary all profess loyalty to the British and are loud in denunciation of Sinn Feiners. However, from indications other than answers to direct questions, Irish constabulary all sympathize with Sinn Fein, and though they will doubtless arrest any man caught red-handed, there will be very few they intend to catch red-handed. Sinn Feiners often speak of their officers as lieutenants and colonels, and just days ago on the occasion of one of them being accidentally (?) shot, a great procession, four companies in military formation—though of course without arms—followed his body to the cathedral where it is to lie in state for two days while great crowds come to do it honor.

The great point of difference between the English and the Irish is after all the English have no sense of humor and the Irish have the keenest sense of humor in the world. It is this difference that makes it impossible for Englishmen to understand Irishmen, and it is an axiom that one must first understand those whom one would govern. . . .

One of the most dangerous symptoms lies in the fact that the whole Sinn Fein movement is tinged with the idea of martyrdom, and it seems to derive considerable strength just from the fact of its hopelessness. The only parallel I have ever seen was in the southern Philippines, where native priests told the Moros that the greatest good that could come of them would be to kill a heathen American and be shot down in turn, for only then would the gods transport them to Seventh Heaven. Irishmen are rapidly getting the same sort of fanaticism and openly declare that they neither fear nor would they regret being shot down for their cause, since every Irishman shot down by the police or by the soldiery means a distinct gain for Ireland, because 20 men will be inspired by the example of the one who has fallen. Of course, this means bloodshed. Nor does the fact that England has some one million troops at her call dismay the Irish; the fanatic would not be dismayed by a hundred million. So I fear that it will not be long before blood is shed in Ireland. It may be that the situation can still be saved by a wiser consideration of the Irish question than has yet taken place, and by a sane policy being firmly carried out, but it must come soon—and very soon—or it will be too late. . . .

So hurrah for Ireland and the Irish, say I! It's the devil of a country to live in or work in but a fine place to play in. And the Irish? I love them as friends and playmates, but oh! how I'd hate to have them as compatriots or relations![32]

With the swirl of Irish politics around him, it is no wonder Koehler had less than a full measure of enthusiasm for his official duties aboard the new subchasers. From the roughness of patrols on the Irish Sea to the pervasive smell of fuel oil, he described twenty-four hours of "drifting patrol" (drifting with no engines for German subs to hear), as "murder."[33] Influenza descended upon crews in leaky ships exposed to freezing surf. Wet clothing, cramped quarters, and noxious fumes were the rule. But there was exhilaration at inventing new and effective antisubmarine warfare techniques, and Koehler was eventually awarded the Navy Cross for his work with the leaky subchasers in Queenstown.

After the war the British commander in chief of the joint British-U.S. antisubmarine campaign, Vice Admiral Sir Lewis Bayly, wrote of the subchasers that, after they learned the intricacies of the Irish coast, "their plucky energy, which declined to see difficulties, and owing to the great ability and tact of Captain A. J. Hepburn, U.S.N., who was in charge of them, they soon grappled with an unfamiliar situation, and would soon have become a great asset in working with the seaplanes of the coast."[34]

"These subchasers," Koehler wrote to his mother,

could determine the direction of the submerged submarine accurately but could not get the distance. Accordingly, three subchasers operated together in a line, each subchaser determining for itself the direction of the hunted submarine; then these three directions were plotted on a chart and the intersection of these three lines of direction gave the exact location of the submarine. Having thus located the submarine, the subchasers immediately rushed to that point and stopped there for a moment to listen with their special instruments, in order to get the direction of the submarine. As the submarine had probably moved during the interval [in which] the subchasers were approaching its location, the subchasers had to get a new location of the submarine, and in this way they ran down the submarine, quite like a hare and hound chase. When the subchasers got to a position approximately on top of the submarine, they dropped a large number of depth charges, which did the rest. On one occasion a group of three of our subchasers chased a submarine (which they had never seen) for seven hours before they finally got into position to bomb her. Yet, one could not help admire the great way some submarines were handled, and though the submarine campaign was ruthless, it nevertheless produced excellent examples of the finest skill and judgment and cool courage.

As a result of our success with subchasers, the British commander in chief decided to put the operation of all aeroplanes in charge of my chief, Captain A. J. Hepburn, and that gave us another splendid instrument with which to work. In addition to various subsidiary stations, we had four large aircraft stations on the Irish coast and, from dawn to sunset, kept up continuous aircraft patrols. The aircraft kept in touch with the nearest group of subchasers by means of a wireless telephone, and as soon as a submarine or its wake was sighted, the location was immediately communicated to the subchasers. This cooperation of aircraft with subchasers multiplied the usefulness of both, as subchasers became ears for the aircraft and aircraft became eyes for subchasers. Operations consequently were a great success and it was almost with a feeling of regret that we received news of the armistice, for it seemed hard to lay down this instrument, which we had worked so hard to perfect, just at the moment it had reached its highest development. I do not mean that we regret the armistice, for every day the war went on meant the world was nearer and nearer to bolshevism and chaos. As soon as the armistice was concluded, our chasers were started homeward, and I went to headquarters, London (Admiral [Williams S.] Sims), for duty.[35]

—❦—

The guns on the western front had been silent less than a month when Koehler again arrived in London. He was in a special position to observe the renewed bustle of the center of the Empire; he had seen wartime London in August, before he reported to Queenstown.

"It is at night one has the most difficulty recognizing the London of old," he had written then,

for the few street lamps lighted until ten o'clock are either screened or painted so as not to show any light upwards, and they are of such low power they seem almost gloomier than utter darkness. All lights whatever are extinguished promptly at ten, and woe betide any unfortunate householder who allows a streak of light to escape round the edge of the window shade, for he is certain to be hauled up promptly and charged with violation of the mighty "Defense of the Realm Act." A few—very few—theaters are still going, but no one seems to care about them. However, I understand that theaters do rather better when there is good news from the front. For that matter, one does not need to read the dispatches to learn the kind of news that has come from the front, for when the news is good, shops are crowded and people seem to have a mania for buying everything in sight, but when news is bad no one will buy anything at any price, and shops and streets are alike deserted. . . .

Every large doorway, arch, and arcade has been made to serve as an air-raid shelter, and in addition, a good many underground shelters have been provided. Of course, the danger of a bomb injuring any particular person is remote, but there is nothing remote about the danger of being in the streets during an air raid. Immediately any hostile aircraft are sighted, hundreds of guns located on every high building and tower available put up a shrapnel barrage so tremendous it soon fills the streets with a perfect hail of shot and shell fragments. The most recent air raid occurred the night we arrived, and we saw the brilliant effect of hundreds of searchlights sweeping across the sky. These searchlights are busy all night long except during moonlight, and one soon becomes so accustomed to them it seems natural to see the night sky lighted with a perfect basket weave of searchlight beams.[36]

— ❦ —

Koehler's upper-class friends endured the war quite nicely—apart from mild discomforts of petrol rationing and evening meals cut to three courses. The two postwar months Koehler spent in London were very far from the bilges and fumes of the freezing subchasers. His next letters from London were written from a blissful reverie of Anglophilia: even after the slaughterhouse of France, Edwardian aristocracy abided.

"I have landed among the very smart and fashionable and the diplomatic set," he wrote his mother,

many of whom I already knew officially: and on the other hand through Lady Scott (wife of Captain Scott* who discovered [sic] the South Pole), whom I have known a long time, I see a great deal of men like Bernard Shaw, Arnold Bennett, and James Barrie, so I don't get too narrow in my ideas about things English. Mike Vanderbilt's sister, the Duchess of Marlborough, has been chaperoning me very carefully and on two occasions has had me all but married without consulting either me or the lucky girl! Rumors of this may reach you, but you are not to take them seriously. Of course, I always take all lovely women seriously— but I shall hardly try to tell you anything about me! I have managed to get away to the country for most of the weekends, for there is nothing more delightful than English country life. I spent Christmas [1918] at Cranmore with Lady Paget, and a more delightful household one could not imagine. It reminded me of home, for we had all the excitement of waiting at the door while Santa Claus put finishing touches to the tree, and listening intently for the sound of the bell that meant the opening

---

* Captain Robert Falcon Scott (1868–1912) was the fifth man to reach the South Pole [after the Norwegians Amundsen, Bjalland, Wisting, and Hassell]. Scott and his four companions all died on their return journey from the Pole.

of the doors and the rush of the children to find their corners. . . . Lady Paget has the most exquisite talent as a hostess, for somehow she manages always to have everyone at their best. This party was quite a heterogeneous one and included every sort of person London produces: from her two brothers-in-law, Mr. Balfour and Lord Gladstone,* to the ambassador from the new Tcheko-Slav republic and the Archbishop of Odessa. You can imagine it was rather a job to handle a party of thirty-seven such diverse personalities, to say nothing of an additional dozen and a half children: but still it was wonderfully managed. One evening at dinner James Barrie was told to construct the most wonderful play he had ever written. He did so the following morning; in the afternoon the play was rehearsed, and in the evening it was produced in seven acts, a tremendous success. It was wonderfully clever, for most of the actors had simply to act their own characters. Mr. Balfour took the part of a Foreign Minister; Lord Gladstone took the part of a Colonial Governor (he had just been Governor of South Africa) and I was a dashing (sic!) young naval officer. The result was a screaming farce. We were there five days and were idle not a solitary moment. Almost every day we had a football game in which everybody took part, men, women and children, and indeed it was a lesson in poise to see the splendid way in which the most dignified old statesmen and haughty dowagers dashed about and scrambled in the mud.

The day after Christmas we had a great partridge shoot, so I was late for dinner and thoroughly starved. I rushed to the table intent on food, for dinner was well under way. I had hardly settled in my seat when suddenly I forgot all about food, for on my right was the most exquisite sweet-young-thing I had ever seen. And though food was rushed to me in great quantities, I hardly looked at it, so intent was I in gazing at that vision of loveliness so near me. Imagine my surprise when on turning to the left I beheld another sweet-young-thing, even more wonderful than the first, if that could be possible. Naturally, after that I starved, but what a delightful starvation it was! The only misfortune of it all was they were sisters—the two daughters of the Marquess

---

* Arthur Balfour (1848–1930), Conservative British statesman, was prime minister from 1902–1906. Vehemently opposed to Home Rule for Ireland, he was more sympathetic toward a homeland for Jews in Palestine, as expressed in his Balfour Declaration (1917). Lord Herbert John Gladstone (1854–1930), Liberal British statesman, was son of "The Grand Old Man," William Gladstone, and close friend of Hugo Koehler. Herbert was an M. P. from 1880 to 1910, as well as first governor general and high commissioner for South Africa (1910–1914).

of Bath.* Of course, two beautiful women at the same time are always a difficulty, but particularly so when they are sisters. I realized I would have to make the dreadful decision sooner or later, so I decided to make it at once, and for the rest of the evening I forgot all else in the world save that the most important thing in life was to be near the most exquisite creature I had ever seen. The night came to an end all too quickly, and I—worse luck!—I was scheduled to go over to Maiden Bradley early the next morning to shoot with the Duke of Somerset.† It seemed a cruel end, especially as there had been no opportunity to say good night except when there was a herd of men about. All during the night I saw visions of the most wonderful eyes I had ever seen, and even when I would wake up I still could see the soft glow of the eyes that had thrilled me so at dinner. To be sure, the next morning when I got up I noticed that my wristwatch with the luminous dial was hanging in the very spot from which the soft glow of the lovely eyes had appeared to come, but still I am sure it was the memory in my heart that made it seem so wonderful—and not merely patent paint of the watch! The next morning as I started out all gay with the prospect of a wonderful day's shooting, and all sad at the thought of the lovely eyes I was leaving behind and that would have disappeared forever by the time I got back, Lady Paget called from her window beseeching me to be careful not to shoot the duke, for he was quite the biggest target in all the countryside and altogether the nicest duke in England. A moment later a dozen other windows flew open and cries of "Oh don't shoot the duke! Don't bag the Duke!" sent me speeding along my way to Maiden Bradley. On the way over I scribbled a note to Lady Paget telling her of the precarious state of my heart and inviting her to come to my assistance. As the shoot was to be over at about five o'clock, I suggested she call for me at Maiden Bradley, and that on our way back to Cranmore we arrange to have a puncture just in front of Longleat (the Marquess of Bath's seat) and we could then go in and have tea with the lovely young things at Longleat while the puncture was being repaired! You see, the sweet-young-things had come to Cranmore only for the ball the night before and they were to return to Longleat early the following morning while I was out shooting. I showed the note I had scribbled to Lady Paget to Mr. Balfour, who in turn passed it to the duke, and they

---

* The fifth Marquess of Bath, Sir Thomas Henry Thynne (1862–1946), married Violet Caroline, 19 April 1890.

† The sixteenth Duke of Somerset, Sir Edward Hamilton Seymour K. B. E. (1860–1931).

5. Longleat. (Photo courtesy of Lord Christopher Thynne.)

roared. The duke asked me what I was going to do about it. I answered that I was going to get them of course! I had been absolutely soaked during the morning of the day's shoot and just at that time I was dressed in some of the duke's old clothes, including a wonderful old greatcoat I had much admired. When I announced that I was going to "get them of course," the duke roared some more and added that he would bet me that greatcoat I liked so much against the bitter end of the cigarette I was smoking just then, that I would not "get them of course." It happened that he had liked my gun very much, so I answered that I wouldn't bet him the cigarette end but would lay him my gun against his greatcoat. So he took me on, and though I was still dressed in his clothes (my own were dripping) I started off on the great adventure. I was rather a picturesque sight to say the least, because the duke is something over six feet four inches tall—and concerning his girth I would not even venture to guess. Some half hour later I arrived at Longleat trembling but happy. Lifting the enormous knocker, I beat a bold tattoo on a door about the size of the gates of St. Peter's and even more boldly announced myself to the footman who came running along a moment later. They seemed not at all surprised when I announced who the great man was and immediately asked me if I had left my suitcase in the motor. This was indeed a surprise, I must admit. I was ushered into an enormous room—incidentally one of the most beautiful rooms I have ever seen—and while I was toasting myself before a fireplace big enough to hold a pair of horses, the sweet-young-thing came down. Her first words were, "I am so glad you have come so quickly." This also surprised me but obviously pleased me more. I lost no time in explaining my plan. The sweet-young-thing was delighted but said her mother would never allow it—and much less would father. Accordingly, I undertook further negotiations with mother and father. Just then an old aunt appeared and I recognized my only chance; I made myself agreeable harder and faster than ever before in my career, and luck was with me. I told her my plan; she said she would prepare the way for me with mother and father and as soon as she signaled that all was propitious I was to come up and see what could be done. The signal was a long time in coming, but I dashed up in a hurry when it came. I may have mentioned that I was somewhat astounded when I first saw the sweet-young-things, but I think I was even more surprised when I saw the old marquess. He is without doubt the most beautiful man I have ever seen—really a perfect Greek god; and the marchioness is exquisite. I have never seen a more beautiful pair. I was really quite overcome, but I managed to tell them my story, and with fire in my eye! Somehow everything happened just as it should, suitcases were packed, and fifteen minutes later we were off for Cranmore. As we drove up to Cranmore, Lady Paget, who happened to be standing out front, called out, "Did you bag the duke?" "No, something much better!" I called back. "What did you bag?" one of the other yelled. "A pair of sweet-young-things," I was tempted to answer but only smiled serenely. And then the mystery of why my suitcase had been expected at Longleat was cleared up, for when I got to my room I found a telegram from the sweet-young-thing asking me to come over to Longleat for the weekend. The telegram had come over while I was at Maiden Bradley, so of course I knew nothing about it when I pounded so boldly at the gates of Longleat. At any rate I have the duke's greatcoat. Since then all my weekends save one, when I went back to the old duke, have been spent at Longleat.

Last week I took one of my old shipmates, a very amusing fellow, Stewart Lee, down to Longleat with me. As Lee was quite overcome with the wonder of it, the marquess asked him what he would do if he had a place like Longleat in America. Lee hesitated for a moment, and then said, "Why I would walk right up to old John D. Rockefeller and tell him to go to hell!" This was somewhat startling, to be sure, but the old marquess seemed to understand perfectly. It is indeed a wonderful old place, a large part of it dating from the fourteenth century. I haven't any idea of the number of rooms and halls it contains, except that it took us all Sunday morning to go through part of it, and we didn't even go near one end that had been turned into a hospital (150 beds) during the war. You would love it, for it is filled from top to bottom with the most exquisite old furniture and porcelain, glass, majolica, marble, and the treasures of the ages. The libraries contain the most wonderful old books, hundreds of old parchments, manuscripts, letters of Queen Victoria and Samuel Johnson, and all manner of priceless things. In my room was an exquisite head of Sir Joshua Reynolds, another of Andre Montegna, and tapestries such as I've never seen outside a museum.

But why do I waste time telling you about places and things when all that really matters in this world is the Lady Emma?* (There you have it!) Of course I think Longleat wonderful; but so would I think the North Pole wonderful if she were there. I adore her; yet all her loveliness is but the tiniest part of her worth—she is pure gold inside. Of course I am in love with life and the world, and all the world is better and lovelier for that she is in it. Oh! Mother—I believe I am in love. Oh! Oh! Oh! But this is a subject with which I dare not continue, for I would expend all my adjectives and this letter would never have any end.[37]

— ❦ —

Whether or not his friends in the aristocracy deserved to enjoy "the fine art of how to enjoy life to a higher point than has any other race in the last few thousand years" Koehler less than neatly squared in another letter to his mother. "I shall grieve as much as any Englishman," he wrote,

when the old order changes, for I cannot help thinking that when all the land is cut up into small farms and the great estates pass out of existence, England will lose a lot more than she will gain by any improvement that may come from men working their own farms instead of being tenants. For instance, Longleat comprises some 68,000 acres. Of course, that seems a tremendous big corner of a small country like

---

* Lady Emma Margery Thynne (1893–?) was daughter of the above-noted fifth Marquess of Bath and his wife, Violet. While he obviously enjoyed her company at Longleat in 1919, Koehler ultimately lost the beautiful twenty-five-year-old Lady Emma to the sixth marquess of Northhampton, whom Lady Emma married on 15 October 1921. For more on the temper of the upper class at this time see Arthur Marwick, *The Deluge; British Society and the First World War* (Boston, 1965), pp. 198–203.

England for one man to own. But no one will ever provide for that land and all the people on it as carefully as have the Thynnes (the family name of the Marquess of Bath) for many generations. And that great and wonderful home—what would become of it? It takes 68,000 acres to support it. And these aristocrats of England, they deserve well of their country—they've poured out their blood and their treasure unsparingly in this war. Take the Thynnes, for example: every one of them did splendidly. The oldest son, Viscount Wells, went to France the first week of the war, distinguished himself, and was killed in action a week after he got the V.C. And the girls saw their job and did it. It was necessary that women, who had never worked before, should go into factories. The quickest way to bring about so revolutionary a change was to make it fashionable. So these girls with the proudest blood in England in their veins promptly took jobs in a munition factory. They stuck at it, and for long hours each day, for month upon month, they worked at their lathes with a thousand other men and girls about them. In the meantime their mother, the Marchioness of Bath, converted her home into a hospital and ran it herself, having asked the government for nothing but medicines—she provided doctors and nurses and all else. So bravo for them, I say! They saw their duty and they did it.[38]

— ❦ —

Koehler's reverie at Longleat was soon put to an end by the Navy Department. It was time to go back to the war, this time to see what it had done to the other side.

2

Germany and Versailles
1919 _____

So thoroughly is the shame of the German Navy felt that the blue uniform is considered almost a badge of disgrace, and except for the uniforms of men on the few ships still in commission one never sees any blue, although the streets are crowded with thousands of men in the forestry gray of the infantry. (February 1919)

Koehler's commanding officer at Queenstown, Captain Hepburn, attended the 18 December 1918 meeting that organized the Allied Naval Armistice Commission. When Hepburn left London for the United States early in 1919, Koehler stayed on as an aide under Admiral Robison. For a month there were dinner parties every night and Longleat on the weekends.

The commission met at Scapa Flow on 5 February. Koehler, as official interpreter, departed with the commission for an inspection tour of the German ports. As his conversations and observations reveal, he was just as concerned with social conditions in postwar Germany as he was with the German ships the commission was inspecting. And those conditions were a shock.

The democracies had managed to demobilize as fast as ships could be found to return the survivors of France and Flanders. By early 1919, a million Britons had returned to their island, many threatening mutiny if they were not immediately brought home.

The shame of a naval mutiny was very real in Germany. As the German armies in the west were retreating in October 1918, the German admirals still retained their essentially unscathed High Seas Fleet. With an unfavorable armistice looming, the admirals conceived a plan to draw out the British Grand Fleet from the base at Scapa Flow and smash it in the Skagerrak, at a time and place of the admirals' choosing.

It was a daring plan and could have favorably altered the fate of Germany during the negotiations in Paris. But as the fleet moved into position on 29 October 1918, war-weary elements on two of the bat-

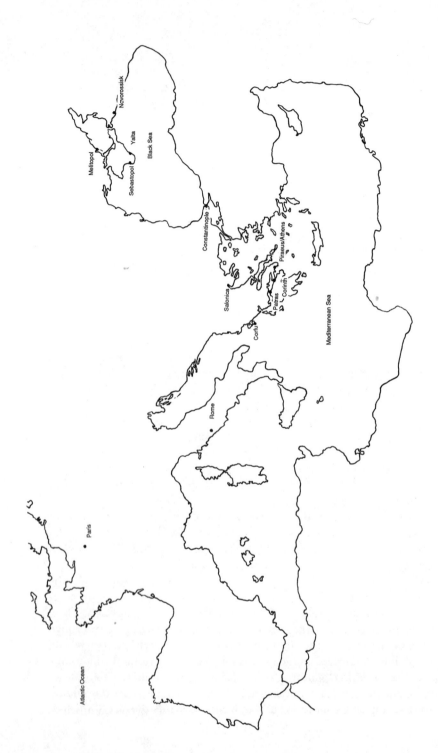

Map 1 Southern Europe

tleships refused orders, and a general mutiny ensued. Admiral Franz von Hipper, in charge of the fleet, arrested the mutineers but was forced to withdraw to Kiel, where another general mutiny broke out. The great fleet of capital ships was incapacitated: workers' and soldiers' councils were formed, and red flags soon flew over the naval bases at Wilhelmshaven and Kiel.

As part of the armistice, the High Seas Fleet was delivered to the Allies and interned at Scapa Flow. But there was no Allied military police force in defeated Germany. After the armistice, the losers of the trench massacres were beset by radical movements of Left and Right.

This was the situation when Koehler arrived in early 1919: the once and future order of Germany was a poor, demoralized chaos of beaten soldiers, weak politicians, and seething radicals. A vengeful France plundered from the west; bolshevism loomed from the east. A German "Red Soldiers' League" fought and defeated a reactionary *Freikorps* of ex-soldiers, for a time threatening a Bolshevik revolution in Germany before the Weimar Republic's army finally put down the Reds.

As Koehler noted firsthand, Germans were outraged by what they considered the Versailles *diktat.* The malaise of defeat saw rusting wreckage where once the vaunted German military machine had been: the ruin of the German navy, especially, was total.

And here it becomes obvious that Koehler is beginning to play on a larger field.

Wilhelmshaven, Germany
12 February 1919

Went ashore [at Wilhelmshaven] with the armistice commission inspection party and almost immediately came across a German officer who insisted on telling almost everything he knew and several things he didn't know. We found the German ships all in a frightful state, both as regards cleanliness and preservation. They had evidently been hastily put out of commission, for there was no one whatever on board, not even a shipkeeper, although a few men (apparently squatters) were living on board simply for the make of a roof. That the ships had been put out of commission in a most careless manner, as well as very hastily, was everywhere apparent, for although some attempt had been made to grease guns and working parts, the job had not been properly done, and guns were already beginning to rust inside and out. The ships that were in commission, as for example, the new light cruiser *Koenigsberg*, were also in a hopeless condition, although they had large crews on board. I

have never seen a ship in commission in as frightfully filthy a condition
as that of the *Koenigsberg*. Before going aboard we asked that the crew
be removed in order to facilitate our inspection. The captain immediately gave the necessary orders, but the crew straggled up by twos and
threes in a most desultory manner. Most of them were smoking the
large cigars, made of cabbage leaves soaked in licorice and tobacco
juice, now very much the fashion in Germany. As we were being considerably delayed by the slowness in clearing the ship, I asked the
captain whether this could not be expedited. He answered that he
would give further orders but that he doubted exceedingly that they
would have any effect since the men did exactly what they pleased and
nothing else. As this rabble came out on deck where we were patiently
waiting, the men crowded around us, so that it was necessary to ask the
captain to have them withdraw sufficiently to allow us breathing space. I
think the literal translation of his words of command describes the
situation, as regards discipline, more thoroughly than could pages of
explanation: "Please, it is requested that the men withdraw, please, just
a little distance for just a few minutes, please." The men moved away
slowly and sulked and muttered. We also inspected the destroyers,
submarines, and the aircraft station. Conditions were everywhere alike:
everything unspeakably filthy, no work being done, everything going to
rack and ruin. . . .

A horse in a passing cart was shot [during a riot], and within
twenty minutes after it fell, every shred of flesh was stripped from the
carcass. This indicates the meat shortage even more plainly than the
empty meat shops do. . . .

Had heard much about ingenious substitutes for rubber tires, so
one of the first things I did was to see what had been done in this
respect. In addition to coil-spring tires, I noted link tires with springs
inserted in the spokes. These had proved effective despite the infernal
racket they made. Most heavy trucks have broad, smooth iron tires with
no spring inserts of any kind. Bicycles and aeroplanes have rope tires,
although a new form of coil spring is said to be a considerable improvement. Many lightweight motorcars use tires of a wood composition.
These do fairly well for use at slow speeds on perfect roads, but lack of
any resiliency causes excessive wear of the cars. I noticed many wooden
shoes in shops and on the streets. Practically no leather except very
heavy sole leather is obtainable. . . .

The great slaughter of cattle on account of the shortage of food
has resulted in accumulation of large quantities of hides in Germany.
The reason for this accumulation is that Germany cannot get hold of

any tan bark and all substitutes so far discovered have resulted only in a waste of hides. This intensified search for substitutes will prove of considerable use to Germany after the war, for many processes have been discovered that will work out very well for peace purposes. The search for motor spirit to take the place of gasoline and kerosene, of which supplies were limited, resulted in the discovery of a process of distillation of a light oil from soft brown coal of such poor grade that heretofore it has been practically useless. There are immense deposits of this brown coal in Saxony and Wurtenburg, and motor spirit can be produced comparatively cheaply by this new process. Were it not for the shortage of tires, motors would be much more plentiful in Germany today than they are in England. There are many similar war industries that will survive and doubtless be a source of considerable wealth.

One notices an enormous number of placards posted in places heretofore sacred. The Rathaus, churches, schools, and even the police station were newly plastered with these placards and showed evidence of former placards that had been torn down. The most conspicuous of these signs was one that read: "We have a right to something besides work! We have a right to bread! Labor, which alone produces wealth, alone has the right to wealth! No more profit!" This was signed "Workmen's and Sailors' Council." There was also evidence that a good many of these signs had been torn down. . . .

Much of the clothing I saw was of woven paper. This is not nearly as bad as it sounds, and I expect the industry will continue after the war. Practically all cotton mill machinery has been converted to spin paper cloth, and even were the supply of cotton increased enormously it would take many months before mills could be converted to use cotton again, as the difference between the two installations is considerable. Even cord is of paper and, strange to say, quite strong. They have now developed paper cloth for dresses, paper sheets, and paper under-clothing, which with care can be washed from seven to ten times. As the government took all linen from hotels, paper sheets and table cloths are used.

During the war all surgical dressings, the absorbent cotton as well as bandages, were made of paper. They gave excellent service and are said to be preferred to the former cotton dressings.

One sees a good many double chins and paunches still, that is, among the men. The women really look emaciated. They have suffered from the food shortage a good deal more than the men have. In good old German style, the men keep the lion's share for themselves. The saddest thing, however, is suffering among the children. . . . Infant mortality has been very high. . . . Not a single millinery shop had anything but black hats and mourning bonnets, and in all women's shops about 90 percent of the cloth displayed was black—here again the difference between provision for men and women. Almost all real cloth that remains is reserved for men's clothes; women use the various substitutes.

I put in a good many hours while at Wilhemshaven in reading German newspapers and the placards and handbills distributed by the Workmen's Council, the Socialists, and the civil government. I also got a number of pamphlets with which every bookshop and kiosk is packed. I asked which pamphlet had been most popular and was informed that one entitled "Tirpitz,* the Grave Digger of the German Navy," by a Captain Persius, had had an enormous sale. A refutation of this pamphlet was also on sale but had not proven popular. Newspapers devoted a great amount of space to outcries against "The Rape of the German Colonies" and to the injustice of inflicting penalties for nondelivery of coal while at the same time demanding a further delivery of locomotives and rolling stock. . . . It was impossible to fulfill the Allied demands for coal since the means of transportation had been taken away from them. Repeated outcries were made against this delivery of locomotives, since lack of transport would mean factories would have to shut down for lack of coal, and resulting unemployment was doing more to plunge the country into bolshevism than all other factors combined. By far the greatest amount of space was devoted to outcries against aggression of Poles and Bolshevik forces on the eastern front. . . . The Germans have in all about 110,000 volunteer troops on the eastern front, and Hindenburg† has just assumed command. They fear, however, that lack of provisions and communications will prevent him from holding out against overwhelming numbers. . . .

At Bremen I got in touch with a number of former submarine captains. . . . One of them had more decorations than anyone, save a bandmaster, that I have ever seen. In addition to the Iron Cross First

---

* Alfred von Tirpitz (1849–1930) was a German naval staff officer and an expert on torpedoes. The grandiose ideas of Tirpitz convinced the Kaiser to invest in a German High Seas Fleet to rival German's traditionally strong army. That investment triggered an Anglo-German naval arms race widely held to be a driving cause of World War I.

† General Paul von Hindenburg (1847–1934) was a German hero after crushing the advancing Russian armies at Tannenburg. After the war he became President of Germany (1925–1934).

Class, he had the "Pour le Merite" and palm, two household orders of the first class, and three other orders I did not recognize. He had made twenty-seven voyages in command of four different submarines, the last two being the U-90 and the U-164. He had spent his entire time in the Irish Sea. He appeared entirely frank, and though some of his guesses missed, I felt confident he was telling the truth. My first question was what antisubmarine measures of ours he had feared the most and which had been most effective. He said that at first all submarine captains were afraid the aircraft would sight the sub and warn the convoy. Experienced skippers who kept their heads could get away from them. Destroyers, like almost everyone else, made the mistake of setting their depth charges for too great depths. His own invariable method was to dive to thirty feet, go ahead full speed with small rudder for about twenty minutes, then run up his periscope for a quick look around and maneuver according to what he saw. On one voyage he counted 164 depth charges, none of which had injured him in the slightest. When asked about the effect of depth charges on morale of the sub crew, he said unless explosives were very close no one but the man at the hydrophone knew anything about them. After the first few attacks, the men got sort of used to them and noted them only for the purpose of making notches on a swab handle. (I cannot help feeling this was simply superlative bravado!) On earlier cruises he had not allowed the hydrophone man to sing out when depth charges were dropped, but on later cruises he allowed the hydrophone man to sing out for every explosion; the crew did not mind, he said. He was of the impression that we used depth charges of two sizes, fifty and a hundred, and said they ought to have been much larger! (We used three hundred-pound charges.)

He said what had really gotten his nerve was when he was chased by three motorboats that looked like submarines. (Obviously our subchasers! Hurrah for them!) They followed him for over an hour, but he doubled back and passed right under them, and was lucky he had turned, because a little later they dropped a number of bombs. . . . When attacked by vessels using hydrophones, silent speed was to be used, but no submarine had been able to get more than four knots at silent speed—and that only when everything was in perfect condition. Experiments were in hand, he understood, to get more speed in silent running. . . .

The greatest danger from depth-charge attacks was when green skippers got panicky and dived too deep. Later German U-boats have to dive at a fairly steep angle (15 degrees), and so it often happened that panicky skippers went down too far and too quickly and consequently got caught by depth charges with deep settings; or, when they heard charges exploding near them they made the mistake of keeping on and so got into great depths. He himself had made that mistake on the U-71. He had been following a convoy on the surface at full-speed for about two hours. He dived deep as soon as he delivered his attack, and when attacked by the escorting destroyer he went to too great a depth. During his long run to get into position for the attack, his exhaust pipe had gotten so hot that when he had got down to a great depth he took on water in such great quantities he had to come to the surface immediately. That time he needed luck and lots of it, and he had it in bunches; when he came up, the destroyer was beating it at four bells in the opposite direction and did not notice him, although he was close at hand. There was a mist at the time, so a few seconds were enough to save him. . . . Giving away his location by using wireless did not worry this skipper in the slightest. He knew about English wireless direction finders but considered that to have his location spotted simply meant a destroyer would arrive some hours after he had been there; that bothered him not at all. About the beginning of November, it suddenly flashed across his mind that the German point of view about wireless was wrong after all, because giving away the location of U-boats, not dangerous to U-boats themselves, enabled the Allies to route convoys to avoid U-boats. He knew of no U-boats with underwater wireless, although he had heard of experiments along that line. They had habitually signaled up to thirteen miles by means of the hydrophone.

He was attacked once by an American submarine off the west coast of Ireland. The American sub fired two torpedoes, both missing narrowly, by less than ten feet. . . . American subs dived quicker than U-boats. He could never be sure of diving to twenty feet in less than forty-five seconds and it often took a minute. . . . He considered it useless to fire a torpedo at anything more than 600 yards away, and if he had the chance he got to within 300 yards. He had been attacked by gunfire twice when within 200 yards of a ship, but the guns could not be depressed far enough and shots went over him. He had been saved more than once by slowness of trawlers and destroyers in dropping depth charges. . . .

The largest submarines carried a complement of six officers; a captain and two deck officers, a chief engineer, and two engineer watch officers, the latter two usually being warrants. The captain did all the navigating and bothered himself not at all about the engines. The officer of the watch always took charge of the diving and completed it before turning over to the captain in case of emergency.

The German navy is finished, finished far more effectively than if every officer and man and ship had been sunk. With the exception of the U-boat men, the navy and everyone in it is in disgrace. The U-boat men were loyal throughout all the revolution and are loyal to the central government today, but even they are ashamed of the navy and now wear soldiers' uniforms. Hardly anywhere does one see a sailor in uniform. So thoroughly is the shame of the navy felt that the blue uniform is considered almost a badge of disgrace, and except for the uniforms of men on the few ships still in commission one never sees any blue, although the streets are crowded with thousands of men in the forestry gray of the infantry. . . .

One finds hardly any interest in the future of the navy and the surrendered U-boats and ships interned in England [at Scapa Flow]. . . . It seems perfectly obvious to Germans that the Allies will make them pay to the limit of their capability, because it appears to them self-evident that if they had won they would have made the rest of us pay right up to the verge of bankruptcy. And every minute I am in Germany makes me realize, more thoroughly than the whole war has done, that if the Germans had won they would have made us sweat blood and sweat blood and sweat blood until there was no more to sweat. This feeling is being so thoroughly ground into me that at times I almost want to fall on my knees in the middle of the street and thank God for the victory. And all that the Germans are servile and boot licking now simply makes one the more certain of how arrogant they would have been were the present situation reversed. There is no doubt the German leaders understand Germany has been licked; neither is there any doubt that the people in general do not understand it and everything is being done to keep them from understanding it. The more one sees of Germany and the Germans, the more certain does one become that all our talk about German character having changed and Germans beginning to realize civilization has gone too far to revert to "Frightfulness" is without any foundation. Germans realize they have made mistakes, but their idea is simply that military blunders were made; they believe in frightfulness as thoroughly today as they ever did. The only thing that could bring home the real truth to Germans is that they once feel the bitterness of a real defeat. They do not feel that now; for their sakes as well as that of the rest of the world it appears necessary they be made to feel it. Their only idea of defeat is that military blunders and bolshevism turned a long succession of victories into a defeat of the military forces. . . .

All Germans agree that [the Kaiser] was weak about use of gas.

They say he had forbidden use of gas but was overruled by the military. No one thinks use of gas was wrong, though quite a good number think it was foolish to start off on a small scale. If the Kaiser had allowed use of gas on the tremendous scale the General Staff wanted at the beginning, they would have won the war before the Allies had gotten gas masks. It is also said the Kaiser opposed air raids on undefended towns in England but was overruled by the General Staff. I have heard a great many criticisms of the German chemists who could not discover a noninflammable gas for Zeppelins, while American chemists did.

Great preparations are being made for an enormous emigration to the United States. Strangely enough, this is being encouraged by the authorities. Their idea is that if they lose their colonies and the greater part of their former markets, Germany will not be able to support the present population, and that the first need for Germany is opening new markets. Accordingly, people are being told the best way to serve the Vaterland is to go to the Americas and there open markets for German goods by the simple process of buying only things "Made in Germany." If immigration is unrestricted in the United States there is no doubt the Germans are coming over in millions.[1]

— ❧ —

After receiving this letter, Adm. William S. Sims, commander of U.S. naval forces operating in European waters, wrote to Koehler:

> My opinion of the value and the interest of this letter is such that . . . I have had it mimeographed for circulation among our forces here.
>
> I am also sending copies to the O.N.I. [Office of Naval Intelligence] and to certain officers in the Navy Department. . . .
>
> As you doubtless know, I have in the past spent many years as naval attaché and as intelligence officer in collecting information, but, unfortunately, I never was able to develop the faculty of observation to anything like the extent that you have shown in the letter.
>
> This is of course a valuable quality for a naval officer and should be given every opportunity for further development.
>
> I should be glad if, as opportunity offers, you would continue similar observations and send them in to headquarters.[2]

Koehler continued his inspection tour in Hamburg.

Hamburg, Germany
24 February 1919

In those questions on which the United States has taken a different stand than the Allies, Germans attribute it to a latent friendship for

Germany—a friendship somewhat disturbed these last years but that still exists. It is difficult to point out that the attitude of the U.S. is not that of favoring Germany but simply the earnest desire to do the right thing and bring about a peace that does not contain in the very peace terms the germs of another war. That the U.S. took none of the surrendered U-boats is well known in Germany and considered a good omen that the U.S. has no desire to take anything from Germany. Extreme bitterness toward the English seems to be lost in their greater hatred of France. They say France has only one idea of peace—to ruin Germany utterly—and the only thing that can keep France from doing this is the British sense of fair play and this latent friendship of America. . . .

A restaurant manager asked the same question that greeted us on all sides: how soon American tourists might be expected in Germany. . . . He was surprised when I mentioned it seemed likely the places to which Americans would flock after peace had been declared were the battlefields at Ypres, the Somme, and Château-Thierry, and not the spas of Germany. . . .

It is not difficult to get inaccurate impressions of the scarcity of food. I heard several of our officers and men mention they had seen dog meat and dog sausages for sale in shops at Hamburg and Bremerhaven. I insisted this was not possible, but they insisted they had seen such placards announcing dog meat for sale and had seen the sausages. I was finally led to a shop where the placard in question was triumphantly pointed out. The sign read "Kaninchen Wurst." He knew that "kanine" meant dog and "wurst" meant sausage and thereby followed the deduction the sausages were of dog meat. Though this officer spoke some German, he apparently did not know that "Kaninchen" happens to be German for rabbit. . . .

On occasion of our sports held on Washington's birthday, the most interested spectators were German soldiers and sailors, who peered through openings in the storehouses on the dock alongside which the ship was lying. I took the opportunity to talk with the more intelligent of them and asked what they thought of our sports. One of the German petty officers broke in with a remark that if the Germans had had games and sports to keep up their interest when they had no work they would never have succumbed to the disaffection that resulted in a revolution; only this disaffection and resultant revolution had kept Germans from going on to Calais when they broke through on the western front last March. He added that if they had kept on through the hole, nothing could have stopped them, for the war would have been over before the great masses of Americans came over and took up the fight with all the enthusiasm the Germans themselves had when they started but that no one could keep for four years. . . . The one fact that stood out clearest to them in all the chaos of the last four months was that there was no wickedness nor any nefarious idea that would not spring from men who were idle. In connection with the remark that they had no games in the German navy, I remarked it was always a matter of comment on our part that every German ship was equipped with parallel bars and similar athletic outfits. . . . This, they answered scornfully, was only another form of drill, which, if possible, was duller and of less interest than any other of this ceaseless round. . . . The sight of our games during Washington's birthday celebration made a more profound effect on the German soldiers and sailors who watched us than any other event or circumstance connected with our stay.[3]

Wilhelmshaven, Germany
16 June 1919

Conditions at Wilhelmshaven were materially the same as during our last visit, but I noticed a distinct improvement in discipline. A few of the German light cruisers are in full commission for duty as minesweepers and communication with the German ships interned in England. Conditions on board these ships are much more nearly normal than three months ago, and the mean appear much happier and more contented than on the ships where there is no discipline. The first effect of a lack of discipline on board ship is the ship rapidly becomes filthy and with it the men. Their self-respect goes and with it every restraining influence; utter chaos results. But now officers feel that in the navy they have been through their worst as regards discipline, for the men realize not only that they cannot get along without their officers, but that life under the conditions they have made for themselves is nothing short of hellish. There are no more soldiers' or sailors' councils, and though it will undoubtedly take years again to build the esprit of the navy, there is no doubt that the reaction has set in. . . . Although they still speak of the "disgrace of the navy," numerous shop windows contained postcards showing the interned German fleet at Scapa. I must confess that I cannot interpret the trait of character this illustrates. . . .

As usual the bookshops contained an enormous number of new pamphlets. The last time I was here I could not find a single pamphlet in defense of the Kaiser, von Tirpitz, or Ludendorf,* but this time the

---

* Erich Ludendorf (1865–1937) was Hindenburg's chief of staff during the Battle of Tannenburg and later planned much of Germany's World War I strategy.

number of books and pamphlets in defense of the Kaiser and von Tirpitz was especially noticeable as they were conspicuously displayed in all shop windows. All bookshops contained a list for subscriptions to Ludendorf's memoirs, which are due to appear on July 1, and I was told that the list of subscribers exceeded that of any book ever published in Germany. Series of pamphlets were entitled "Hints for Emigrants," "Helpful Guide for the Intending Emigrants," and "Why We Should Emigrate and Where To." One of the most interesting pamphlets was entitled "How We Are to Regain our Lost Wealth."

The whole harbor of Kiel was filled with decaying men-of-war. It is almost impossible to conceive how complete is the ruin that comes to men-of-war in just a few months of neglect, for these splendid ships of only six months ago are even now almost beyond recall. . . .

The first step in undermining discipline was withdrawal of the best young officers from the fleet to man the U-boats. For this service only the best young officers were taken at first, but the drafts soon became so frequent that by the beginning of 1918 the fleet was practically without any of its younger officers of the regular navy. Their places were taken by retired officers who had been in the reserve and by petty officers who were given commissions from the ranks. At the same time, all the older petty officers were drafted from the fleet for U-boat service, and their places were taken by newly promoted seamen. The fleet was then filled with the latest drafts of recruits, all of whom were very young, and with old men who have outlived their usefulness on board ship. When such a motley assembly is in the charge of retired officers who have lost touch with the navy and men promoted from the ranks who lack experience handling men and for whom the men have no respect, we have the most frightful state of affairs it is possible to have in military service. The higher officers were entirely out of touch with their men, and the men had for their immediate superiors incompetent officers who likewise were out of touch with higher officers. The men were cooped up on ship, with nothing but drill to keep them busy (and there is always a definite limit to the amount of drill that can be given to men to any advantage). It was all a state of conditions that could lead to only one end—mutiny. So collapse of the German fleet is not to be wondered at. On the contrary, it appears remarkable it did not happen sooner. . . .

Almost everywhere in Germany, I heard a good deal of discussion concerning the policies of Bismarck and comment to the effect that whenever Germany had departed from these policies she had gone wrong. Bismarck is quoted as having advised an entente with Russia and Japan, and the great advisability of such an entente is mentioned on almost all occasions when the future of Germany is discussed. Of course this is at present mere talk, but the only occasion on which I have seen a German kindle with the old enthusiasm has been when the discussion was on this project. The question of the union with German Austria seems to be receiving less attention than it did three months ago, but it appears more than likely it will be revived before long. The question of Poland and the so-called Polish aggression still looms large in the German mind and leaves no doubt in my own as to what would happen to Poland the very first time that Germany had a chance at it.[4]

— ❧ —

Less than a week after Koehler wrote this report, the Germany navy, in an act of supreme defiance against the dictated terms of peace, scuttled most of its ships interned at Scapa Flow. The peace treaty itself was signed finally on 28 June.

A month later, the Weimar Constitution was adopted, which established the new German Republic. In September, a German Workers' party of little note inducted its seventh member, a fanatical Austrian-born German nationalist and incoherent anti-Semite. Adolf Hitler was unalterably opposed to Weimar and the "betrayal" of Germany at Versailles.

Paris, France
4 July 1919

Arrived at Wilhelmshaven about noon [Sunday, 29 June 1919], and immediately put ashore and began the inspection. . . . All Germany and particularly naval officers are jubilant about the sinking of the German ships at Scapa Flow. I gathered that the reason none of the ships remaining in Germany, still to be surrendered to the Allies, were sunk was simply because the Germans did not wish to block up their own waterways; and I have a very strong feeling that the Scapa Flow incident will be duplicated in some form when the remaining ships are turned over, unless we take very definite steps to prevent this. . . .

Everywhere in Germany I heard the cry against the clause in the peace terms that provides for the trial of the Kaiser and others responsible for the war. The former officers base all their outcries on the ground that it is an insult to the nation. But I suspect that a good many of these outcries were based on dread that they or some other of their U-boat colleagues might themselves be called before the tribunal. However, I also heard a number of merchants, who in no way could be personally affected by this clause, refer to it as the bitterest and the most cruel stipulation in any treaty in all history. . . .

I had not been many minutes in Berlin before I came across signs of the recent upheaval, first in the scarred walls of the police station, then in the bullet marks and broken doors of the palace. Even the great cathedral showed traces of vandalism—the doors had been smashed in. Berlin was in the throes of a transportation strike, and no trams, buses, or conveyances except a few antidiluvian carriages could be seen. There were no disturbances, but . . . food is more scarce in Berlin than any city I have ever visited, and [this] again demonstrates the unequal food distribution in Germany. . . . The most conspicuous thing in Berlin is the Hindenburg statue, and though a few of its many thousand nails have been pulled out, it is still remarkably impressive in its position at the head of Sieges Allee, which it so completely dominates. In Berlin I again heard the echo of the report that Italy was seeking a rapprochement with Germany. . . .

On the journey from Berlin to Dusseldorf an elderly man and his wife came into my compartment and asked me various questions about general conditions in England and America and talked to me at some length on numerous subjects. He appeared to be a man of some importance judging from the very marked deference with which he was treated by all the railroad officials. As the train filled, other passengers required the space in the compartment where he had left his luggage, so he turned to his wife and suggested that she get their baggage and bring it into the compartment where they now were. She promptly got up and a few minutes later returned with a number of small handcases, which I then helped her to stow in the racks, her husband meanwhile continuing calmly to smoke his cigar, although he appeared momentarily somewhat surprised when I got up to help his wife. He appeared unusually broadminded for a German and discussed numerous questions with a very real and very keen intelligence. Finally he turned to me and asked what it was that had made Germans so generally disliked and even hated; he added that when all the world was bitter against the Germans one could not help feeling that there must be some very definite and fundamental reasons for it. The frankness of the question rather staggered me for a moment, but he was evidently so much in earnest that I answered him. I said I thought the fundamental reason for it was perhaps best illustrated by his attitude to his wife just a few minutes previously when he had remained in his seat because it was the most comfortable place, while his wife got up from her less comfortable seat to bring in the baggage. He seemed not a little surprised at my comment, so I enlarged somewhat on our idea of the German character; for instance, that the German father would work and slave in order to provide every possible advantage for his children, such as music lessons and better schooling, and would otherwise make efforts for them that would in most countries be considered quite beyond his capacity. On the other hand, he would be unutterably rude to his children, and no matter how much he might love them at heart, his manners to them, as to his wife, would be execrable. I continued that we felt the German was a bully in his home, because he was master there; and in the same way, the reason the Junker officers had been bullies was because they had been the masters in their country; so it came about that the reason the world would not and could not accept German rule was they realized that once the Germans were masters they would also be unutterably arrogant bullies. I added that I had given this opinion only because he had asked for it, and as he obviously knew Germans better than I did, he must know best whether or not my opinion was accurate. It was quite some time before he answered and then he said the German women were brought up in that way and that they liked it. I then asked whether he really thought his wife had liked dragging in the baggage and whether he really thought that one of the commonest sights in Germany, namely that of the wife carrying a child while the husband carried only his cigar, really represented what the wife liked or what the man found most comfortable for himself. I also suggested that he might ask his wife about it, she in the meantime having said not a word, although she looked very thoroughly startled and just a little frightened. But all at once she spoke up, and then there was no doubt at all about her idea of the matter, for she poured forth all that she and about all the other women in Germany thought about it. She ended with many blushes and said that although it was perhaps true that women liked to be mastered by men, the pleasure of such mastery was confined to a few very private moments and in no way applied to the daily manners of life—to such incidents as getting the baggage or carrying the baby while the husband puffed a cigar. It was again a long time before the man replied and then he said that it was a difficult point of view for a German to get but that perhaps there was something in it after all. At any rate he added, there must be something radically wrong in a system that had brought on its followers the hatred and condemnation of the whole world; which comment convinced me that he was the greatest German I had ever known and that if he could persuade his countrymen of the truth of his idea, he alone was worth more to his country than all the millions of the war indemnity.[5]

During this inspection duty, when the commission reached Hamburg on the British cruiser *Coventry*, the English officers did not wish to go ashore—the city was under martial law, machine guns were every-where, and Koehler was warned to stay aboard the ship. Hugo, how-ever, was not about to sit on the *Coventry* when stories were to be had ashore. With notebooks and pencils in hand, he and his newly acquired yeoman, Walter Dring, strolled down the gangplank and walked to the gate of the Hamburg-American Line pier. As Dring recalled later, they pushed through a crowd clamoring for sugar and cigarettes to the main street of the city. The commotion attracted attention from two M.P.'s cruising along in a three-wheeled motorcycle. Koehler tried to explain, but the M.P.'s hauled the two of them to headquarters, where three German admirals lined up to question them.*

Koehler explained about the *Coventry* being the first inspection ship to arrive in Hamburg after the treaty of peace was signed, adding that the British officers preferred to remain aboard and that only he and Dring had landed.

The British would not come ashore! The Germans loved that, Dring remembered, and gave permission for the American navy spy and his scribe to go about Hamburg as they pleased. That was hardly good enough for Koehler, who asked for and received permission to go to Berlin by the night train, provided the pair remain locked in their compartment all night.

At 7 A.M., they arrived as the first Allied officers in Berlin. Koehler flipped a coin to decide who would be the first American to set foot in the city, but they "both landed on the platform at the same time in a heap."

Koehler hailed a cab—an emaciated horse, wheels with iron rims, no leather, no rubber—and told the driver to take them to the Adlon Hotel. There he asked for Louis Adlon, and Koehler and Adlon remi-nisced about the times before the war when Koehler had stayed there with his grandfather. They gave Adlon two bars of chocolate, soap, and some cigarettes.

After breakfast, their sightseeing was interrupted by three policemen who took them back to the Adlon. With no papers to show but their orders from London, they were ordered to take the six o'clock train out of Berlin. Koehler had no intention of going back to the *Coventry*, so instead he took Dring to the best hotel in Dusseldorf.

After Dusseldorf they boarded a train to Hanover, then went on to Cologne, where Koehler said he must speak to British officers of the

---

* According to Dring, the three admirals were von Scheer, von Reuter, and von Hipper (*Memoir*, p. 86).

army of occupation. The officers appeared and promptly locked them up, convinced Koehler and Dring were spies. Complained Dring, "Hugo looked like the Kaiser with that damn little mustache." Koehler told them to call the First Lord of the Admiralty, as well as the American Embassy, and offered them chocolate and cigarettes. Shortly the British officers received this directive: "Release these two men, apologize, and see that their plans are expedited."

Once released, they took a train to Brussels and Paris. On arrival in Paris, Koehler said he was "going to duck for three or four hours before reporting to the embassy." Dring was left to face the Red Cross in the Gare du Nord. He was hungry and stood in line with officers and men waiting for breakfast. He was questioned and replied that he had just come from Germany. Red Cross officials were unable to believe he had really come from Germany, so M.P.'s, sure he was a spy, arrested him again. He continued hungry.

Dring finally reached the American Embassy, where they asked, Where is Koehler? The Commander showed a few days later and wrote his report on conditions inside Germany. On 7 July, the adventure over, Dring was ordered back to London.[6] Before he left, Dring introduced Koehler to Admiral Newton McCully, who had recently arrived from operations off north Russia.

In Paris, Koehler became aide to McCully, the senior U.S. Naval member of the American Peace Commission. On 6 August, Koehler was sent on another tour of Germany, this time a rudimentary inspection of floating dry docks. Before he returned to Paris, the Commander was called to London to present a briefing on conditions inside Germany to Winston Churchill at the War Ministry.[7]

The peace negotiations themselves were moving rapidly into dry dock, and working for the diplomats at the Crillon was doing little to improve Koehler's mordant worldview.

"I used to think that if there was anything particularly outstanding in my makeup it was that I was a confirmed optimist," he wrote to his mother,

but somehow or other my greatest difficulty here has been to keep from becoming a hopeless pessimist. Of course, if one keeps one's eyes open here one simply cannot help knowing the details and the real facts of just about all the many questions that are troubling the world just now. And unfortunately, to see the new statesmanship and diplomacy at close range is frightfully disheartening. This is simply the battleground of greedy and unutterably selfish interests, made still more distasteful by the fact that they are invariably presented in the light of high ideals and altruism. I know there is much dissatisfaction in America because it is felt that some of our representatives at Paris have been led by the nose . . . but still I think that about the most hopeful sign is that our people have not been so beastly self-seeking and greedy and grasping as have practically all other diplomats here. . . . But I had better leave this subject alone because it always makes me rather pessimistic, and I'll try to stick to the more general news, which even if it isn't very cheerful at least isn't so actively depressing as is the thought of what was really in the backs of the minds of the men who had the most to do with this document that is to be the world's guide in the next generations. . . .

I really think that the most popular country with the peace conference just now is Germany—in the first place because the Germans make no insistent demands for an indemnity for Germany or for a slice of Germany or Austria, and in the second place because Germany is the only country in Europe that has really settled down to sawing wood. . . .

About three times a day I hear a tremendous rattle at the other end of my corridor, which announces that the prime minister of Poland has arrived; and a few minutes later M. Paderewski,* with hair a good deal sparser on top but ever more flowing neckwards, comes steaming down the corridor followed by two clanking orderlies, who have developed the art of coming down on their heels so as to make a tremendous racket, to a higher point than ever yet attained by any other two men. He haunts the Crillon and the Quai D'Orsay, and the cooler his welcome the more assiduous his attendance. Poor Poland is spending an enormous lot more on her army than she could afford if all her industries were going full blast and everything was rosy. So like her neighbors, she is living on loans, the printing press, and on the dread that the Allies have of the complications that would result from still another revolution. . . . [Paderewski] is a very decent fellow, but it is wasteful to spoil a good pianist to make a bad politician.[8]

— ❧ —

It is easy to read here just how much Koehler longed to return to his duties with the American fleet: yet it was not to be. Civil War was raging in Russia, and, as we shall see, Admiral McCully was the best "Russia man" in the Navy: he was ordered to go there and find out

---

* Ignace Jan Paderewski (1860–1941), concert pianist and Polish statesman, led the new republic in 1919, as well as the Polish government in exile, 1940–41. His remains lie in a chamber at Arlington National Cemetery in Washington, D.C., awaiting burial in "free" Poland.

6. Hugo Koehler, at the time of the mission to South Russia, 1920. (Photo by Bill Warren; photo courtesy of Clarkson N. Potter.)

what was going on. Once more, destiny found Koehler with the right person at the right time.

Koehler and McCully journeyed from Paris to Constantinople on their way to south Russia. For the admiral the trip was routine, but for Koehler it offered another opportunity to flay the more fulsome Europeans he met, as this excerpted account of part of their journey describes.

"The Peace Commission shut up shop on December 10th when all hands left Paris," Koehler wrote to his mother, "all others proceeding to the United States and Admiral McCully (my chief) and I on to London." (They later took a train from Paris to Italy, boarding a steamship there for Greece.) "In Corfu," he continued,

I gathered that the English had done much for it during their occupation. So had the Turks; but the Greeks—nothing at all. The Achilleion, the ex-Kaiser's villa just outside of Corfu, has been taken over by Greeks. They, in true Greek fashion, charge five drachmas admission but let the place go to rack and ruin. The gardens are exquisite, and the house—built by the former Austrian Empress—is pleasant, but some of the Kaiser's improvements are a bit doubtful, as, for example, the decoration of the dining room ceiling, which consists of numerous cupids blowing soap bubbles—said soap bubbles being opalescent electric lights.

From Corfu, we left for Patras, a dull and flourishing city on the shores of a beautiful bay encircled by gentle purples and grays of hills and snowcapped mountains beyond. Small wonder Byron loved it. It inspired his struggle for Greece, for he lived on the opposite shore— near enough to see all the beauty of the bay, not too close to the city and the modern Greek. . . . Its principal monument is the ruin of an old Turkish fort on the crest of a hill holding a magnificent view across the bay toward Byron's valley. In the rear of the fort are ruins of a Roman aqueduct. The few remaining chambers of the fort are still packed with Bulgarian prisoners of war, guarded by soldiers whose rifles are choked with rust and mud. The German blood of the former queen is shown by her experiments in forestry, which though only recently undertaken, met with considerable success, as thick pine growth covers some of the usually barren hills. Several old mosques were shorn of their minarets and converted into Greek churches. I attended a Greek service, which I understood not at all, since my ancient Greek—of which I was once proud—helps me not at all, except with street signs. I was somewhat bewildered by the continual crossing of the breast, the increasing stream of prayers *en haute voix* and the kissing of numerous pictures of saints and icons in gold and silver plate. Outside of the church, in the middle of the square surrounded by the graceful pepper trees so plentiful here, a bagpiper was holding forth. . . . (Our idea that bagpipers are suffered only by the Scotch is not entirely accurate.) The very popular debtor's prison nearby seemed to appreciate this exotic noise. . . .

Here, as elsewhere in Greece, coffeehouses were innumerable, all crowded with Greeks busy at the national sport of gorging themselves with inexpressibly sweet sweets and fondling beads. These beads illustrate the temper of modern Greeks, for the men, including soldiers and officers, carry these circular strings of beads, which they continually fondle. These are not prayer beads nor counting beads nor ornamental beads; their purpose is solely to be fondled. Greeks apparently do not drink much; their vices are sweets, beads, and inertia. Native wines are very sweet, the most famous being a too-sweet port. Mesticka, a distillate from grape pulp, which resembles absinthe in appearance and slightly in taste, is very popular among the over-gold-laced, bead-fondling young officers. I had hoped that the great popularity of the cafes might be counted for in part by the fact that there is no coal in town and that wood costs five cents gold per pound, but I understand that on the most sweltering hot days the cafes are packed as per routine. As I strolled about in these towns, I was accosted by all sorts of people, disreputably dressed, who ingratiatingly informed me either that they were American citizens or that they were very shortly going to America. I'm afraid my lack of enthusiasm seemed overtly conservative to some of them!

I talked to . . . a professor at the University of Athens, [who] spoke at great length about Greek claims and aspirations, about Greek claims to Smyrna. I asked what these claims were and what they were based on. They were all based on historical reasons, he answered but was vague as to the exact historical reasons. I commented that the principle of territorial aspirations based on so-called historical claims was a delicate question for many of us; on this score England would have historical claims to a large part of the United States, and France and Spain to whatever remained. In the same way, Italy, via Julius Caesar, had historical claims to England, and France, via Napoleon, historical claims on most of Europe, [and] Spain, via Phillip II, etc., etc. My professorial friend became slightly confused but answered that historical claims on Smyrna were different. Just how they were different he could not explain but repeated that they were so. . . . I commented that . . . what Greece needed was raisins rather than historical reasons—raisins and olive oil to pay for her tremendous imports being paid for only by loans and paper. . . . But apparently the Greeks believe that there is no need for such mundane things as raisins and olives while loans are plentiful and they can get flour and automobiles for paper money. . . .

En route to Piraeus, we passed through Corinthian Canal. It is gradually filling up, as no effective means are taken to prevent earth from the side of the cut falling into the canal. As for the most part the cut is through rock, and as the earth is solid, the slide is comparatively very slight and could without too much trouble be prevented from filling the canal. But Greek interests are now political; canals and industries do not interest them. The result is that the canal, originally 26 feet deep, now will not take ships of more than 21 feet draft. In places where the cut is through rock, the surface has been chiseled to imitate stone masonry, but in other places where real stone masonry would have been advisable, nothing has been done. I noted a goat climbing a stone embankment that was precariously near the perpendicular. I would like to believe this a typical example of Greek energy, but it is a better representation of the agility of the late Greek politicians. . . .

Aside from those concerned with the shipping [in Piraeus], everyone else was sitting behind a basket of oranges or alongside a brazier of roasting chestnuts, waiting for customers, or sitting behind a shoe-shining box, waiting for muddy boots. Emphasis on the sitting!

As the day was remarkably clear, I was soon on the Acropolis and enjoying the glorious view. I was much interested in comparatively recent discoveries on the Acropolis of the work of the Pelasgians of about 1200 B.C., work which is easily distinguished by its being entirely of limestone instead of the white marble of the Periclean Age. The Acropolis Museum contained numerous new finds, many of them having been located even since my visit of ten years ago. A considerable quantity of Parthenon material has recently been discovered . . . sufficient of the original material to effect a considerable restoration or a replacement, which would add greatly to the beauty of the Parthenon. My Greek friend answered, yes, undoubtedly, but with a sigh added that Greece was too poor to undertake the work. I could not resist the comment that the cost of the rusty-gunned and over-gold-laced army for even a single month would be more than enough to effect marvels on the Acropolis and would have the additional advantage of removing great numbers of loafers from the streets and wine shops.

Greece is more prosperous than Italy, and though some of the prosperity may be artificial, the Greeks undoubtedly made great earnings during the war, particularly in the merchant marine. Along curbs stand innumerable cabs and new motorcars—mostly American. Fresh paint is in evidence. But I doubt whether any country can long remain prosperous where the greater part of its manpower of all classes of society spends most of its time and apparently all of its energy loafing in coffeehouses and playing with beads. . . .

From Athens we went to Salonica, a purely Turkish city now in Greek hands . . . numberless tall minarets scattered over the city, which crawls irregularly up a gentle slope, a large white Venetian tower in the foreground and an old fort with high-walled enclosures in the hinterground. The harbor was filled with shipping, and again I saw four fine new American merchantmen. In the last six months it has been the exception not to see an American flag whenever I've entered a foreign port from the Baltic to the Aegean. Some ten years ago, I went around the world without seeing a single American merchantman. The British and the French still maintain small forces here. . . . The Greeks have a very large force but still less does anyone know why they are here, except, of course, because of "aspirations on historical grounds." I explored part of the town and found it full of interest and also terrible smells and the mud and filth of ages. . . . As a result of the practically continuous warfare of the last nine years, the entire district along the coast from here to Constantinople, formerly the most productive of all this region, is now practically depopulated. Fields and villages are alike deserted, the people driven out or killed. A tiny green garden and a modest villa on the outskirts of the town is the retreat to which ex-sultan Abdul Hamed had been forced to retire after the last Balkan war. And with only twelve wives to share his troubles! Poor devil! What an anticlimax it must have been, twelve instead of some two hundred and in addition all the first families of Turkey striving to bring up daughters worthy to be added to the collection. This scheme of things is rapidly dying out. But what a shame to see these good old customs perish. I am no Abdul, but just on general principles I hate to see such fine old customs come to an untimely end![9]

— ❧ —

The same jaunt through the Greek isles was described by McCully as follows: "After leaving Brindisi, [our ship] called at Valona, Corfu, Patras, Piraeus, [and] Salonica and arrived Constantinople January 6, 1920. . . . In Greek ports food conditions seemed good, but harbor facilities were congested and labor conditions were difficult. The Greek army is not yet demobilized, and many soldiers were everywhere in evidence, and loafers were numerous."[10]

With descriptive powers of such meager dimensions, it is no wonder the admiral wanted Koehler along to paint the canvas of what they were about to witness in Russia: for if it was not properly recorded, it would never be believed.

3

Novorossisk, Russia

January 1920

We were Americans; and, somehow or other, Americans and Russians seem to get along together splendidly. Whenever I saw Russians and Americans together, in work, in play, in business, they got along splendidly. (January 1920)

Newton McCully, whose Annapolis graduation took place twenty years before Hugo Koehler's, was in important ways Koehler's moral polar opposite. Koehler, in his mad haste to observe and understand *everything*, seemed at times almost analytically fascinated by the cruelty one person, one group, or one nation could inflict upon another. The soft-spoken admiral from South Carolina, on the contrary, was more flesh than steel, more humanitarian than gunboat diplomat. In a world where human beings were rapidly becoming statistical "force structures," where the value of human life was being constantly cheapened, McCully was moved to action by starving children and suffering villagers. He was also arguably the most knowledgeable man in America when it came to Russia and the Russian people.[1]

Lieutenant and assistant naval attaché in St. Petersburg in 1904, McCully traveled from Moscow across Russia to Port Arthur, where he witnessed the Russian Pacific Fleet in operation during the Russo-Japanese War.[2] When Czar Nicholas II abdicated in 1917, Captain McCully, who had returned to St. Petersburg (Petrograd) as naval attaché after the outbreak of the First World War, was the only U.S. official left at the American Embassy who could speak Russian. Through the spring and summer he watched the disintegration of A. F. Kerensky's inept provisional government. In September, McCully was ordered to France for duty. Just weeks later V. I. Lenin and his relatively small group of twenty thousand Bolsheviks seized power, causing affairs in Russia to deteriorate even further and creating problems on two fronts for the western Allies.

First, with Lenin in Moscow, anti-Bolshevik resistance groups began

7. Newton McCully as a Vice Admiral in 1928. (U.S. Naval Historical Center Photograph, neg. no. NH47954.)

to coalesce around former czarist generals Lavr G. Kornilov and Mikhail V. Alekseev. And the still-powerful German army in the east advanced through light resistance, its eye on two million tons of Allied military supplies there, on the north Russian ports of Archangel and Murmansk. The Allies, ostensibly to protect their stockpiles from the Germans, sent warships to the area. As historian Charles Weeks describes:

To carry out this assignment, the senior naval officer in North Russia, British Rear Admiral Thomas W. Kemp, sent 200 British and

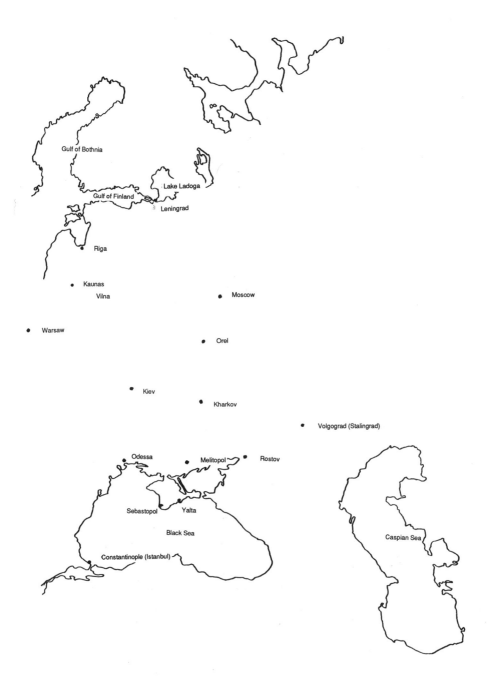

Gulf of Bothnia

Lake Ladoga

Gulf of Finland

Leningrad

Riga

Kaunas

Vilna

Moscow

Warsaw

Orel

Kiev

Kharkov

Volgograd (Stalingrad)

Odessa

Melitopol

Rostov

Sebastopol

Yalta

Black Sea

Constantinople (Istanbul)

Caspian Sea

Map 2   Russia

100 French marines ashore at Murmansk on 9 March 1918, thereby initiating the Allied intervention in the Russian Civil War. By July a state of undeclared war existed between the local anti-Bolshevik governments (supported by the Allies) and the Bolsheviks. In August President Wilson reluctantly approved the dispatch of nearly 4,000 American troops to North Russia solely to protect the military supplies. But once U.S. troops had landed in Archangel, the British high command diverted them to combat areas where they soon suffered casualties. At this point, the Navy Department deemed it necessary to send a flag officer to command American naval forces in North Russia. Again, because of his experience in Russia and familiarity with the language, Newton McCully, who had been advanced to Rear Admiral in September, was selected for duty in Russia.[3]

McCully deftly walked a diplomatic/military tightrope in north Russia. Official instructions stipulated that his naval forces were not to become involved, thus restricting the admiral to the status of an observer. Nevertheless, McCully issued immediate warnings to Washington, pointing out that the reactionary anti-Bolsheviks the Allies were now supporting offered little hope for the suffering Russian peasants and their clamor for a concrete program of land reform, education, and *habeas corpus*. In addition (and more important to Washington), U.S. soldiers, on the verge of mutiny, would soon break into open rebellion if they were not brought home immediately. As a result, by the end of June 1919 the Americans were hastily evacuated but not before ninety-six of them were killed in action against the Bolsheviks and entombed in the frozen Russian earth.[4]

Bolsheviks, however, were seemingly on the march in more places than Murmansk. For some in America in 1919, a "Red Scare" so terrorized the United States that in January 1920 Attorney General A. Mitchell Palmer authorized raids without warrants on private homes and labor groups, resulting in the arrests of thousands of Russian immigrants, many of them refugees who had fled the Bolsheviks. McCully, at the Paris Peace Conference, repeatedly asked his government for humanitarian aid for the Russian people, but given the temper of the times, his pleas for relief supplies were ignored. At this point, he must have welcomed meeting Hugo Koehler, who was in Paris to write dispatches for the Paris diplomats on his wide-ranging inspections of Germany, where after the war a Red revolution had been quickly squelched.

But the Russian storm refused to go away. There, a civil war was being fought, in the words of Richard Luckett, "amongst, and with, the military and political debris of a world war."[5] By late 1917, that scattered debris comprised over five and a half million casualties, including at least one million Russian soldiers killed in action.

On the western front on 11 November 1918, the Germans had finally agreed to an armistice, and then began their long, slow withdrawal from Russia. On the eastern front, however, there was no peace. Throughout the fall and winter of 1918 and into the spring of 1919, Lenin's forces for revolution were under relentless attack from all sides.

In the spring of 1919, the armies of Admiral Kolchak, organizer of the White resistance in Siberia, advanced rapidly toward the Volga. In the north, a Russian general with the unlikely name of Eugene Miller took over the anti-Bolshevik forces and harassed the Reds as far as the approaches to Petrograd. From the west, a small army under Gen. Nikolai Yudenich also advanced on Petrograd, while in south Russia, Gen. Anton Denikin, began to advance on Moscow.

The Allies, with the exception of Winston Churchill at the War Ministry, were loathe to stumble into the Russian pit. Infiltration by Bolshevik agitators was the last thing their armies needed, since many were on the verge of mutiny. It was difficult for those soldiers, men who had just defeated one Kaiser, to understand why they were now being asked to fight against Russians who had just overthrown their own Emperor.

As for the politicians, few quite fathomed the unsettling new power that confronted them from the east, again with the ringing exception of Churchill. The future prime minister declared warnings that were both immediate and explicit. "[Bolsheviks] destroy wherever they exist," he told the House of Commons on 25 March 1919, "but by rolling forward into fertile areas, like the vampire which sucks the blood from its victim, they gain means of prolonging their own baleful existence."[6] The foreign intervention in the Russian Civil War could not have proceeded as far as it did without the British war minister's insistent prodding. As for the rest, however, bolshevism and its murky ideology was and remained an enigma. At the very least, the politicians at the Paris Peace Conference recognized that the many newly independent states needed to be sheltered from the Red wave poised to break over them. Encouraged by the early successes of the White armies in 1919, the Allies backed their efforts to overthrow the Reds. However, at Versailles in May 1919, the extent of the Supreme Council of Allies' recognition of Denikin in south Russia and Kolchak in Siberia was to send them not only obsolete tanks and airplanes but also hundreds of troops, "volunteers" previously marked as unfit for service on the western front.

By seizing the chance to move into the vacuum created by the departed German army in the summer of 1919, newly independent Poland complicated the Russian morass further. Advancing where the Germans had left off, the Poles occupied parts of Lithuania, eastern Galicia, and Ruthenia, before moving against light opposition into the western Ukraine. There, Nestor Makhno, an anarchist brigand with a following of disaffected peasants, was harassing and killing both Red and White troops wherever his men encountered them.

Then almost as suddenly as they had advanced—and nearly simultaneously—the various White resistance factions were beaten back. Trotsky, successful in rebuilding a Russian army the Reds had so assiduously destroyed with the infamous "Order No. 1," took advantage of interior lines of supply and communications and concentrated his forces where the fighting was most intense.

Under pressure to get their troops home, the British withdrew from the north, leaving Miller's army to its fate. Miller himself escaped. Yudenitch pressed into Russia one town too far and the Reds forced him back into the Baltic states, where his army wandered about for a time before disbanding.

To the east, Kolchak's overextended forces were crushed before they reached the Volga and began a tortuous and cruel retreat to Siberia, forced to strip corpses of shoes and clothing along the way. The small American contingent sent by President Wilson to guard the trans-Siberian and protect Czech legion tried to stay out of the line of fire. A larger force of Tommies, freezing alongside the Czechs, retreated, fighting almost as much amongst themselves as with the Bolsheviks. To add to this grim picture, a million refugees were pushed eastward ahead of the retreating White forces.

Within two hundred miles of Moscow, Denikin tried to decide which horse he would ride into the great city when it was captured, but once again, overextended and weary troops were savaged by the Reds, and Denikin's front dissolved in a matter of hours. His troops, driven southward from Orel, were forced to surrender Kharkov to Bolsheviks on 13 December 1919.

Thus began a disastrous retreat by the Whites to the Black Sea and the port of Odessa, and it served them little that along their paths of retreat they committed many small-scale pogroms. The Jews, held to be widely responsible for the spread of bolshevism, were obvious scapegoats for a defeated army. The prominence of several Jews on the

Bolshevik Central Committee only served to confirm White suspicions. Better in deed only were the Allied interventionists. As the Whites retreated, London began to consider renewing ties with the Bolsheviks. Maj. Gen. Sir Alfred Knox, British military representative at Allied headquarters in Siberia, expressed the opinion of Allied and White officers alike when he cabled home that "suddenly the whole of Russia is informed by wireless that her Allies regard the brave men who are here fighting for part of civilization as on a par with the blood-stained, Jew-led Bolsheviks."[7] For the Allies, with no intelligence "assets" inside Soviet Russia, the situation had completely unraveled.

Before bolshevism devoured everything in its path, the United States needed an agent inside Russia as quickly as possible to measure this new malignancy—much as Bruce Lockhart and Sidney Reilly had done for the British. The decision was made to send a special naval intelligence mission to south Russia to link up with Denikin and assess the situation. Its leader would be Admiral McCully.

McCully himself thought he was too old to be chasing around the back end of a shooting war and so requested that Hugo Koehler accompany him to do the legwork. Koehler, whose Russian was limited, then retired from his rounds at the Paris Conference to study Russian language, history, and literature.

On 23 December 1919, Secretary of State Robert Lansing cabled McCully designating him Special Agent of the Department of State and instructing him to proceed with Koehler and a detachment of nine others, "to the south of Russia with a view, first, to make observations and report to this Department upon political and economic conditions in the region visited, and second, to establish informal connection with General Denikin and his associates.

"Admiral McCully had been furnished with a code of the Department of State and has been directed to telegraph directly to this Department. [signed] Robert Lansing."[8]

On New Year's Day, 1920, Koehler and McCully sailed for Salonika aboard the steamer *Karlsbad*. Six days later they arrived in Constantinople. From the American Embassy there, McCully, as we have seen, wrote Lansing a terse, officious three-page report about the journey from Paris. Koehler wrote to his mother.

8 January 1920

Dear Mother:
It is long since I've been able to send you any word except by cable, but you know the trend of events in general at least. We arrived here in

Constantinople just a few hours ago and as it appears that unless we hurry we will arrive in Russia just in time to see the Bolsheviks push Denikin into the Black Sea, we are proceeding immediately. . . . In preparation for Russia, I've let my beard grow, and find that it is much more gray and white than brown! I've rather suspected that each day was costing me a week, but all this white hair reminded me of it rather forcibly. . . . We did not choose this time, just before Christmas, because we thought it would be particularly pleasant to spend Christmas and New Year's on a dusty train, but because we wanted to get to Russia as soon as possible."[9]

— ❦ —

McCully and Koehler were in the Black Sea port of Novorossisk by 21 January, and by the end of the month, they had met with General Denikin. January had not been a happy month for the White general and his Volunteer Army. After the defeat at Orel, one town after another had fallen to the Reds. Refugees flooded the south Russian Black Sea ports. Denikin, who had never doubted his eventual success, had made no provision to embark them; refugees, crowded along the quays and certain of their fate under the Bolsheviks, committed suicide in panic.

The U.S. mission met also with Baron Peter Wrangel, the brilliant young White general. There were many in south Russia calling on Wrangel to save them both from the Bolsheviks and from Denikin's inept leadership. Wrangel, however, feuding with and unwanted by Denikin, resigned and with his chief of staff departed Russia for Constantinople.

Koehler described the U.S. mission's first days in Novorossisk.

We took quarters here in an old second-class railway coach in a corner of the railway yards, and although it was about the filthiest place I had ever seen, it was also about the most favorable situation in town. Our neighbors, also in coaches and abandoned freight cars, were beggars and princes, ragged refugees, Grand Dukes who had lost everything they owned except their ballet dancers and a few jewels, railroad officials, a few stray Grand Duchesses, and more refugees, so bruised and beaten by all that they had suffered these last months they seemed mere lumps. Poor devils, what could they have done to deserve all this! Their sins were surely not positive and active—they had not really done anything definite that deserved so horrible a fate—their sins were almost entirely sins of omission; it must be they had sinned simply in not taking steps necessary to prevent all this. There was much food for thought through all this misery and ruin, through cattle cars crowded with sick, dying, and sometimes even the dead, all sprawling on un-speakably filthy floors in station rooms and halls and corridors of prac-tically every public building. Hotels, hospitals, stables, stores, and bar-racks were crowded to the very doorsills with sick, dying, and those about to die, simply because they could not fit into the existing order of things. All had a patience so exquisite it was maddening more than pathetic. . . .

Our nearest neighbor in the squalid freight yard was the former president of the Vladikavkaz Railroad, the best system in Russia, who, with his children and grandchildren, occupied one small coach. Grand Duchess Marie Pavlovna* with members of her former suite and their families also had a single coach, while her son, Grand Duke Andrey,† with his son of oddly indefinite parentage and said son's mother, a famous ballerina in her day, likewise lived for months in a tiny railroad coach on the opposite side of our mudhole. The Grand Duchess was a charming lady, nor did the terror of her situation and the utter squalor of our surroundings take one whit from her delightful sense of humor and her quality of *une grande dame*.

Novorossisk marked a definite change in my point of view. Re-turning from a visit to Grand Duchess Olga, the czar's sister, a very nice, simple, and gentle lady, I picked my way through the mud and filth, and commented feelingly on the terrible tragedy of this poor old

---

* "Born Princess Maria of Mecklenberg-Schwerin . . . she was known after her mar-riage as the Grand Duchess Maria Pavlovna (or sometimes simply as the Grand Duchess Vladimir [after her husband, Vladimir, brother of Alexander III, the czar who was suc-ceeded to the throne by Nicholas II]). It was said that as a young girl in Germany she caught sight of the eligible Russian prince and never stopped pleading and intriguing until Alexander III forced his brother to end his carefree pleasures and marry her. Her unprecedented refusal to convert to Orthodoxy then greatly angered the tsar, who also found her overbearing intellectually and socially. . . .

"The grand ducal couple had four children between 1876 and 1882, Cyril, Boris, Andrew, and Helen. . . .

"The Grand Duchess . . . had spent harrowing days in peasant disguise in the Cau-casus during the Revolution. Having proudly refused rescue by her Rumanian relatives, she found herself fleeing Russia with her sons, Boris and Andrew. [It was at this moment that Koehler met her in the "mudhole" in Novorossisk.] . . . The onetime brilliant leader of St. Petersburg society stepped from the train [in Switzerland] a ragged scarecrow of a woman, and Maria Pavlovna died soon after in 1920" (John D. Bergamini, *The Tragic Dynasty: A History of the Romanovs* [New York, 1969], pp. 374, 463; hereafter cited as *Tragic Dynasty*).

† "Andrew [Andrey in Russian] at last married the mistress he had shared with [Nicholas II], Matilda Kshessinska, in Cannes in 1921" (*Tragic Dynasty*, p. 463). Andrey died in 1956.

lady who had spent her life at court, everyone bowing abjectly before her. Now her court was reduced to a single, feeble old servant, who still addressed her mistress as "Imperial Highness" as she laid before her the proceeds of the last visit to the pawnbrokers.[10] Later that evening, discussing the situation, the whole company expatiated loudly upon the tragedy of the poor Grand Dukes who were now living pathetic existences, with no suite and only a single pair of servants—and no amusements, no diversions! All the fine times they used to have! Oh! it was terrible, terrible! So echoed one and all. Then suddenly the folly of it all came over me and I suffered a complete revulsion of feeling. Why was her case, or that of the Grand Dukes and other former great personages now idle in Novorossisk or in comparative ease in various capitals of Europe, so much more tragic than the thousands of other Russians suffering much greater hardships in their attempts really to do something for Russia? A look of startled horror came over the company. The only tragedy of the Grand Duchess Olga, I said, was she was an old lady separated from her family, many of whom had suffered a still unkinder fate. Except for that she was not deserving of greater sympathy than all these other people who were suffering more, even if the contrast with their past was not as great.

As for the Grand Dukes, with one or two rare exceptions, they had never done one useful thing for themselves or their race or their country. Had they not helped to bring about this very state of affairs of which they complained so tearfully? With a single exception, had one ever heard of a Grand Duke going out to fight for his country? Did one know of a Grand Duke ever doing anything except to become more profligate and a greater waster? Had any ever contributed a single idea that helped country or civilization or any of the people on whom they battened fat? In a torrent of passion I recounted the various things I knew of these Grand Dukes, facts far from secret among these people who knew them better than I did. Nor did I omit the account little Lupokova, the famous Russian dancer, had given me of orgies each year when the famous Kojinska, a former dancer, would give a party at her palace for young girls of the imperial ballet school who had finished their training; girls raised almost as in a convent and then turned over to the Grand Dukes—nothing more than throwing children to the wolves. Of course, this was all true, they said, but what will one have? These wolves were after all Grand Dukes; and even my friends looked at me with mixed surprise and horror—surprise, because what did I expect of Grand Dukes? Did I not know what a Grand Duke was? They wondered how a man with such unorthodox ideas ever arrived in their august assembly. This was a pernicious form of anarchy, they felt. With such ideas I must be as dangerous as if I carried a bomb.

We delayed little in Novorossisk and hurried to Ekaterinodar, capital of the Don Cossack province and General Denikin's headquarters.[11] We saw the general almost immediately, and after a long interview, during which the general explained his ideas frankly, we dined with him. He and his numerous staff and friends were extraordinarily cordial. This welcome was not only pleasant, it was also prophetic of the Russian attitude toward us during the year to follow. Although Russians are the most hospitable race under the sun, their attitude toward us seemed more than cordiality, for even from the beginning their friendliness had a naturalness and spontaneity that betokened a real understanding. This was due in large part to the fact that we were Americans; and, somehow or other, Americans and Russians seem to get along together splendidly. Whenever I saw Russians and Americans together, in work, in play, in business, they got along splendidly; more than can be said for most other Russian-foreign combinations.

There were many examples of this fact. For instance, the British were pouring millions of pounds sterling worth of supplies into south Russia to support Denikin; in fact, they were almost the entire support of the Denikin effort. There was a large British mission, political and military, with Denikin, and the hundreds of British officers were splendid fellows—I have rarely seen a finer lot of soldiermen. But still, save in exceptional cases, they never seemed to get along at all well with the Russians. This is not the fault of either the British or the Russians; it is merely a fact.

Nor were the French particularly successful with the Russians. Although many more Russians spoke French than spoke English, one rarely saw French and Russians together—they had little in common. Next to Americans, Italians mixed with Russians better than anyone else, although they were doing nothing for Denikin and were even strongly suspected of trafficking with the Bolsheviki. Yet Russians found them agreeable and sympathetic, always on excellent terms with all classes. They liked Russians and in turn were liked.

This question of two races getting on together does not always have a logical explanation, or perhaps the logic is fundamental and not on the surface. We do not always like the people who do the most for us, although we usually like those who like us. In our own case, the attitude of my chief, Admiral McCully, had a great deal to do with the Russian attitude toward us. At a time when most other people were impressing the Russians with their own particular importance and the absolute necessity that the Russians provide them with special quarters, private cars, and goodness know what, Admiral McCully was busy explaining to the Russians that he himself was of no importance whatever, with no power or influence, and was only there to see what was going on simply because Americans were very much interested in the Russians and the future of Russia; as for quarters, he insisted that as in the towns the people were crowded at the rate of about one family per room, we not only needed no more room than the Russians, but under no conditions would we accept more. The result was that no matter how crowded the Russians, they were always trying to do for us. Month after month we jammed ourselves into quarters our orderlies considered far beneath their dignity. The admiral ate tinned corned beef, which he had brought along, simply because he felt it was not playing the game to buy food at the market when it was scarce, even though the rate of exchange would have made it possible for us to buy the whole market for nothing had we cared to.

General Denikin proved to have as much charm as good looks, which is no faint praise, for he is a very handsome man and indeed looked the part of the courageous leader he was. He is typical Russian—shaved head, full beard, long flowing mustaches, broad of shoulder, broader of waist, natural, cheerful, and friendly, and with it all, dignified and without the slightest trace of snobbery, or what we call "side." His dominant characteristics were honesty, sincerity, and obstinancy. He seemed undismayed by defeat and showed every confidence in his eventual success, but my impression was definite that he was neither brilliant nor receptive to new ideas and much less a creator of ideas. He was an honest man and a patriot, and he was reputed to be a good soldier, but he certainly was not a great leader. In the months that followed, when I saw a lot of him, these impressions became convictions.

I was worried when I saw his beautiful sweeping mustaches with every hair so perfectly and exquisitely trained in place; I revolted at the thought of the enormous cost in time and effort; it seemed to indicate a lack of sense of proportion in anyone who, during such a crisis, would be willing to spend that amount of time on mustaches. However, I dare say, fine mustaches and that sort of thing are very important to a Russian general, no small part of whose stock in trade is swank and swashbuckling; so it may have been worth it.

I was much interested in General Denikin's entourage. Like the general himself, his ministers were forceful men and patriots perhaps,

8. General Anton Denikin. (Photo courtesy of Hoover Institution Archives.)

and there were good soldiers on his staff, but all had one fundamental in common. Not one of them realized there had been a revolution in Russia—a revolution that had affected the thought of the people no less than it had affected things political. These generals did understand, and very thoroughly, that there had been some sort of disturbance, a violent one to be sure, that they themselves had lost their estates, that everything was going to rack and ruin in Russia, and certain evil beasts called Bolsheviki had to be wiped out before they could ever get back their estates and live the fine old life of the imperial days. Yet I doubt a single one of them knew there had been a real revolution; and I doubt, too, whether any of them *could* realize it. I never got from them the faintest trace of any idea broader than the thought that the Bolsheviki had to be smashed somehow or other, and the good old days would automatically come back.[12]

4

Odessa, Russia

February 1920 _____

One trait in common I noticed among these commissars: they were all men who had more or less fundamental qualities of leadership; not merely spellbinders, they invariably had a certain charm of simplicity and earnestness. Yet not one of them impressed me as believing what he said. (February 1920)

_____

On 7 February 1920, McCully and Koehler sailed for Odessa aboard the American destroyer *Biddle*, while on the Siberian front that same day, Admiral Kolchak, "Supreme Ruler of All the Russias," as he had dubbed himself, surrendered to the advancing Bolsheviks. After a prolonged interrogation, the admiral was placed in front of a firing squad: a few minutes later his body was pushed through a hole in the icy Angara River.

Denikin's situation, so recently spectacular, was now nearly as hopeless as that of the late "Supreme Ruler," for the White armies were in headlong retreat. One of Denikin's commanding officers, General Schilling, had shamelessly abandoned the port city of Odessa to the Bolsheviks without a fight.

McCully and Koehler received this news en route but nevertheless grimly sailed on, anchoring in Odessa harbor on 10 February. Chaos reigned on the quay, where the desperate citizens of Odessa were attempting to board any ship that could deliver them from the advancing Reds. A note in McCully's diary records that they "picked up three praying women on end of pier."[1]

Amid this storm, Koehler, alone and unarmed, went ashore into the now Bolshevik-occupied city. His report on his meeting with twenty-four-year-old Red Army commander I. P. Uborevich is an epic of naval intelligence.[2]

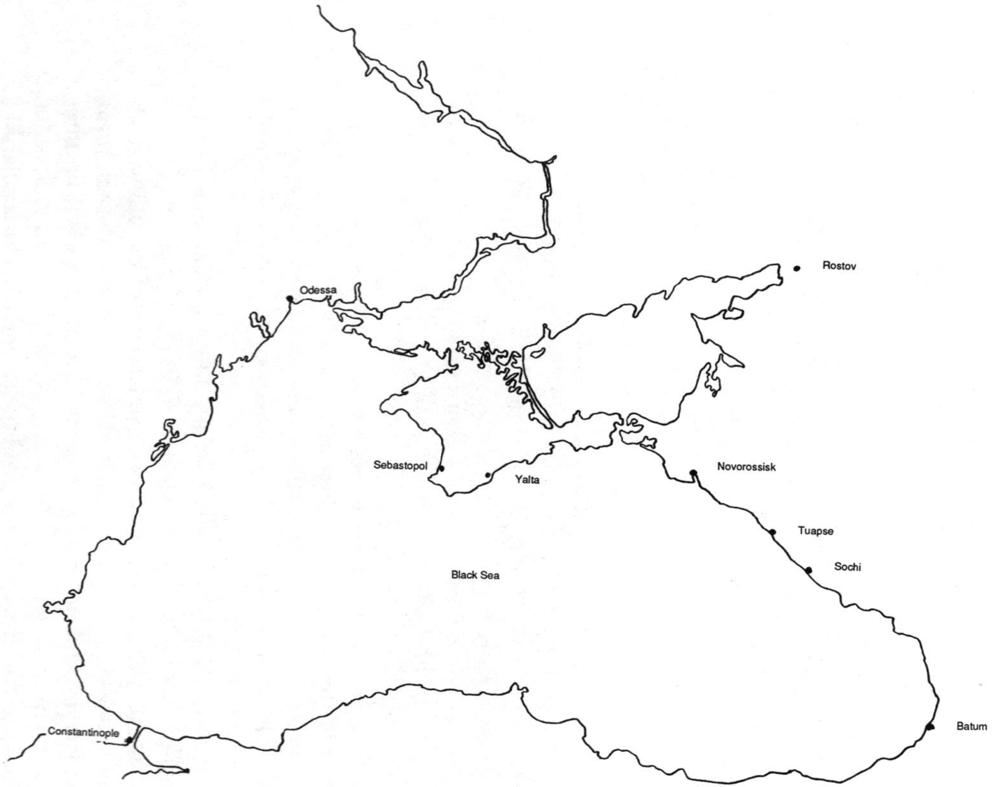

Map 3 Southern Russia and the Black Sea

78

Odessa, Russia
10 February 1920

FROM: Lt. Cmdr. Hugo W. Koehler, U.S. Navy
TO: Rear Adm. N. A. McCully, U.S. Navy
SUBJECT: Report of interview with Bolshevik commander in chief in Odessa relative to safety of American citizens there.

In accordance with your instructions, I landed at Odessa lighthouse at about 10:30 A.M., 10 February 1920, and immediately began negotiations with the lighthouse keeper with a view to persuading him to go to the town authorities, or at least to the nearest outpost of Red troops, with my request that I be allowed to communicate with the commander of the forces of occupation concerning the safety of three or four American citizens believed still to be in town. The lighthouse keeper was loath to go, as he had not been in town for four days, did not know what was going on there, and was fearful of what was happening, but he was finally persuaded to carry my request to the nearest Red post—just at the end of the mole and immediately under the guns of the [destroyer] USS *Talbot*. About half an hour later he returned with word that the captain of the Red guard there would talk to me and, if it seemed advisable, would furnish me with a guard as far as the headquarters of his immediate superior.

Arriving at this first post I met a very swanky officer in red hussar breeches, high hussar boots, and a British overcoat festooned with bows of red ribbon on the right breast and shoulder, and an enormous, white Cossack fur cap. I explained my mission to him, and after some hesitation and consultation with other officers he agreed to take me to the battalion commander. We then entered a house nearby to await the arrival of the automobile that he said he had ordered. Some thirty men were quartered in this small house, in addition to the large family that ordinarily occupies it, and the disorder and filth were extravagant even for Russia under the present conditions.

During the conversation a commissar entered and immediately took part by asking me pointedly what the men-of-war were doing in the harbor and why they had fired on the Bolshevik troops. I replied they were concerned with the evacuation of refugees, and understood the reason they had fired was that prior to the entry of the regular Red forces the town had been full of marauders and thieves. He then continued his questions—all more or less of the same tenor—and then branched out for himself in a long recital of the outrages perpetrated by Denikin's army. A number of other officers joined the group and alternately fired questions at me and argued among themselves. Their attitude toward me was neither particularly hostile nor friendly.

After waiting some time, I explained that if agreeable, I would prefer to walk rather than wait for the automobile, because I wished to dispatch my business as soon as possible and because I would enjoy the exercise. This created some merriment; I was told they were all sick of walking [and] had been doing nothing else for five months. They explained that during the first part of the time they had been retreating before Denikin, but at Orel the retreat had been suddenly interrupted by their taking up the advance themselves. They added that the advance had been even more unpleasant than the retreat because it had been more rapid. Shortly afterward, when they mentioned all was normal in town, I suggested if we started out on foot we would probably be able to get a droshky before long, and thus finally persuaded them to start. I was accompanied by a commissar, an officer, and a motley squad that followed in the rear. Their complaints about being footsore were evidently not imaginary, for I noticed that most of my companions hobbled and stumbled as if their feet were in bad condition. At this point they asked why it was that the American Red Cross, supposedly neutral, helped only Denikin's army: they said their sufferings from typhus were worse than those of the Denikin forces, and they had no medicines whatever. Another commissar now joined us, a very intelligent, earnest, and forcible-looking man, who in mentioning the Denikin army, commented that their greatest mistake had been that in their advance they robbed and plundered peasants, who were now so hostile that the advance of the Red Army had been easy. His comrade then rambled on [about] outrages perpetrated by Denikin's army: for example, cutting out of the tongues of some 4,000 soldiers of the Red forces, chopping off hands of an even greater number, lining the streets of a certain village with rows of men strung up on telegraph wires, etc., etc., many of the stories bearing a striking resemblance to the stories of German outrages in Belgium current not long ago (including the famous story of the well full of baby hands). This commissar went on to say he was sick of war, [and] so were all the others; he was fighting because Denikin's army killed his wife and child, but, so far as he was concerned, one army was just like another; he would just as soon belong to Denikin's army if they would not kill him and really meant peace and would allow a man to go back to his house and farm. He continued on the same strain for some time, and his comrades apparently all agreed with him, for several interrupted him with their own accounts of how sick they were of war, and nothing really mattered if only they would have peace. After a walk of about a mile from the docks toward the center of the city, during which time I saw hardly any soldiers, we arrived at Bolshevik headquarters, and from there proceeded to the headquarters of the regiment guarding the port.

Upon explaining my business to the colonel in command, he agreed to proceed with me to division headquarters. This regimental commander was a general—a quiet, well-mannered man of about 34, evidently a former officer; his bearing was unmistakably not that of the new school and he still wore the old uniform, though without the shoulder straps. He was the only one of the higher officers I met who did not speak either French or German; but I never quite believed he did not understand all three and guarded myself accordingly. German was more useful than French, for all the commissars and many higher officers spoke it fluently. No commissars spoke French. The division commander was . . . not over 34 years old, very quick and energetic in speech and manner, and had a harsh and unpleasant voice. But he had a certain force in bearing, and appeared the type of man one would not like to meet in a lonely place on a dark night. However, he received me pleasantly. While we were talking he excused himself to go out to greet the commander in chief just then arriving and in a few moments returned with General Uborevitch, who entered with much swagger and greeted me in a rather hail-fellow-well-met style. I judge he is not more than 28, and in appearance is hardly more than 23 or 24. Excepting his youth, he came close to usual ideas of a Bolshevik leader: small, beady, close-set eyes, cruel lips, alert manner, a mind sharp as a whip, quick to seize an advantage, vain, with a braggadocio and flippant manner of talking and not a trace of intellectuality in face or expression. Perhaps his most definite characteristic was of utter unscrupulousness and the impression he would stop at nothing.* His staff were all older than

---

*This was Ieronim Petrovich Uborevich (1896–1937), who, after distinguishing himself in the Russian Civil War, rose to become army commander first-class in 1935. He was one of the prominent army commanders arrested and executed by Stalin during his purge of the top military leadership.

A lieutenant in the czar's army, Uborevich after the Revolution joined the Reds and fought against Allied forces in northern Russia. Near the conclusion of the Civil War, just before Koehler met him, Uborevich commanded the Ninth (Kuban) Army in the Caucasus, and it was Uborevich's army that broke through the White lines near Nikolaiev and drove the resistance into the Crimea.

An interesting counterpoint to Koehler's description of the general is provided by Joseph L. Wieczynski, ed., in *The Modern Encyclopedia of Russian and Soviet History* (Gulf Breeze, Florida, 1985, 40:138–40 (hereafter cited as MERSH): "Bespectacled and scholarly in his appearance, Uborevich became known as a dedicated military commander who

himself and of widely differing types—the most striking being the
commissar with the figure of a boiler-maker but a very weak face. . . . I
was surprised at the pride that all who could do so took in announcing
they had been officers under the old regime. The chief of staff never
disagreed with the commander in chief but several times later in the
conversation expressed views diametrically opposite to those previously
expressed by his chief, and [they were] invariably the more sensible.
The commander in chief told me he had been on the Archangel front
and was well and favorably known there to the Allies, though at that
time had been only a colonel. I gathered from the sinister laugh of his
colleagues that his record is not savory. No officers wore insignia of any
kind, except a red star of cloth or metal on their caps and occasionally
festoons of red ribbon on the breast and shoulder. The commander in
chief had a single medal on his breast, a red enamel design made of a
star and flag with inlaid silver lettering—the Soviet equivalent of the
Cross of St. George, he told me.[3]

I stated my errand, namely, I understood there were three or four
American citizens still in Odessa, and I would like to communicate with
them and, if they were in danger and it was agreeable to the commander
in chief, to take them to the ship. He replied he would let me know
whether this could be done upon receipt of instructions from Moscow
and asked whether I had any other business to transact. I answered no, I
was concerned only with the safety of American citizens, but if he
wished to tell me anything of his position in Odessa and his aims and
purposes there, I would make a report to my superiors. He stated he
had come from Moscow, from the heart of Russia, to clear the borders
of Russia of the bandits of Denikin's army, who were under the protection of England and "a little bit also" ("*ein bischen auch*") of America.
He added that for the moment I was his guest and would be treated
accordingly, nor would I be taken as a hostage though he knew there
were enemies of the Bolsheviks—spies and men who had committed
outrages against Red forces—who were out in the harbor on ships
sheltering behind the guns of the Allied squadron. He asked why armored ships were in the harbor when, according to the new treaty
between Russia and the Allies, ships were to come only for purposes of
trade. I answered I could speak accurately only concerning the American destroyer, in Odessa solely for the purposes of securing the safety of

---

dabbled in political affairs only when he felt constrained to defend the interests of the
army. (He clashed heatedly with Trotskii concerning the latter's proposals for reorganization of the Red Army.)"

American citizens and aiding the evacuation of refugees if necessary. Upon his repeating the question concerning purposes of British men-of-war in the harbor, I answered I understood their purposes were similar but I could not speak for them. He asked pointedly why, if these ships were interested only in the safety of refugees, they fired on Red forces. I answered there had been no firing since we had been in port, so I could not answer definitely, but I understood this firing previous to our arrival had been because there were at that time no regularly organized forces in town, and the town was consequently terrorized by bandits and marauders. He then got out a map, pointed to the position of Odessa and then to another location some six or seven miles away, and said it seemed evident there must have been some extraordinarily bad shooting, since, while aiming at marauders in Odessa city, shots had accidentally hit Bolshevik forces some seven miles away and in an entirely different direction! I was, of course, more or less at a loss for a rejoinder, so I simply reminded him of my previous statement that I could tell him accurately only what concerned Americans and the American ship, and no firing had taken place since our arrival. He added whoever had directed those shots had information about Red movements, and numerous Red soldiers had been killed and their advance delayed. He asked what was the position of the navel squadron here with regard to Denikin's army. I replied again I could answer only for the American ship, and so far as the military situation went we had no connection whatever with Denikin. He appeared to doubt this, and I then added that although we had had forces at Archangel they had been withdrawn, and I understood that our forces along the Siberian railway were also being withdrawn. He commented that this was a timely move, for Admiral Kolchak had been taken prisoner and, with his gold, was being shipped to Moscow. He asked whether there was a destroyer of Denikin's army or any army force in the harbor. I answered I did not know. He stated there was—a Denikin destroyer had come in during the night. He asked whether we wished to take any further refugees out of town. I answered we would like to take such American citizens as would like to leave. He replied he would have to refer the question to Moscow and would let me know the answer in three days.

A commissar, listening all along, joined in and asked what I thought, what America thought, about the Bolshevik victories. I answered I did not know American opinion at present, but my own impression was that the recent Bolshevik advance was rather an example of the weakness of Denikin's army than a test of strength of the Bolshevik army. No one made any comment on this reply, and I became

definitely of the impression that at heart they agreed. In the discussion
that followed, the commander in chief stated boastfully that the Reds
now had an army of more than 4,000,000 and when Russia was thoroughly organized they would fear no one—not England, nor America,
nor the whole world. . . . He brought the conversation back to the
men-of-war in port and asked why they were remaining there. I replied
so far as the American ship was concerned we were interested only in
the safety of our citizens. He replied by asking me please to deliver a
message to the British man-of-war, that if they did not leave port
within three days' time, he would bombard them from shore and bomb
them by aeroplane. I did not undertake to deliver this message and
made no comment whatever concerning it. I again asked whether it
would be agreeable to him to allow me to communicate with the Americans in town. He had previously stated he would have to refer the
question to Moscow, but he was now in a more agreeable mood, for he
said he had no objections to my seeing them but could not give me an
answer until tomorrow whether they would be allowed to leave the
town; that is, his reply would depend on instructions from Moscow. I
asked what assurances I could give these Americans concerning their
safety in the meantime. He replied they would be safe; under no circumstances would anyone except spies or robbers be shot, he intended
to restore order, and the town was already quiet. I then asked him,
categorically, whether he considered himself sufficiently in control of
the town to be able to guarantee the safety of our citizens and whether
he would do so. He answered in the affirmative in both cases. I asked
whether I might proceed to get in touch with the Americans, as I was
anxious to return to my ship as soon as possible. He agreed but stated
that a photographer had just come up and would like very much to have
our picture. I answered I did not feel I could wait, as photographers
invariably take a long time, and I would have to start out at once to
locate Americans I town as I anticipated some difficulty finding them.
He repeated the picture would take only a moment, but nevertheless I
managed to avoid it. He had previously offered me his motorcar, and
when I now started out he said the motorcar was not yet ready but
would be in about a quarter of an hour. I answered I would be glad to
walk; but he would not have this and himself accompanied me to the
motorcar. I noted while we were waiting for the motorcar two photographers were busy taking snapshots. I was annoyed, though there was
nothing to do but sit on my annoyance; but I suspect I took myself too
seriously, for I noticed later I was never snapped when alone, though I
was snapped twice again with His Excellency. Later I learned he had a
special weakness for photographs of himself.

Accompanied by a general, an orderly, and a guard, I went first to the address of Mrs. Eli Keyser, and after some difficulty located her. She stated she was an American citizen, born in England but married to an American, and all her family were Americans in America. She had been in Russia three years, practically the entire time in Odessa, her husband having died about a year and a half ago. She is a concert singer but appears a quite respectable woman. I repeated the result of my interview with the commander in chief and told her it appeared likely arrangements could be made to take her off to the ship, and in the meantime the commander in chief assured me she would be safe. She said she would like to leave if she could go direct to America. But, rather than go to Constantinople, or to any place other than directly to America, she would prefer to stay in Odessa if she would not be killed. She added she spoke Russian as well as she did English and could probably earn her living better in Odessa than in any place other than America. She then told me about her various troubles, her consumptive husband, etc., and in doing so became quite hysterical, but ended by saying if she were not in danger in Odessa she would rather remain there. I asked her if she had sufficient money and said I would be glad to give her whatever was necessary. She answered she was alright, she had some jewels, and besides God had given her a great gift and she could sing very well and had no trouble earning her living. On leaving I spoke to a Russian woman who lives with her, and asked about her condition. This woman said that she was a very courageous woman, but at the moment she had no money, although she doubtless would be able to earn some as soon as conditions were better. Accordingly I left money with this Russian woman, with the understanding that it would be used for Mrs. Keyser.

I then went to addresses given for Mr. Tate and Mr. Barnet Young but at both places was told they had left some days ago and had left no addresses. I then looked up Mr. Rubin at his address and on not finding him there went to the former American and English Red Cross headquarters and thence to the Russian Red Cross headquarters, where I was told that Mr. Rubin had been there two days previously to volunteer his services to the Bolsheviks and, in fact, had been the first to do so. His present whereabouts was not known, but he was supposed to be somewhere in town. From all that can be learned Mr. Rubin is strongly suspected of pro-Bolshevik leanings. . . .[4]

I was then taken back to headquarters of the Red commander in chief and again was pressed to have my picture taken, in such a way that it was impossible to avoid the invitation. I had previously been invited to dinner but had been able to decline on the plea of being pressed for time, but now, my business having been finished, I was asked to have tea while awaiting the motorcar being made ready for me. It was not possible to decline again, so I accepted with the best grace possible. Tea, however, proved more or less a supper, but as it was becoming late I left on the plea the darkness would make it very dangerous for my boat to get in to me. I was escorted out with marked friendliness; as I left the commander in chief told me he would allow me to take out the Americans to the ship. [Because of] approaching darkness, and the fact that it would surely take them some time to get ready to leave, I made no attempt to get them that night; and with a view to making the best of the situation, I added that if he assured me he could and would protect them, I had no desire to take them out at that time.

I was impressed that all the officers I saw were Russians; in fact, I saw not a single Jew. I was told, however, that shortly a group of administrators would arrive, which I dare say means Jews are flocking in. I was also impressed that at supper none of the officers had wine or spirits of any kind, although a few had beer, but little of that. En route to town in the morning I noticed a commissar who, having noted the bulging pocket of a passing soldier, seized the bottle of vodka, smashed it on the pavement, and soundly berated the man.

I entered two food shops and although there was not a great abundance of supplies, both shops had customers buying food. All money is current: Soviet, Romanov, Kerensky, even Denikin army money, in accordance with the decree to the effect that shopkeepers are required to accept every kind of Russian money tendered them. The plan of making this money current is an inexpensive and simple way of winning over peasants and shopkeepers, who of course have laid in stores of Denikin money, and whose only allegiance to Denikin is the desire to give their money some value.

Streets of the town were in deplorable condition. Numerous dead horses and dogs were lying about, but I saw no human bodies, although we met a cortege of some five or six carts, which, I was told, had gone around the city to pick up all bodies in the streets. Numerous windows were broken, but I saw at least six glasiers at working mending them, and other than this there were no signs of rioting, for bullet scars on windows seemed old. I covered at least ten miles of street and the main part of the town, for fortunately the Americans I was endeavoring to locate lived in widely separated quarters of the town, so I was able to go practically everywhere I wished. I saw no crowds, nor were streets deserted, although traffic was less than one would expect in a city the size of Odessa.

I was particularly on the lookout for signs of German influence, German officers or munitions, any trace of German activity, but failed to discover anything I could put my finger on as in any way German. Many officers carried Austrian Mauser pistols. The men seemed well clothed, and their boots were fair for the most part, but there seemed to be a great scarcity of gloves, even amongst officers. Many officers went about bare-handed, certainly not from choice. I noted numerous English uniforms, and the orderly of one of the generals who escorted me had an American overcoat, which he described to me as Polish.

One of the commissars asked why Denikin's army destroyed so many railroad cars on leaving, for though in the early days the Reds had destroyed the fittings of some of the cars, it was their principle never to destroy railroad cars, bridges, and things necessary for the country. The same commissar asked when I thought America would go Bolshevik. I answered, "Never." He smiled and added, perhaps not now, and never in the same way Russia was Bolshevik, because Americans were different and more educated, but in fifteen or twenty years the whole world would be Bolshevik, because the greatest principle in the world was "all for all." He went on to say that because some people work with their brains and others work with their arms, there was no reason why the former should receive more than the latter, for they both were doing the same thing—both were by their work paying the price of their existence, though they were paying in different ways. Evidently foreseeing my answer to this, he continued that the fact one man was not getting more pay than another did not mean there would be no incentive for good work and greater effort—it meant only that incentive would be not money nor a soft seat but pride in one's work, pride on doing a thing well, in work for work's sake!

One trait in common I noticed among these commissars: they were all men who had more or less fundamental qualities of leadership; not merely spellbinders, they invariably had a certain charm of simplicity and earnestness. Yet not one of them impressed me as believing what he said—all seemed stamped with the same mark of insincerity. But some of the simpler soldiers, and the company leader who escorted me to town, really believed in the theory of "all for all," which they repeated over and over again.

There appeared to be a discipline of sorts, perhaps not exactly the variety we are used to, though there was still some clicking of heels by orderlies, and salutes between officers were numerous. Frequently authority appeared to rest with the one who could scream the loudest, but despite this, things were being done, there was a substitute sort of discipline, and some sort of organization was functioning, apparently functioning very well, considering the circumstances. I tried particularly to read in the faces of the men I saw some indication of what was the strength of this movement. For whatever one may say of it, and however conclusive the proofs against it, the simple fact of its having arrived at its present position, however precarious, must mean it has a certain strength. But I could see no gleam of conviction, no inspiration of a great idea, nothing except a sort of faith made up mostly of hope, which some of the soldiers had in the "all for all" idea. I could not get away from my impression of the insincerity of the leaders and lack of enthusiasm of their followers. Yet the Red forces have an organization that actually functions, clumsily perhaps, undoubtedly with great waste, and certainly after a fashion of its own, but the wheels do run even though they grind little meal.

Hugo W. Koehler[5]

In the days that followed Koehler's masterly exit from Odessa, Red radio broadcasts issued the obligatory charges that the *Talbot* had bombarded the Black Sea port and accused Koehler of being a spy for the British.[6]

Four years after the singular dialectic between Koehler and Uborevich, men from worlds so vastly different, Edwin C. Denby, then Secretary of the Navy, received the following letter:

Dear Sir:

I wish to describe to you a real, heroic act of an officer in your Navy, whose name I was fortunate enough to learn upon my return to the United States from Russia.

The story was as follows—it happened in Odessa, Russia, in the month of February 1920. When Odessa was evacuated by the Allies, I happened to be sick in bed with pneumonia and tonsilitis, and I wrote a letter to the American mission, imploring them to save me as I had suffered enough. Lieutenant Foster, who represented the American mission, came in answer to my letter, and he promised to take me with them. He failed to do so, however, as the Bolsheviki happened to get in [sooner than] expected. My sufferings were indescribable when I found this out, and my surprise was great when, four days later, one of the neighbors ran into my room and said that an American officer was coming up the stairs, looking for me. I could not believe my eyes when I beheld a tall man entering my room dressed in a black cloak, conveyed by two armed Bolshevists.

Is it possible? An AMERICAN OFFICER, I exclaimed. When the American officer, whose name I have been fortunate enough to learn—Lt. Cmdr. Hugo W. Koehler—came close, he said, "Yes, it is possible; here I am to help you, as I know you are sick."

I broke down, crying like a child, and begged the kind officer to take me to America, to my Mother, as I had no one in Odessa but my beloved husband's grave. . . .

During the sad scene one of the armed Bolshevists took stations at the door, and the other, evidently knowing the English language, came closer to hear the conversation. Lieutenant Commander Koehler tried to quiet me, explaining that he had orders to take the refugees to Constantinople only. The neighbors, hearing this, advised me to remain, as I was too ill to travel. Lieutenant Commander Koehler, also finding this best, advised me to stay. . . . Thinking that I was in need, he offered me money . . . and he assured me that I was not in danger, and if he found out that I was, he would come and take me with him.

After he left, my friend explained to me that his [Koehler's] life was in danger, as there was no government to be responsible if anything should happen to him. I worried very much about it, especially because he had risked his life for me. The next day, I read the Bolshevist newspaper (which I have with me), which stated that an American officer had been to see them regarding the foreigners. Learning that he had got away safely, I thanked God for sparing this nobleman's life, and also prayed to be in a position to come to the United States some day in order to find Lieutenant Commander Koehler and to thank him personally and to tell the world that there are still some noble and kind people who will endanger their lives to help a little, weak woman, a mere stranger.

Yours very truly,
Annette Keyser[7]

The Secretary of the Navy wrote to Koehler that his "chivalrous efforts" were "the kind of service that makes life worthwhile."[8]

In a letter to his mother, Koehler wrote:

You heard, did you not, of my landing at Odessa after the Bolsheviks had taken it? I believe the State Department gave out some few details, for several people wrote that they had seen it in the London papers. But the aftermath was never published, for about a week after my return the Bolshevik government sent a long wireless dispatch to

President Wilson and also to the League of Nations to the effect that although they had allowed me to leave only after my having given my word that I would not fire on the town, no sooner had I regained my ship than a murderous fire was opened up from our entire squadron and hundreds of innocent women and children were killed thereby. Of course the whole account was ridiculous—in the first place because our "entire squadron" consisted of one small torpedo boat destroyer, and in the second place, because not a single shot was fired. Inasmuch as we naturally knew this and would so inform Mr. Wilson, one might think it strange that the Bolsheviks would lie so stupidly. But the answer is that although the message was addressed to President Wilson and the League of Nations, the Bolsheviks didn't care a hang whether the President or the League of Nations ever saw it or what they thought of it, for the message was intended simply as propaganda for their own people.

And incidentally, although this message described me as a very terrible and very wicked man, I've always been grateful to the Bolsheviks for it, for in the light of these tactics I was able to understand many things not clear to me before.[9]

5

Novorossisk, Russia

March 1920 _____

*Ships lying alongside the docks crowded on human cargo almost to
the last inch of space and then, fearing the fire, moved away from
the piers into the stream, although they made almost no impression on the multitude seeking to board. (March 1920)*

After the ordeal in Odessa, Koehler and McCully returned to
Sebastopol, where clearly demoralized remnants of various White units
wandered the streets. The mood of defeatism was hardly diminished
when a certain Captain Orlov led a mutiny against Denikin by occupying Simferopol. Eventually driven into the hills, Orlov reorganized his
band of mutineers and led a raid against Yalta.

When the Americans, after a short visit to the Crimean front, returned to Novorossisk on 20 February, they were met only by more
suffering and disorganization, with the Russians now resorting to mor-
bid humor to comfort themselves. A Novorossisk paper published "A
French Course"—a macabre satire of the conventional phrase book
dialogues. It concluded:

Q. It is true that your uncle is a remarkable man?

A. Yes, he is, indeed, a remarkable man. He has been ill once with
ordinary typhus, twice with spotted typhus, and three times with recur-
rent typhus. He is impatiently waiting for spring, in order to fall ill with
cholera.

Q. Do you like walking in the cemetery?

A. Yes, I like walking in the cemetery, because all my friends and
acquaintances are there. The day before yesterday my last friend in
town died. In order not to have to visit the cemetery every day, and so
wear out my last pair of boots, I want to remove my residence to the
sexton's quarters.[1]

Rapidly losing control of the situation, and with the fiasco of the
Odessa evacuation weighing heavily upon him, Denikin lashed out at

his subordinates, blaming Wrangel for the military setbacks, spreading scurrilous rumors among the British. But when he banished Wrangel to Constantinople, the military situation only worsened.

Denikin's last chance was to concentrate his forces in the Crimea and fight it out there—a solution Wrangel had proposed in December but Denikin had rejected out of hand. Now it was his only hope of escape. But while a retirement into the Crimea in December could have been covered in an orderly manner, now in March at the port of Novorossisk, it became a disastrous, headlong retreat. Denikin had made no provision for the sudden increase in refugees. Families of White officers, as sure as those in Odessa of the fate that awaited them at the hands of the Reds, fought for space aboard freezing ships. "There were [also] Cossacks, nomad families with their black tents, Caucasian tribesmen and families from the Caspian shores. Their route was marked with bodies, stripped naked and frozen; dead horses, mules, and camels; abandoned guns, field-kitchens, and vehicles, together with all the debris of an army in flight."[2] Denikin was forced to appeal to the Royal Navy for enough ships to evacuate both populace and army.

McCully's indictment of Denikin's leadership is explicit in a report to the Secretary of State. "During his advance in the fall of 1919 Denikin's forces were welcomed with flowers; this feeling changing within a month to detestation." He continued:

With good will everywhere evident personally toward the general . . . there was every reason for him to win, time and time again, in each case suffering defeat instead, due to his political ineptitude. He realizes his mistakes afterward, publicly confesses them, professes to reform, and then repeats the same mistakes. . . .

The old imperial military forms were retained, much attention is given to saluting, and subordinates and private soldiers were punished with death for military offenses that could be dealt with otherwise, while high-ranking officers who show inefficiency or betray their trust are dealt with leniently, in cases even being promoted. . . .

The evacuation [of Odessa] was unnecessary and due to incapacity and cowardice of the officer commanding, General Shilling, who failed to organize means of defense before the city was attacked. Even before his troops had ever been in conflict with the numerically inferior enemy, Shilling himself was first to abandon the town. This incapable officer was retained by General Denikin as commander in chief of the Crimea, even after a protest by principal officers of the Russian army and navy, who were themselves relieved from their duties for making the protest. . . .

The evacuation was carried out without any order or plan, nearly altogether in Russian vessels, the British naval authorities employing such means as could be found and meriting principal credit for any good accomplished. Weather was very severe, temperatures ranging from minus 5 degrees to plus 20 degrees, with fresh winds and rough seas. Helpless refugees had to remain afloat under these conditions for days without fuel, water, medical attendance, or provisions. When loading the ships, it was at one time necessary to spray machine guns on masses of refugees, men, women, and children, to prevent them rushing already overloaded vessels. On board the *Vladimir*, a 6,700-ton vessel, were nearly 7,000 refugees for over a week. Conditions accompanying this evacuation were a reproach to all so-called civilized Powers. On evacuation, the storehouses at Odessa were left full of wheat, barley, wool, bristles, and other valuable stores. . . . Although White forces in northern Crimea were holding their own, weaknesses in command, communications, and supply indicated the organization could not remain effective for long and promise little hope of a definite result in favor of the Whites. The rear was hopelessly paralyzed, and no authority seemed capable of remedying the situation. . . .

During these events there arrived in the Crimea General Wrangel, who had first been appointed commander in chief of the armies in the field after the reverses of 1919, and who shortly after resigned this post on account of differences with General Denikin. A movement began in the Crimea involving most of the army and navy to get rid of General Shilling, on account of the general lack of confidence in him, and to substitute for him General Wrangel. However Wrangel would not consent to act against General Denikin, who nevertheless requested him to leave Russia, which Wrangel promptly did.

— ❧ —

As the American mission returned to Novorossisk, they found the port city "flooded with refugees from Kharkov and Rostov:"

All matters of administration were in a state of disorganization, the streets were full of skulkers from Denikin's army, mostly officers, and no authority had any control over them. No one would work even to provide himself with food, and the feeling everywhere was panicky. . . .

A chicken in the market cost 600 rubles, while the pay of General Denikin himself was 6,000 rubles per month, and the Minister of Foreign Affairs, Mr. Neratov, lived, ate, and slept in a corner of a bank office. . . .

On March 17, Ekaterinodar, capital of Kuban Province, about 80 miles northeastward of Novorossisk, had been captured by Reds, and it was evident that Novorossisk would soon fall. . . .

On March 26, Red forces appeared in vicinity of Novorossisk, advancing along the railway, and shelling Denikin detachments in the outskirts of the town. The British battleship *Emperor of India* and cruiser *Calypso* and French cruiser *Waldeck Rousseau* used their heavy guns throughout the day to cover retreat of Denikin forces, but Red forces remained well under cover, advancing all the time, and the fire from naval vessels did not seem effective. Through Novorossisk moved a constant stream of retreating troops mingled with refugees, soon causing a jammed mass of people along the entire waterfront of the city for three miles. On the piers troops began throwing overboard forage carts, automobiles, bicycles, machine guns, ammunition, and other military material. Thousands of horses were turned loose to wander aimlessly about the streets. Nearly all the artillery had to be abandoned. . . .

Everywhere was gross disorganization, but people and troops were remarkably patient and self-restrained and there was no serious disorder. During the day the storehouses along the waterfront were set on fire and burned day and night. Water transportation was entirely insufficient, although everything that could float was pressed into service. Everything was packed to the limit, one 3,000-ton steamer being stated officially to have embarked 7,600 people at one time. Fortunately weather was calm and mild, otherwise some of the means of transport would undoubtedly have foundered.

The evacuation continued all through March 26, and the night of March 26–27, but there still remained about ten thousand troops and a large number of refugees who had to be abandoned.[3]

— ❧ —

Luckett puts the total number of troops abandoned at Novorossisk closer to twenty-two thousand, adding: "Several officers shot themselves on the quay; more drowned trying to swim out to the ships."[4]

In a letter to his mother, Koehler described the same drama played out from his vantage point aboard the USS *Galveston*.

March 26–27, 1920
Novorossisk

The evacuation of Novorossisk has been going on for several days. Many ships had already left, carrying officers' families, sick and wounded officers, and a few civilians. Most had gone to the Crimea, but many, especially women and children, had been taken on British and American ships, as refugees to the camps just established on the several Princess Islands, just off south Constantinople.

All week, troops from the fading front poured into the town, but instead of being organized for defense, they were embarked on ships and sent to the Crimea as rapidly as possible. It early became evident that no hope was held for making a stand in this section, and the date of the fall of Novorossisk depended entirely on how quickly Reds could bring any considerable force against the town.

On Monday, March 22, the Bolshevik radio station in Moscow broadcast the information that their army would take Novorossisk on Saturday, the 27th. Nevertheless, few believed it could be accomplished so soon, and even lawless elements in town, who customarily rob, plunder, and carry on other excesses in such critical times, remained in the background and quiet.

Thursday night it was reported that Bolsheviks had completely surrounded the town, occupying principal points in the hills that encircle the city and bay. Ships alongside the docks were rapidly boarded by those fortunate ones assigned to go, and many vessels, including the ship carrying officials of the government, sailed during the night.

Friday morning broke calm and clear and conditions appeared to be no different from on the proceeding day. The American cruiser, USS *Galveston*, flying the flag of Rear Admiral McCully, U.S.N., lay just off the docks. In addition to several Russian merchant ships, fighting ships of England, France, and Italy lay peacefully in the inner harbor. Outside in the bay lay the mighty *Emperor of India*, flying the British admiral's flag, and the French battlecruiser *Waldeck Rousseau*.

With powerful glasses we scanned the surrounding hills from crest, down the winding roads, to the base, but no moving bodies of men could we see, except to the northeastward, where small cavalry units could be seen making their way down the slopes. These we knew to be Volunteer Army forces and so gave them scant attention. Nevertheless, early in the forenoon, the *Emperor of India* opened up with 13.5-inch turret guns, firing directly over us toward a village perhaps seven miles up the valley. From then on, all day, either she, the Frenchman, or one of the British destroyers would keep up a ranging fire toward that vicinity, while a scouting aeroplane flew back and forth to watch and report results. The Bolshevik was following closely to his schedule.

About noon, fires began to break out in the vicinity of the railway yards and waterfront, whether incendiary or otherwise we could not ascertain. Soon an uncontrolled and vicious fire was raging, consuming everything in its path, buildings, warehouses, ammunition, oil supplies, and rolling stock worth hundreds of thousands of dollars.

Ships lying alongside the docks crowded on human cargo almost

9. Rear Admiral McCully aboard the USS *Galveston* in March 1920, at Novorossisk, Russia. (Note Marine at left and caissons for 3″ landing force guns in foreground.) (U.S. Naval Historical Center photograph, neg. no. NH 50275.)

to the last inch of space and then, fearing the fire, moved away from the piers into the stream, although they made almost no impression on the multitude seeking to board. Packed on the docks and beach, surrounded by raging fire, were thousands who had hoped and expected to be taken away but who had been left behind for lack of ships to embark them. These were mostly soldiers just arrived from the vanished front, but many women and children were seen among them.

Intermingled with the human element were hundreds of pieces of personal belongings, guns, and war material. Several small boat trips were made from the *Galveston* in a last effort to rescue a few more women and children, but it was impossible to get any considerable number of them through the throng. This unfortunate mass, which had been waiting for many hours, growing larger and more confused every minute, spent the night there hoping against hope for a chance to get away. Some few did get hold of small boats and make their way out into the stream, where they would be taken aboard the nearest ship. The harbor waters were covered with empty drifting boats of every description. The big ships, crowded to their utmost capacity, stood out to sea and turned westward toward Crimea.

Just before dusk, the *Galveston* moved out of the inner harbor and took a new berth outside the mole, for no one knew what might develop during the night.

Saturday morning we were awakened by the sounds of firing. Going on deck, we could immediately see that the last struggle for the defense of the town was on. Advance guards of the Red forces were already in the outskirts and larger forces could be seen making their way down the winding roads from the hills into the valley. The last stand was not spectacular, the only determined effort being made by two Russian destroyers that sped into the inner harbor and there opened a heavy fire into the foremost enemy forces. Reds were now approaching from every direction, and machine-gun fire soon drove these valiant little boats outside the mole. At 11 o'clock the Reds were in possession of the town.

Soon after, batteries were brought down to the shore and fire was opened on the ships still lying in the outer harbor. We were nearest to the beach and soon 3-inch shells began to strike or pass perilously close to us. Of course we made no attempt to man our guns to answer their shots, so they soon directed theirs against other ships. They made no hits, but soon all ships were scampering to sea. The *Galveston* had got underway immediately after the shore battery commenced firing, and although shots were no longer coming in our direction, still there was nothing we could accomplish by remaining any longer, so we sailed out of the harbor. Looking back we could see the crowd along the waterfront, rapidly thinning, now that their last hope of escape in that direction had gone. Some were making their way aimlessly toward the town, while many others were fleeing into the hills or eastward down the coast. Behind in the railway yards, flames of many fires leapt to the sky while a deep, black smoke hung ominously over all, obscuring the scene entirely as we passed out into the open sea.

Of those left behind, probably very few escaped. . . .

No one can tell what the ambitions of the leaders of the Bolshevik movement are today. If they get over their ideas of world revolution and internationalism, we need have little fear of them; if they still cling to these ideas, it is only a question of a short time before they will be invading neighboring countries, such as Poland, Rumania, and Persia, and stretching their claws still further, and the world will be faced with another terrible war, the lineup of sides for which we scarcely dare hazard a guess.

Certain it is that we must recognize that the Bolshevik party controls Russia today, and we must face this as a fact, not as a theory, for practically the last semblance of opposition was swept away with the driving of Denikin's forces from their holding grounds in the Kuban and north Caucasus region, of which the fall of Novorossisk was the last chapter. Although Denikin succeeded in moving something like 25,000 troops to the Crimea, which he still holds, neither the final result nor the quickness of its coming has been changed. These ill-equipped, war-worn, and demoralized men will no more make a stand here than they did in the Kuban, especially as they realize the only consequence of such a stand would be that those behind the lines would escape but they themselves would be left to their fate. The idea that a few troops can permanently hold the necks leading into the peninsula against any number of troops the Reds can throw against it is ridiculous. When the Bolshevik is ready to strike, he will make short work of this ragged remnant.

The Soviets got down to brass tacks before their enemies. If Denikin or Kolchak had been able to organize their rear and keep it contented or even under control, their fighting energies could have been devoted against the enemy at the front. The story today would have been far different. Not at the front but in the rear did these representatives of Old Russia lose the struggle, for they tried to apply Old Russian methods of red tape, noncompromise, political corruption, and graft, not to mention unkept promises, upon a people who, having been freed from them, even for a short time, would not stand for their reimposition. Not one constructive policy did the anti-Bolshevik groups bring forward; the only watchword they lived up to was "Down with Bolshevism," and in attempting to carry out this motto they frequently exceeded the Reds in the harshness of their methods. That was not the way to win; it required some definite ordered program that would show the people that their conditions would be bettered, their interests protected, and their freedom, gained by the Revolution, maintained. Such a program was never put into effect, only promised, and the people, tiring of promises, ceased to support the movement they had at first welcomed, and the natural result followed.

For the future of Russia, we can only be optimistic. She is such an enormous country, with such a wealth of undeveloped resources that, though she stands today absolutely demoralized and nonproductive, a few short years of peace should see her on her feet and make her once more one of the great, perhaps the very greatest nation of the world. Education and hard work, combined with square business and honest governments, is all that she requires. If the above results from this present upheaval, then it will not have been in vain.

To reach such a stage, she must cast aside the impractical in Bolshevism and then, though her government may be Bolshevistic in name, it will not be bolshevism as we understand the word, i.e., anarchy and destruction. If the present leaders cannot cast these aside, then another party must arise from within and overthrow them, perhaps in a bloodless revolution, and establish a new government that shall incorporate virtues of both the old and the new regimes but without the faults of either. In Russia alone lies her salvation; the time is past for interference from the outside, and those who have already tried to have a hand in her affairs have severely burnt their fingers.[5]

Hugo

— ❦ —

From McCully's report to the Secretary of State:

On April 1, General Denikin published a proclamation announcing final dissolution of the democratic government agreed upon on February 4 with representatives of the Don, Terek, and Kuban, and abolition of the Council of Ministers organized under the February 4 provisions, but making no provisions for representative institutions except for local needs. This in effect constitutes a military autocracy, or a distinct reversion to reactionary methods. The forms had always been preserved, and under pressure from time to time certain liberal concessions had been adopted, but always under protest, and never having the confidence of the people, "GORBATAVO ISPRAVITSA MOGILA." (Only the grave straightens the hunchback.)[6]

6

Yalta, Russia

April–May 1920

General Wrangel had the former commandant of Yalta, who surrendered the city without fighting, hanged over the door of a railway station, so that people had to duck to avoid hitting his feet with their heads. (April 1920)

On 3 April 1920, McCully and Koehler reached the Crimean port of Yalta, where, McCully noted in his diary: "Fruit trees in bloom and everything most delightful. I must get a house here and Koehler expects to do the same."[1]

The debacle at Novorossisk finally discredited Denikin, and he fled the Crimea on 21 March. His last act was to grudgingly appoint as commander in chief the one man who could possibly salvage and energize what was left of the resistance, the same man he had banished from Russia—General Baron Peter Wrangel.

In Constantinople, Denikin and his staff were put under British protection, but even so, Denikin's chief of staff, Romanovsky, was assassinated. Denikin himself escaped under the protection of the Royal Navy and found his way to England.

Wrangel wasted no time in transforming the Crimea into a virtual White island, the last parcel of Russian soil held by the anti-Bolshevik resistance. His methods were simple: ruthlessly restore discipline at and behind the front by shooting all looters, agitators, speculators, and commissars. On one memorable occasion, Wrangel's forces captured nearly three thousand Bolshevik prisoners. Wrangel had all Communist officers and NCOs—370 in all—rounded up and paraded in front of him; then he ordered them all shot. The Baron then offered the remaining men the chance to redeem themselves by joining the White Army. As Luckett wrote: "If there was an alternative to this choice he did not make it explicit."[2]

At the end of April, McCully and Koehler telegraphed the Secretary of State to report that, after three months in south Russia, "the prin-

10. General Baron Peter Wrangel. (Photo courtesy of Baron Petr Vrangel Collection, Hoover Institution Archives.)

cipal conclusion evident is that all of Russia is sick to death of war and its accompanying disorganization, desolation, and suffering" and somewhat naively suggested a cease-fire.[3] But Wrangel and Lenin, locked in a fight to the finish, neither expecting any quarter from the other, knew better.

As for the United States government, which had managed to extricate itself from northern and eastern Russia in 1919, a renewal of hostilities in south Russia in 1920 was hardly part of its postwar program. This telegram from the Special Mission, a copy of which was sent to the President, went on to say:

> For the great mass of the people any solution at all would be welcome that would establish peace and order. . . . No practical interest has so far been shown in the great body of the patient, lovable, suffering Russian people. . . .

Foreign intervention in Russian affairs has accomplished nothing useful either for the Russians nor for the interests of the powers intervening. The Russian people have never been convinced that foreign intervention had any other aim than the self-interests of those powers. . . . There is no evidence of organized German propaganda, but there is a strong sentiment among the humblest types of Russians that if any external influence is necessary, that of Germany is the only one capable of restoring peace and order. . . . This idea comes from experience of German occupation in 1918, when a comparatively small German army occupied south Russia, lightly disposing of any Bolshevik resistance. . . . Each Russian peasant knows that the appearance of German uniforms was the signal for disappearance of Bolsheviks and that in a town of 50,000 or 60,000 inhabitants, peace and order was maintained by detachments of 50 or 60 German soldiers.

This is compared with the discouraging Allied intervention, which, through its confused and halfhearted policies, brought only increasing disorder and usually ended in abandonment of such Russians as confided in them to the mercies of the Bolsheviks. . . .

A cessation of fighting by all elements at this time is most desirable in order to avoid suffering to innocent populations and during a peaceful interval to give, if possible, the Russian people themselves a chance to be heard and to choose the side with which they will ally. . . . It will be a power whose goodwill will be invaluable and with whom it would be wise to be friends.[4]

— ❧ —

Later, McCully and Koehler cabled a report, "Conditions in South Russia, April 1 to July 1, 1920," describing the ghastly last days of Denikin and the first hopeful weeks of Wrangel:

In March, Denikin's army, superior in numbers and equipment, was through incompetent leadership forced to retreat 180 miles to the sea, and then under attack of insignificant detachments was hustled aboard ships and forced to sea when sufficient shipping to embark it did not exist. Denikin abandoned all his horses, his tanks, most of his artillery, his wounded, and about 15,000 of his men, including a gallant little rear guard that was doing what it could to cover the embarkation. Automobiles, carts, bicycles, machine guns, ammunition were dumped overboard, and about fifteen million dollars' worth of British supplies was destroyed by fire. It did not seem possible for the army to recover from this catastrophe, which as a military scandal was second only to the evacuation of Odessa. . . .

About 30,000 troops in all were transferred to the Crimea, while 20,000 left behind had to shift for themselves, some going over to the Reds, the remainder retreating down the east coast of the Black Sea, hotly pressed by the Reds. Troops transferred to the Crimea were accompanied by large numbers of refugees, the transports being fearfully overloaded—on one 3,000-ton vessel there were 7,600 people. Had the weather been anything but fine and smooth, there would have been ghastly disasters. . . .

When Red troops entered Ekaterinodar on March 17, a portion of Denikin's cavalry . . . about 30,000 Cossacks . . . retreated by way of Maikop, joined on their march by about 30,000 refugees, women and children with their cattle and such household effects as they could take with them. This column made a march of 150 miles under conditions of great hardship and finally arrived at Tuapse on the Black Sea coast, where it joined up with remnants of the forces retreating from Novorossisk. Reds continued to press down on this chaotic mass of troops and refugees, who were almost without food or ammunition, driving them further and further south, first to Sochi and finally to Adler, harassing them continually and giving little mercy. A portion of the troops and refugees was brought over to the Crimea, but transportation was not sufficient for them all, and being prevented from entering Georgia by Georgian troops, the 15,000 or 20,000 remaining on May 3 began negotiations with the Reds for surrender. The Reds promised immunity to all except malefactors, on the condition the troops would march against the Poles; but immediately on the surrender being accomplished, the Reds began the usual slaughter of officers and stripped the soldiers of their clothes. The Cossacks again took to arms, about 10,000 taking to the hills and about 2,000 escaping across the Georgian border. Unable to take them along, about 700 children were drowned at the beach by their mothers, who then took to the hills with the men.

On account of the Novorossisk evacuation, General Denikin was completely discredited in public opinion and in the army. His life was threatened. Only the British seemed to have any further confidence in him, but even this support, which had been instrumental in keeping him in power (since to Denikin were consigned all munitions), was now insufficient to save him. On demand of his senior military commanders and against his will, General Denikin gave up command of the armed forces of south Russia to Lieutenant General Baron Peter Wrangel, whom shortly before Denikin had ordered out of Russia, but who, in a council of seventy of the principal officers of the army, navy, and administration, was named the only man capable of the task. General

Denikin then sailed on a British war vessel for England. On April 3, General Wrangel arrived in Sebastopol, and on April 4 assumed duties as commander in chief, armed forces of south Russia, in accordance with the last order of General Denikin. General Wrangel announced simply that he had assumed command.

Conditions would have dismayed any ordinary man. Wrangel's troops were only a handful against hundreds of thousands in the Soviet forces. Morale was low, typhus was ravaging their ranks and the question of maintenance and supply was hopeless. There was popular discontent from lack of food, and public opinion was panicky. In every direction disorder, confusion, lack of confidence, and lack of unity were evident. Many, who with every reason to fear death if Bolsheviks should take possession, yet harried and harassed by months and years of suffering, looked with equanimity on almost any solution that would mean an end. Sebastopol, and practically every other town in the Crimea was overflowing with a mass of refugees for whom there was neither food nor lodging. Crimes were frequent and treasonable organizations actively at work. Streets were crowded with thousands of loafing officers and soldiers recognizing no authority, unpaid, reckless and disorderly, openly declaring they would fight no longer (this class probably never had done much fighting). However, certain elements of strength were evident. The Crimea was a natural fortress and could by wise administration be made self-sustaining. Naval forces, although low in morale, were still loyal and controlled the Black Sea. Certain portions of the officer regiments and the gallant little force under General Slashchev,* which had held the Crimean isthmuses through winter, could be relied on. The Soviet government made the error of estimating that the south Russian force was eliminated. Most of all, in the new commander in chief, the anti-Bolshevik forces had a young man of undaunted personality, indomitable will, [and] fiery energy, and a brilliant soldier. On the very day of assuming command, General Wrangel received a notice

---

* Yakov Alexsandrovich Slashchev (1885–1929), who was promoted to lieutenant general in the White Army, was later stripped of his command by Wrangel. Although he had led many brilliant campaigns against the Reds, Slashchev became increasingly dependent upon alcohol and drugs, to the point where it began to impair severely his command abilities. "For example he always had a caged crow carried after him, for he believed that the animal would bring him luck. He would have people hanged unceremoniously just because they aroused his ire. In the spring of 1920 . . . he had himself surrounded with more and more birds, laughed at inappropriate moments, and unexpectedly burst into tears" (Peter Kenez, *Civil War in South Russia, 1919–1020: The Defeat of the Whites* [Berkeley, 1977], p. 263 [hereafter cited as Kenez].

from the British, that by decision of the Supreme Council, the Allies would undertake mediation between him and the Soviet government, and if he did not accept this mediation, no further support would be given his forces. Characteristic of the spirit of the man, even under such circumstances Wrangel's resolution to carry on the fight was unshaken. On April 10 he began his first offensive against the Reds. His accomplishments during the next two months over almost insurmountable obstacles were little short of superhuman.

Members of the former Russian Senate, although they no longer have an official status, on April 6 passed a resolution requesting General Wrangel assume all power, civil as well as military, without any limitations. This General Wrangel did in the Proclamation of April 13, becoming dictator over territory occupied by his forces. . . .

On April 10, General Wrangel left by sea with an expedition to . . . Perekop, and at the same time another landing force was operating in the Sea of Azov. After six days' hard fighting, a slight advance was made sufficient to give the Crimean forces an exit to the northward when the occasion should be opportune for an offensive. The results of the operation did much to revive morale of the troops and to restore public confidence.

Next was to restore internal order, suffering from general demoralization, in particular from a mutiny in February of a small detachment under Captain Orlov. Troops at the front for months had been fulfilling their duties under difficult circumstances, but the rear was badly demoralized and no authority seemed capable of dealing with this evil. The new commander in chief set about ruthlessly to correct these conditions. The former commandant of Yalta, who surrendered the city without fighting to the Orlov mutineers, was hanged over the door of a railway station, so that people had to duck to avoid hitting his feet with their heads. The only courts that functioned were military field courts, whose sentences were usually death. Batches of 10 or 15 men at a time were hanged or shot. Passing through Sebastopol, men could be seen hanging on telegraph poles near the railway station. In Sebastopol during one week, two officers were shot and three others publicly hanged for committing robberies and crimes of violence. Some small boys were hanged for ridiculing officers, and a Sister of Mercy was hanged for beating a wounded soldier. Public executions were so frequent that they were simulated in children's play. Undoubtedly many persons suffered unjustifiably, but it is equally certain that by the end of April there was order, and by the end of May conditions appeared almost normal. . . .

Wrangel's naval forces in the Black Sea, although always control-
ling the sea as far as Red naval forces were concerned, nevertheless had
suffered more in morale than the army. Vessels were inadequately man-
ned, officers apathetic, and crews discontented. Under Shilling and
Denikin, they were looked on more as possible means of evacuation
than as fighting forces, some vessels being already loaded with personal
effects of high officials. They undertook some activities along the east
coast of the Black Sea during March, but cooperation with military
forces was halfhearted and insufficient, and usually they went to sea or
not as pleased them. . . .

Practically all the . . . former Black Sea Fleet had been sunk or
had their machinery so damaged by French and British in April 1917
that they could no longer be considered serviceable. However, guns and
mounts remained serviceable, and there was undestroyed a large
amount of ammunition for the naval guns. . . .

Vessels were repainted by direct order of the commander in chief,
their appearance so improved their crews were no longer ashamed of
them, and people could hardly convince themselves they were Russian
vessels. Crews were new and inexperienced but composed of very intelligent young men immediately put under intensive training. Vessels
were cleaned up, brightwork polished, batteries put in good order, and
regular routines established. Subcaliber practice is carried on, and the
[battleship *General*] *Alexseev* has been to sea and tried out her battery.
On account of lack of fuel, larger vessels steam up only once a week,
and lack of light and sanitary service makes living conditions on board
difficult. Three more destroyers, several gunboats, the dispatch vessel
Almaz, three torpedo boats, and a submarine have been placed in commission, and several other vessels are being made ready. The old battleship *Rostislav* was towed to Kertch and took station as guardship. A
number of light draft barges had 6-inch guns mounted on them and
were sent up to take part in defense of the Crimean isthmuses. Naval
guns were established ashore at both Perekop and Sivash as part of their
fixed defenses. Many motorboats were fitted out with machine guns and
took part in shallow-water operations. . . . At Sebastopol, docking and
workshops are sufficient to look out for the fleet but are troubled by
strikes.

To oppose these, the Reds have very few naval vessels. At Odessa in
February was left the modern cruiser *Admiral Nakhimov*, about 75 percent completed, and two submarines of the type supplied from America
in 1916, the submarines being sunk in the harbor before the city was
abandoned.

Russian naval authorities do not believe that the *Nakhimov* can be completed by the Reds. At Nikolaev were left three other cruisers of the same type as *Nakhimov*, about 50 percent completed (but it is considered impossible for the Reds to complete them) and six of the submarines constructed in America, whose completion is possible. One of these submarines is said to be ready for sea at this time and may be expected soon in operation. . . .

There was much constructive work in other directions. Government material and property was inventoried, and commercial vessels were released from naval requisition, returned to their owners, and placed on regular routes. Bureaucratic institutions were reduced and useless officials sent to the front. Secret Service was overhauled and cleared of its criminal elements, school buildings were released from requisition and courses started again, railway administration was reorganized so trains were on schedule, and sanitary conditions were improved so that a threatened epidemic is under control. . . .

General Wrangel announced that the land question would be settled on the basis of turning over land to those working it. A commission began work on details, and on June 6 the new Land Law was promulgated. The Law is rather prolix and complicated with qualifications and conditions not easily understood by the peasant, even if he could read its terms. Most look on it as a mass of words, and after being repeatedly fooled by both sides, they are extremely skeptical of words. . . . A law expressed in simple terms, without qualifications, giving the peasant unqualified possession of all the land he could work, would have spelt the end of bolshevism. If in addition they could have assured the right of habeas corpus, of free education, of the 8-hour day and the right to strike, 90 percent of the Russians would have been at Wrangel's disposition, and he could have won even without fighting.[5] Any progress toward really liberal democratic ideas comes awfully hard to a Russian whether he is a Bolshevik or anti-Bolshevik.

Economic conditions were in a chaotic state. . . . Shopkeepers secreted their stores, and only pawnshops were doing a thriving business in the few remaining articles of value left to an unhappy population. In the windows of these pawnshops were large numbers of wedding rings, officers' decorations, children's ornaments, worn articles of clothing sold and replaced by even more worn articles bought more cheaply at another pawnshop. . . .

Money is spent as quickly as possible as there is no confidence in it, and each person endeavors to immediately convert it into any kind of material value. Certain kinds of money, or even certain denominations issued by the same government are preferred on account of the more artistic design or coloring. The Don currency is not based on any more real values than the Denikin money but is worth about three times as much as Denikin, principally on account of the more artistic coloring and design. It "looks more like money." . . .

With the reorganization of the army, there were on June 1 about 80,000 men, of whom about 50,000 were available for operations. These consisted of the First Corps under General Kutepov* at Perekop . . . comprising about 7,000 infantry, 46 guns, 12 tanks, 21 aeroplanes, and 500 cavalry. The Second Corps, under General Slashchev, organized for a combined naval and military expedition to a port on the Sea of Azov, was composed of 58 guns, 3 aeroplanes, 5 armed motorcars, and 400 cavalry, in all about 10,000 men. The Third Corps of General Pisarev,[†] at the Sivash Isthmus, was composed of 1,960 cavalry, 19 guns, 9 aeroplanes, 3 armored trains, in all about 11,000 men. The Fourth Corps was composed of dismounted Cossacks, 14 guns, and about 16,000 men in reserve near Sivash.[6]

— ❦ —

These battered and freezing troops, trapped in a situation not terribly disimilar to that faced by the men of Washington's Continental Army at Valley Forge 142 years earlier, were about to rally for one great battle to decide the fate of their country. The White Army's Baron von Steuben had arrived in the person of Baron von Wrangel, and the final battle was about to be joined.

---

* Aleksandr Pavlovich Kutepov (1882–1930?), whom Koehler later described as his "sworn brother," had attained the rank of colonel in the Imperial Army. After the Revolution Kutepov joined the Volunteer Army and was appointed commander of the Kornilov Regiment by Kornilov himself in March 1918. Under Denikin, Kutepov rose to the rank of major general. He covered the evacuation of Novorossisk and then became one of Wrangel's senior commanders. Wrangel awarded Kutepov the rank of General of Infantry. Kenez describes him as a man "completely without appreciation of political issues and needlessly cruel."

† General Pisarev is described briefly by Kenez as commanding a "mixed corps which was made up largely by Kuban Cossacks . . . by far the weakest of the four [main groups of Wrangel's forces] (Kenez, p. 265).

7

Melitopol, Russia

June 1920

General Tsichetski was busy receiving reports and eating eggs at 70 rubles per dozen instead of 300 rubles each—the Crimean price, which for long had lifted eggs above the competence of a mere general. (June 1920)

The "Black Baron," as the Bolsheviks derisively called Wrangel, was encouraged in his boldness by a Polish invasion of the Ukraine, which had forced the Reds to divert thousands of the troops menacing him in the Crimea. Taking advantage of this, Wrangel attacked into the Tauride during the first week of June.

Prior to Wrangel's expedition, Koehler made the rounds of Yalta and Sebastopol and met briefly with Wrangel's staff, then journeyed to the Sivash. His reactions to the situation are clear from an entry in McCully's diary of 20 May: "Met Koehler, who had just been up to the Sivash front—says things looked good, but spirit not so good."[1] And again on 27 May: "Koehler arrived during night, having come over by automobile. He had a most interesting visit to front and considers things in excellent shape."[2] But the Commander was not content to observe the fighting for brief periods of time. He left Sebastopol and headed for an extended visit to the newly formed front in the Tauride on 9 June. McCully noted in his diary that same day: "Koehler leaves to try and get in with Slashchev; if he does he should see some interesting things."[3] He did precisely that, described in his extraordinary naval intelligence report of 23 June 1920.

On 9 June 1920, I arrived at Kirilovka, a small village a short distance inland and about five miles from where General Slashchev's troops had put ashore three days previously. . . .

A small cargo steamer hastily converted into a troop transport by the simple process of marching troops on board in great numbers, and a few days later converted into a hospital ship by the still simpler expedi-

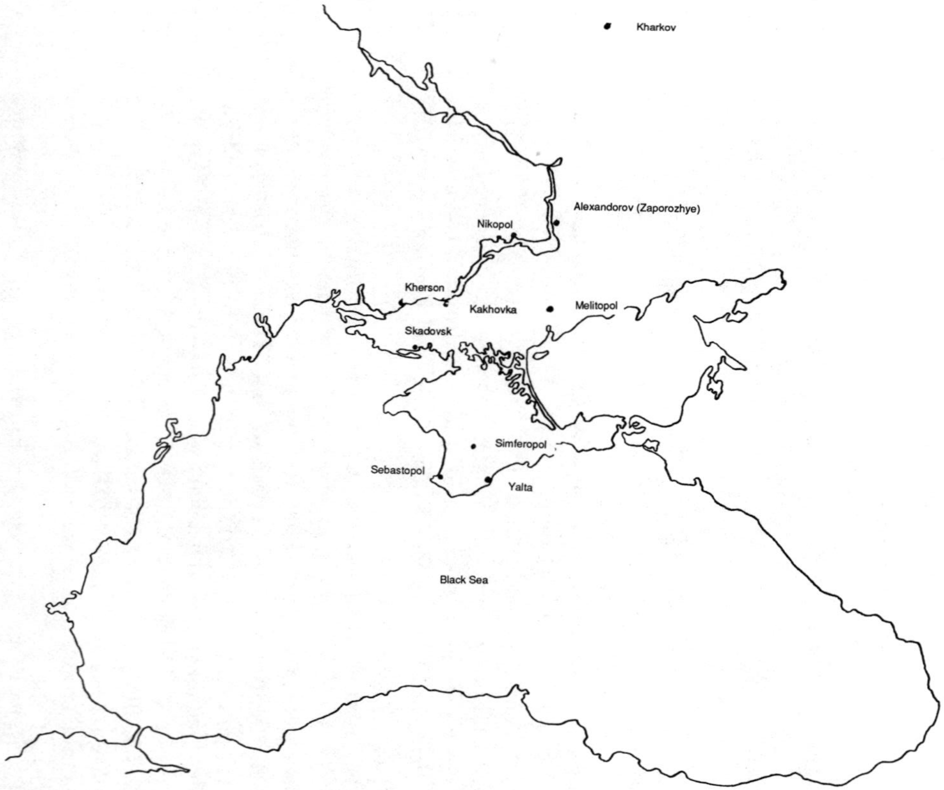

Map 4   Southern Russia and the Black Sea

Kharkov

Alexandorov (Zaporozhye)

Melitopol

Nikopol

Kherson

Kakhovka

Skadovsk

Simferopol

Sebastopol

Yalta

Black Sea

ent of hoisting the Red Cross flag, was stationed at Kirilovka. Wounded arrived in a steady stream, and though arrangements were crude, the wounded were attended to quickly and made comfortable on heaps of straw in cargo holds. Although the front line was then some 40 versts* distant, none of the new arrivals had been wounded more than a day before, and had received prompt first-aid attention. They were rapidly sent to the rear by requiring each village to transport them to the next village, thus interfering as little as possible with work of the peasants and making to their interest to expedite travel. . . . Patience of sufferers during these operations without anesthetics was extraordinary, and it made one feel all the more keenly the wantonness of all this useless additional suffering caused by the great shortage of medicaments of every kind. The proportion of deaths to wounded is very small on the battlefield, but the number of deaths due to lack of simple medical necessities is wickedly large in the hospitals.

Early the second morning I proceeded toward Ephremovka with a detachment of General Slashchev's cavalry. Along the entire route we passed through splendid grain fields and saw many large herds of cattle—at one time eleven herds being in sight, none having less than 150 cattle. I made detours en route to talk to local officials and to groups of Bolshevik prisoners being sent to the rear, usually with one or two guards for a hundred or more prisoners. Villagers were bitter enough in denunciations of Bolsheviks, but I noted no great enthusiasm for Wrangel's forces—the attitude was one of indifference—of a people who had known the worst and cared little one way or the other. . . .

Many prisoners, probably 30 percent, were without footgear of any kind, and none had anything approaching a military uniform, nothing but simple peasant costume. Underclothing was apparently unknown, and even the fortunate booted had their feet bound in rags instead of socks. Despite the heat, many men wore overcoats, for the simple reason that that was the only garment they had. . . .

At Ephremovka, I caught up with General Slashchev, the corps commander, and proceeded with him and his staff to Radionovka. His adjutant, who came with us, was practically unconscious by the time we arrived in Radionovka, as he was suffering from a severe head wound he had received the previous day. This is the third adjutant General Slashchev has had in as many months, the first having been killed outright and the second having died of wounds; in both cases the

---

* A verst is a unit of measurement equal to 3,500 feet.

general was within a few feet when the accident occurred. The previous day a shell had landed beneath the general's horse but had not exploded. The general attributed his luck to a large black crow, which, with two ducklings of which he is very fond, shared the front seat of the automobile with a very plump young lieutenant who had given up skirts for red breeches and Hussar boots, and never stirred without rifle and revolver. The general had in person led the attack on Radionovka two days previously and had occupied the town but, on account of counterattacks by the Reds, had moved back his headquarters. On our approach to Radionovka we heard heavy firing in the direction of Melitopol, and this continued until almost midnight and commenced again in the early morning—apparently a most unusual proceeding here in these days when artillery attacks are confined almost entirely to after-breakfast and before-supper hours. Although Reds had been cleared from town only a comparatively few hours, excellent communication with advanced lines by field telegraph and telephone had already been established, and a portable wireless set maintained contact with other corps commanders and the rear, pending the repair of the regular telegraph lines, which the Bolsheviks had left practically intact.

At daybreak, I joined a small cavalry detachment, which, on our approach to Melitopol, scattered in different directions as it was composed of scouts who were endeavoring to locate the many small bands of Red cavalry separated from their main force during the retreat and now behind south Russian lines. These isolated groups were desperately trying to break through to the northeastward, and several transport trains and small signal parties had already suffered severely from these roving bands of Red cavalry. Upon arrival at the outskirts of Melitopol we found Reds still held Melitopol station and were bombarding the town from armored trains at a distance, but the south Russian forces had occupied the main part of the town. I continued on into the town and went at once to headquarters, where I found General Tsichetski* installed in the building hurriedly vacated a few hours previously by the Bolshevik Central Committee. The general was busy receiving reports and eating eggs at 70 rubles per dozen instead of 300 rubles each—the Crimean price, which for long had lifted eggs above the competence of a mere general. He was much annoyed because the Bolsheviks, although evidently departing in haste, had nevertheless knocked a leg or two off every chair not only in this office but also in

---

* "General Tsichetski," at least as Koehler spells his name, is absent from the English language accounts of the Civil War.

every other public building in town. However, although he had no place to sit down, and was consequently much annoyed, the price of eggs soon cheered him up again, and he finished his ninth with great relish. He scribbled a permit for me and gave me three Cossacks with whom I proceeded at once to an address I had previously obtained from a prisoner as the Melitopol headquarters at the Bolshevik Tchresvichaika.

The address proved correct, for in a few minutes we arrived at a steel-barred and locked building on the principal square. The Cossacks made short work of the locks, and within a few minutes we were in a large room whose walls were completely lined with shelves stacked high with papers and pamphlets—all in the most terrible confusion. In the middle of the room were sacks filled with more pamphlets and papers, all evidently being prepared for a very hurried flight and left behind at the last moment. I started in by collecting such of the papers as seemed of value, and turned the Cossacks to sorting for me a copy of every pamphlet there. They did their work thoroughly—they loved it. On an expedition on which all looting had been forbidden, this was the nearest approach to it they had seen, and poor stuff [though] this paper seemed to them, it nevertheless soon acquired some value in their eyes when they saw how anxious I was to get it. But I could not hold them down to taking only a single copy of each—they simply had to take armfuls. We were getting along very well, however, when we were interrupted by a great clatter outside, and on looking out saw a troop of cavalry dashing by in a great hurry. Asked what was up, some half dozen troopers shouted at us, but all we gathered was that Red troops in force had entered the northern end of the town and that this hurrying troop was the last to leave town. Fortunately a wagon came by just at this time, and though it was loaded, we soon unloaded it and even more quickly loaded it with our sacks of papers and pamphlets, and in a few minutes we were galloping after the retreating cavalry. But it quickly disappeared, and as the town was new to all of us and the streets suddenly deserted, doors and windows barred, we were somewhat at a loss. However, as the Bolsheviks were entering from the northward, it took me very few seconds to decide to set a course for the southward, and at best speed possible. I considered lightening the load by tumbling off a few sacks, but I realized that it would mean the sacrifice of the loyalty of my Cossacks, for these worthless pamphlets and papers had now achieved the dignity of loot—and, drop loot with the enemy on our heels?—it is not done! We plunged along at this rate nearly tc the outskirts of the town when suddenly we heard a heavy fire directly ahead of us, so without further ado we headed into the first open courtyard. Here we ran our wagon into an old stable and well out of sight, and then, having unhitched the horses, took them with us to a point behind a flour mill nearby—a position chosen by my Cossack friends because of its chances for a better getaway as well as for its freedom from entangling pamphlet evidence. Here we stood by for some three hours, during which time the firing became more distant, and on one of the Cossacks making a reconnaissance and learning that the Red troops that had entered the town had retreated hastily on noticing cavalry on their flank, we came out of our retirement and proceeded quickly on to Radionovka. We were received there with much enthusiasm though with few congratulations on our loot, which was examined by many of the curious and pronounced pretty poor stuff to make such a fuss about. All this material was later turned over to the Intelligence Section of the headquarters staff, with the understanding that all of it, together with such similar material as the Intelligence Section had, would be at our disposition. Two days later, when the town was actually occupied by south Russian forces, I returned to Melitopol and with an officer of the Russian Intelligence Section visited all the former Bolshevik offices and gathered much additional material, all of which is now being inventoried. A rough estimate is that there are several thousand pamphlets in which there are probably four hundred or five hundred different kinds, and probably a thousand newspapers from between twenty-five and thirty different districts. Most of the papers and pamphlets are printed in Russian, but some are in Hebrew, Ukrainian, and Polish, and others are even in dialect. In addition, there are some two hundred posters and placards, files of proclamations and similar matter, statistics, photographs, and correspondence. Pamphlets written at the time of the French Revolution, postcards, placards, etc., of the same date, were also found there. Some days later the Russian staff sent orders that all such material be removed from these offices and forwarded to Sebastopol, but it was discovered that during the night certain Jews had removed all that remained, and the posters, proclamations, orders, etc., had also been systematically removed from bulletin boards by these same Jews.

I heard numerous reports of Red atrocities and whenever possible investigated by going personally to the scene and interviewing witnesses. In most cases I was unable to get any definite verification, usually because of the scattering of the witnesses and the burial of the victims, and also very probably because the accounts given in many cases contained interpolations and suppositions not supported by actual circumstances. Nor were the accounts given me by the headquarters staff much more accurate than the gossip of soldiers and peasant women, when the subject of atrocities was touched. Though I had many categoric statements from people who said they had been witnesses and who stated that they themselves had seen certain definite and specific atrocities, I did not credit them, though I would perhaps have been perfectly willing to except as truthful the statements of the same men on any other subject; for on the subject of atrocities it appears most honest people become extraordinarily extravagant liars! Nevertheless, three cases I consider definitely established, for I myself saw the bodies of the victims. On June 13, at Darmstadt, a German colonist village, a small party of telegraphers, busy repairing the lines, were attacked by Red cavalry and literally hacked to pieces. I arrived on the scene within two hours of the attack, while the dead were still on the field and before the wounded had been cared for other than by the villagers. The attack in itself was an atrocity, for the men were mostly unarmed, and as they could offer no resistance, surrendered immediately. The body of the officer was some 500 yards distant from those of the others, having evidently been dragged along the ground. One hand had been hacked off, and both eyes were out of their sockets—apparently having been kicked out. On June 16, near Melitopol, I saw the body of an officer whose arms had been hacked off and whose ears had been cut off apparently by repeated sword strokes. I was unable to get information more definite than statements of peasants in a farmhouse nearby, to the effect that Red cavalry had left this officer there the previous evening. A Bolshevik prisoner told me that on June 10, at Ivanovka, the Reds had shot 30 Wrangel officers and 8 other prisoners; the Russian staff report and two Red prisoners confirmed this statement in its details but not in numbers. I considered it a reliable report. The statements of many Red prisoners and interviews with officials and others who have lived under the Bolsheviks strongly confirm my impression that the organized atrocities against officers that undoubtedly existed in the Red Army at first are no longer carried out, but inasmuch as no measures are taken to prevent such atrocities, they continue on a small scale. However, according to prisoners, very extensive executions are carried out in the towns and cities by the "Tchresvichaika," or counterrevolutionary inquisition.

In all I talked at length to some 50 or 60 Bolshevik prisoners and briefly questioned several times that number. During the first period, when a Russian officer was with me during my conversations, I obtained little information of any kind; but when I was allowed to talk to them by myself, I found they talked much more freely. My plan of procedure was to pick out the stupidest from each batch of prisoners, ask each one to tell me his story, [and] follow this up with questions I had thought out in advance and then with any others suggested by his own narrative or answers. My reasons for picking out the stupidest was that though each man told me much less than would an intelligent man, yet in the aggregate the stupid told me much more, and they agreed in the main, while the accounts of some of the intelligent were at great variance. After I had obtained a certain basis of information I found I could question the intelligent to much greater advantage, for their answers to a series of questions on which I already had accurate information gave me an opportunity to estimate how much confidence I could put on what they said on other subjects. In this way, my later conversations, even with commissars and Jews who were evidently trying to mislead me, became of value.

The general attitude of the simple Red soldier is first and foremost that he is sick of war and wants only to go back to his farm, invariably in some distant part of Russia, for apparently the greatest care is taken to send mobilized men to a front as far as possible from their native province. These men have no interest in bolshevism, or communism or socialism, or Russianism, for that matter, and a day after they are captured they are put into south Russian regiments and sent against the Bolsheviks. And they do very well—regimental commanders are glad to have them and, in fact, infinitely prefer them to the recruits gathered by the south Russia mobilization. When asked why, since they dislike the Bolsheviks so heartily, they have not previously come over to the south Russian forces, they say that they were afraid to, for the Bolsheviks have published much propaganda about the treatment that those who go over to the south Russian army receive there. When asked why, since they are so bitter against this forced military service, forced requisitions, and the many other things of which they complain most grievously, the peasants themselves do not rise up against the Bolsheviks, they answer that they cannot organize, that they are afraid of spies, who are everywhere, that they have no arms, and that if they are even suspected their whole village is burned to the ground by the Communists. And more to this general effect. But of a great national idea, I failed to discover even a trace. Perhaps the nearest approach to a national idea is the firm conviction that the old government was very bad. The statement often made here that at heart the peasants want a monarchy because a monarchy—a czar—represents order to them, is a delusion; they want no monarchy, and on the contrary, they will have none of it. They have no idea of what the south Russian army represents; they were told, and they evidently have believed, that the Volunteer Army was wiped out and that the present advance is by a few Cossacks who are looking for loot and by foreign troops.

Although there are certain regiments made up entirely of Communists—and these are by far the best regiments the Reds have—the real Communists are in an extraordinarily small minority in the army and are mostly spies. There are no Jews, except doctors and pharmacists, in the Red Army—even the Jew army commissars have disappeared. And comparatively few workmen are in the army except in the purely Communistic regiments. If one asks, why then do they not rise against this tyranny they all profess to hate so thoroughly, the same answer is repeated—no organization, they are far from home, if they go over to the south Russians or themselves undertake rebellion their families will at once be killed and their villages burned. In short, they are prostrate—they writhe, to be sure, but they remain prostrate.

This attitude is perhaps best illustrated by that of an aviator captured near Radionovka while I was there. He was a former Volunteer Army officer, very well and favorably known here and captured by the Reds in February when he had to make a forced descent behind their lines on account of an accident to his motor. It was thought at first that he had come over voluntarily from the Reds, and he was greeted enthusiastically. But he quickly dispelled the illusion by saying that his engine had stopped, otherwise he never would have landed. He then explained that in his squadron were twenty aviators divided into groups of five each. Whenever a machine went out over enemy lines, the four other aviators of that particular group were placed under surveillance until the machine returned. If it descended behind enemy lines, the four were summarily shot. As a result of this system these aviators had bound themselves to each other by a most solemn oath never to come down behind enemy lines no matter what their sympathies or what the risk. Consequently, the consternation of the aviator just captured; his non-return at sundown would mean the summary shooting of his four comrades.

I talked at length with a Captain Tretiakov, who had escaped from the Reds during the attack on Melitopol. He is related to General Tretiakov, who commands a division in the First Army Corps of the south Russian forces.* . . .

---

* Brief mention is made of an S. N. Tretiakov, a "former Provisional government member" in Brinkley, *The Volunteer Army and Allied Intervention in South Russia, 1917–1921* (Notre Dame, Ind., 1966), p. 105 (hereafter cited as Brinkley).

He said Bolsheviks made effective propaganda of the visit of the English Labor Commission, and promises of help by this commission had been given enormous publicity.* He himself had been convinced by them, for at a great parade given in honor of the visiting delegates, one of them announced the Labour party in England stood shoulder to shoulder with Russians in this fight for the rights of the working man.

Talking to Captain Tretiakov, I was again struck with the great difficulty of getting a general view of the situation or of accurately sounding the general feeling. This is obviously due to the fact there is no free press and to the entire lack of communication, which makes an accurate general view impossible. No newspapers exist other than those controlled and actively directed by the government, and similarly no books or pamphlets except those endorsed by the government are printed. Communication by post is difficult and dangerous; the telegraph is reserved for government use. So no man knows what is happening beyond his own horizon. For example, I asked whether the Polish advance and the Bolshevik efforts against them had developed any feeling that this was a national war. His idea was that General Brusilov's† appeal to old officers to join in the fight against the Polish invaders had given rise to rather complex feelings. For no matter how bad the internal situation, it had somehow gone against his grain to see Poland taking advantage of Russia's troubles to steal Russian soil, and he had finally decided that even if it meant joining the Bolsheviks he would do his bit against the Poles; and this though he was far from being an admirer of Brusilov, whom he considered a self-seeking windbag. He thought that as it had been with himself, so it had probably affected many old officers, for only the advance of the south Russian forces and the possibility of joining them had kept him out of the Bolshevik's ranks. . . .

In answer to my question concerning the spirit of the Bolshevik army, Captain Tretiakov said there was no such thing—the army consisted of Communists, Latvian and Chinese mercenaries, and great masses of peasants mobilized against their wills and held in the army

---

* England was at this time pressuring Eastern European states, notably Poland, to make peace quickly with the Bolsheviks. See Brinkley, pp. 249–51.

† Aleksei Alekseevich Brusilov (1853–1926), was one of the few high-ranking imperial commanders to enter the service of the Bolsheviks. He did so, not especially because of the Polish invasion, nor because he was particularly enamored of the Reds, but because Denikin's Volunteer forces had executed his son in December 1919. "Brusilov's true feelings toward the Soviet government are still a mystery" (John D. Basil, cited in MERSH, 5:201–5).

only by fear of what would happen to them and their families if they deserted—spirit did not exist, though Communists would fight to the death, for they knew defeat meant death, and Latvians and Chinese gave good service for their pay and privileges; but there was no fight in the mobilized peasants, nothing that even resembled spirit. In regard to officers and discipline, he said that although there were many former Russian officers in the Red Army, promotions were reserved for Communists insofar as possible. He said there was a discipline of sorts, which had begun by abolishing all the formal salutes, etc., but that of late the old "adanichesti"* had been reintroduced with the single difference that the word comrade was always used instead of the rank of officer. Later, to verify this, I asked a prisoner to salute me just as he would a commissar. He saluted just as would a soldier of the south Russian forces and used the same words of greeting except that instead of my rank he used the word "Tovarish." Epaulets and shoulder marks have been abolished by the Bolsheviks, but distinctive sleeve marks are now worn by officers. These sleeve marks consist of a five-pointed red star about four inches in diameter, with a black or gold scythe and hammer embroidered on the star.† Below the star are hollow red squares (about one inch high) or triangles, according to whether the officer belongs to infantry or cavalry. . . . This uniform is almost entirely a Moscow affair, for not a single one of the hundreds of prisoners I saw had anything resembling a military uniform. . . .

I talked at length to the mayor of Melitopol, though during my first conversation with him, Red troops reentered the outskirts of the town, whereupon the mayor's hysterical, and very large, wife fell upon me, and seizing my notebook ran with it to another room, where she tore out all pages she thought might contain notes that might implicate her husband. The mayor was not much help in the crisis and contented himself with explaining that his wife thought he might be compromised if I were captured by the Reds, and he dared not interfere with her. However, he later recounted the entire history of the occupation of Melitopol by the Reds, and his wife added many gruesome details, so we are friendly again. He said the last occupation, in December 1919, was the third time the Reds had come, and each time with increasing violence. The first step was to requisition all large houses and furniture, without payment—much of the furniture being sent away. This was

---

* By "adanichesti" Koehler apparently means "otdanie chesti," which means "salute" or, more literally, "rendering honor to."

† Koehler has confused the scythe with the sickle.

followed by "mandate" requisitions, i.e., an order for the commissar to select such things as the Soviet government required, and which meant, in short, that almost everything of value would be taken. No receipts were given—no payments of any kind were made. On the first and second occupations, all persons suspected of counterrevolutionary ideas were arrested, and many—not less than eight hundred or nine hundred—were shot; on the last occupation, many were arrested but all were sent to Alexandrovsk or Ekaterinoslav for trial. The mayor knew of no one who had ever returned. . . . All material in shops was requisitioned, all shops and factories were closed, [and] all private trade and industry was stopped. Although Melitopol is the center of one of the richest grain districts in Russia and the harvest was excellent, there was a great shortage of bread, which was procurable only by cards, or from Jew speculators at exorbitant prices. For purposes of bread cards, the population was divided into the usual three categories: first, Red officials and clerks, workmen, children under 9, women with children; second, the sick and unable to work, widows of Red soldiers or officials, women who worked, i.e., had no servants; third, all others. No definite amount of bread was given to any category, but the second and third received fractional amounts of that given the first category. When the factories were first nationalized, i.e., taken away from the owners and turned over to the Soviet Council, the control was vested in a committee of workmen, elected by all workmen in the factory. This committee was later replaced by another committee of workmen appointed by the Soviet Council. This committee was in turn supplanted by an expert administrator appointed by the Soviet Council, and the workmen had no voice whatever in regard to the management of the factory, pay, or working hours. The only strike attempted was punished so summarily it was not repeated. Small wonder the workmen before long lost their enthusiasm for the Red regime but were helpless against the Communist troops.

All schools had been closed and the buildings used mostly for offices for the hordes of officials arrived from the north. Bolsheviks announced excellent plans for creation of orphanages, schools for small children, and soup kitchens for small children, but only the last had been carried out. For a long time, instead of newspapers, bulletins were posted three or four times a week. This was doubtless due to shortage of paper, for I saw some of these bulletins and they were printed on odds and ends of paper, all of it already used on one side. The last questions I asked were whether Bolshevism could continue its existence in Russia, and what single good thing it had accomplished. The mayor answered he could not see how Bolshevism could continue, for no work of any kind was being done, and none could be done under such conditions—bolshevism had lasted this long only because it had the accumulations of other generations and systems to live on. When such accumulations came to an end—and the end was in sight—it must perish because it cannot produce. As for good Reds had done, he said there was no single good thing he knew of, save they had announced splendid plans for the care of young children, plans that were never carried out.

Nothing was known in Melitopol concerning Wrangel forces; people all believed they consisted only of refugees, Cossacks, and monarchists, and were without any real force. Nothing was known of General Slashchev's descent or the advance from the Crimea until the railroad was cut near Vladimovka, some twenty versts from Melitopol. Bolsheviks themselves were taken quite unawares, for they made no preparations for departure and abandoned all their gear.

Each corps of Wrangel's army has with it a chief of civil administration, whose function is to organize the civil administration of the newly occupied territory as quickly as possible. I talked at length with an enormous, red-bearded, fiery-eyed giant with a voice like a bass viol, who occupies this post in General Slashchev's corps. He said his guiding idea was that this is a civil war, a struggle between Russians—Russians of widely different ideas, to be sure—but still Russians; in short, the occupied area is not to be treated as conquered territory but must be administered so the people will understand that the new regime is working for them and with them, not against them. I went with him to a number of villages where he addressed the peasants and explained his plans, particularly in regard to the distribution of land. . . . Mikhailof stated the first plan had been to give the land to the peasants without payment of any kind, but peasants would not believe that land received for nothing was actually theirs; they became convinced of the honesty of the administration's intentions only when they could pay actual money for the land, receive a receipt for such payment, and take home a paper with a large red seal that said the land was theirs. . . .

The day I started back for the Crimea, Trotsky arrived in Alexandrovsk and announced in no uncertain manner that the Tauride had to be retaken at all costs; and he at once set to work on the task. He began the campaign by picturing another winter of starvation if the north were denied access to the great stores of grain in the Tauride. His picture is doubtless a true one. A Red offensive will not be a surprise— for though it will doubtless not be made in force for another three or four weeks, preparations to receive it are already well underway. For the south, too, will go hungry without this grain, and the army would be the first to starve. The army understands, and, moreover, it understands that all hope for clothing for the winter also depends on holding this territory. An army that has known cold and hunger as has this army, will fight hard before it leaves plenty to go back to cold and hunger.[4]

Hugo W. Koehler

After such extended and demanding experiences, Koehler turned to the less taxing matter of writing his mother.

Dear Mother:

My latest contact with the Bolsheviks occurred just a few days ago at Melitopol, during General Wrangel's advance into the Tauride—as gallant and brave and well-executed an operation as any in all the Great War. I was with the advance detachment of Cossack cavalry that entered Melitopol, the main objective of the entire movement. The whole affair was such an entire surprise to the Bolsheviks, who, of course, enormously outnumber General Wrangel's forces, that we entered Melitopol literally on the heels of the retreating Reds.

— ❦ —

Koehler spared his mother none of the grim details of the tenuous escape from Melitopol, nor of the wry Cossack humor that was revealed once he had persuaded them they had obtained a cache of "loot," he could not persuade them to give it up.

This stuff had now acquired the dignity of loot, and let go loot? Never!! So we finished loading the wagon . . . and then started out at a furious pace, but slow nevertheless, after the cavalry that had long disappeared. . . .

So I made the best of my way to Sebastopol, some 200 miles to the southward, and have just arrived, with all my loot—and have been much kissed by everyone in sight, from the admiral to the Russian General Staff. . . .

I have been almost everywhere, these last six months, from the interior of Russia to Mesopotamia, from the Caucasus to the Caspian, and Turkestan to Jerusalem. I am grayer than ever I remember my father, and there is more white in my beard than shows in that picture of my grandfather (your father) you've always had in your room. Do I frighten you with the story of the white in my hair? But no—I am very well and fit and, I suspect, pleased as punch about my venerable air; for always I have been too young; and now I am always taken for the admiral and he for my chief of staff—which pleases him mightily, for he is content to be young. . . .

Although there are hundreds of stories and accounts of all sorts about what is happening in Russia, no one in our State Department or in any of the chancelleries of Europe has any real and definite ideas of what is in truth happening there. And the situation is so complex that it is very doubtful whether the people in the very midst of it all have the slightest idea of what is really happening all about them. So our task is to find out what is really happening, what is at the bottom of it all, what it will lead to, what it means, whether bolshevism is a real force, a workable idea, one that will endure, or whether it is the false doctrine that it appears to be. Obviously, our purpose in finding out all this and a hundred and one more similar things, is to indicate what would be a sound policy for our government to follow. . . . So you see why it is necessary to examine this from every angle and why one must see it near to in closest intimacy and also from sufficient distance for a perspective.

The outward facts are not difficult to establish if one takes the trouble to be certain that one's information is accurate and not simply the opinions of too careless observers. In Russia, bolshevism has been an absolute failure as a system of government so far, for the country is ruined, the people are starving, there is no industry; in large cities infant mortality has reached nearly 100 percent at times and at best averages about 80 percent. And instead of freedom, it is the most absolute tyranny that has ever existed in any part of the world, in any age: there is no free press; every single newspaper has been taken over by the so-called government and is simply an organ for the spread of Bolshevik propaganda. No public meetings, except those called by the Communist officials, are allowed. If there is a strike, the men are sent to work at the point of a bayonet, after the leaders, or those suspected of being leaders, have been shot. In small towns, strikes are punished by burning the town to the ground. There is no personal liberty or security for even the clothes on one's back. Requisitions are endless: everything from bed linen and underclothes to furniture and pianos are taken, and, of course, all gold, silver, jewels, furs, valuable papers, and pictures are taken. And this is not by pirates or by pillaging hordes of any army advancing through hostile country but by the organized and authorized officials of the government, which takes these things from its own as well as enemy citizens. . . .

As it is now, the Soviet government is an absolute tyranny—a system of government founded on an unsound economic principle—

and temporarily continued in power by virtue of a very clever and thorough propaganda, and supported by a military system founded on the very simple and at least temporarily effective principle of giving the soldiers the very best of everything—enormous pay and plenty of food while all others are starving—so that they will resist any effort to change the existing conditions, since they know that no other regime will ever give them the cream of everything with a minimum of work. Such a system can last for a time, but only for a short time, and then it must collapse. And bolshevism is falling—it cannot last; the only question is how much it will drag with it in its fall. The Jews are in absolute control, though there are of course exceptions like Lenin, Tchicherin, Krassin, and others; but the great mass of officials are Jews—and they are in their heyday. But their time is coming . . . when once Russia gets on her feet again there will doubtless be the most glorious "pogroms" that the world has ever seen.* . . .

                                                        Hugo

P.S. Of course I leave the important to the postscript . . . for your birthday I send you a tiny present. It is a miniature model of a decoration I've just received from the Russians. I don't go in much for decorations, though it has happened that my service has been where decorations were hanging around, so I've accumulated enough of them at least to make [my sisters] laugh at me for being pompous when I'm all dressed up. But this decoration I like: it was given me by General Wrangel and presented by General Kutepov, who is the finest soldier-man I've ever known and one of my greatest friends. It is the Order of St. Anne, with swords—the "with swords" meaning that it was for a personal exploit. The little miniature I send you was given me for you by Baroness Wrangel.[5]

---

* Koehler's statement is substantiated to a certain extent by the situation then existing in Russia. The Soviet Central Committee of twenty-two in 1917 was approximately 65 percent Jewish; in 1934, 30 percent of the committee's seventy-one members were Jewish. In 1935, U.S. Ambassador William Bullitt had reported to the State Department: "Extraordinary numbers of Jews are employed in all the Commissariats. Only one out of each sixty-one inhabitants of the Soviet Union is a Jew; but twenty of the sixty-one Commissars and Vice Commissars are Jews" (*Foreign Relations of the United States, Diplomatic Papers, The Soviet Union, 1933–1939*, Dept. of State, 1: 294). Then the storm Koehler so accurately predicted hit the shore: fifty-seven Jews were out—natural death, shooting, disappearance, removal from office, exile, demotion. Of the original twenty-one Jews, the two Kaganovich brothers alone remained. The pogroms Koehler predicted did arrive, but in 1936–37, and brought not by Russians but by a "foreigner," the Georgian Djugashvili, Stalin.

11. Order of St. Anne, awarded to Hugo Koehler by Gen. Wrangel, June 1920. (Photo courtesy of the Division of Numismatics, Smithsonian Institution.)

After this letter to his mother, Koehler wrote to Dolly Gladstone.

Dear Dolly:

I'm afraid your experiment in backing Denikin has been much more costly for you and for Russia and for the world than the simple £400,000,000 (in stores, etc.) you ventured on the project. . . . Poor old Denikin—simple, honest, and a patriot, but undoubtably one of the stupidest men who ever came into power in any country. Surrounded by incompetents and dishonesty, badly advised by his allies, he distinguished himself by not one single sound or wise measure. If he had thrown dice for every decision he would have improved just 50 percent.

General Wrangel is of a different caliber: fine soldier, good general, honest, capable, full of courage and initiative, no great statesman, but he knows it and surrounds himself with men who can take care of that end of the game. . . . His miracles continue. But he cannot beat bolshevism by force of arms—nor can any army. Bolshevism fattens on military opposition. It will collapse without it. . . .

Bolshevism is the most utter tyranny the world has ever seen—there isn't a free newspaper from the Vistula to the Pacific. . . .

Koehler told her about the Melitopol adventure.

So now you know what I've been doing. . . .

I have been . . . much farther into the interior of Russia than I've ever told anyone! . . . You see . . . in matters of this sort, agents, even the very best agents, are useless, because they can't stick to the facts and always give their own conclusions as facts instead of simply as stupid deductions and obvious ones, as they usually are.

I like the Russians, immensely so, in fact, and we've become great friends. . . . General Kutepov (the commander of the First Corps) and I have become sworn brothers. He is about the finest type of soldierman I've ever seen—and I'm very fond of him. Many other of my friends are not as estimable, I am afraid, for about all the brigands, thieves, murderers, and similar pleasant scoundrels that disturb the peace hereabouts count themselves among my intimate friends. And I confess I am fond of them, for they're a brave and honest lot even when they thieve. Sometimes I have an odd sensation, as when, for example, Shkuro* gave me a great dinner and at the end drank a toast to the Church of the Redeemer at Rostov from which he had stolen the gold plate that furnished the proceeds for the dinner. And I still show a little embar-

---

* Andrei Grigor'evich Shkuro (1887–1947), was a Kuban Cossack leader and the stuff of legend. Koehler's account of the Rostov church heist matches a similar account of Shkuro and his "Wolves" by Brigadier H. N. H. Williamson. "Never without his wolfskin cap and the red, blue and white ribbon of the Volunteer Army on his sleeve, he was a Caucasian from one of the mountain tribes, savage and cruel as the best of them, and his regiment of three to four hundred cavalrymen all wore wolfskin caps instead of astrakhan wool. They had their headquarters in their own special collection of railway trucks, on which were painted a pack of wolves in pursuit of prey, and they were a particularly fierce and relentless collection of mountaineers, carrying the usual armoury of a *kinjal* or dagger at their waist, a sword slung over their shoulder, a revolver whenever possible, and rows of cartridge cases for rifles across each side of their chests. Shkuro was undoubtably a great cavalry leader but, as we'd been told, he was also a bit of a brigand and, on one occasion, accompanied by three or four of his officers, he entered the ballroom of a big hotel in Rostov where dancing was in progress and invited all the guests to contribute in jewellery or cash towards the maintenance of his Wolves. Confronted by glittering eyes beneath the shaggy wolf's hair and remembering the Wolves' reputation for ruthless pillage and lack of mercy, no one argued. He made a very successful haul" (John Harris, ed., *Farewell to the Don; The Russian Revolution in the Journals of Brigadier H. N. H. Williamson* [New York, 1971], pp. 68–69). "Throughout the Civil War Shkuro and his Cossack partisans became known for their atrocities, lootings and debaucheries not only in Bolshevik lines, but in areas occupied by Whites as well. William Chamberlain claims that Shkuro 'rolled up atrocity records that would compare fairly with those of the worst provincial Chekas.' The notorious reputation of Shkuro's partisans actually led to the surrender of towns without a fight" (Alex G. Cummins, Jr., cited in MERSH, 35: 8).

rassment on occasions such as the name day of one of my Cossack friends, who celebrated it by giving me a large diamond earring he had taken from a Jew whose throat he had slit during the advance a year ago. But when I was offered a pair of boots with the assurance that the man to whom they had belonged would be shot the following morning and obviously would have no further use for them, I accepted hurriedly without a quiver, for boots hereabouts are above diamonds and fine pearls. . . . It is difficult to keep things in a land such as this, when the need is so great; one has almost a guilty feeling if one owns a sheet or an extra shirt. So long ago I gave away all I had, and now if I had a sheet or an extra shirt I wouldn't know what to do with it except to give it to some poor woman to make a child's dress. . . .

I'm afraid I've given you rather a chaotic picture of it all—but you might take the chaotic effect simply as a bit of realism, for life is indeed chaos here; it resembles reasonable conditions just about as much as that famous cubist picture *Nude Descending a Stair* resembles anything real.

In the first months I was here I accumulated great stacks of loot, from pictures and furs to old earrings and relics. But I've decided to take none of it from Russia. I've given it all away again.[6]

— ❧ —

Koehler's appeal on behalf of the destitute Russians he met found its way back to Dolly and to the rest of upper-class Britain. In fact, it reached as far as those wonderful planets called Cranmore Hall and Longleat. Admiral McCully's 15 July 1920 report to the Secretary of State noted: "Recently representatives of a British Fund established by Lady Muriel Paget have established a hospital in Sebastopol, and a British Red Cross and Children's Relief Organization are also at work."[7]

"Reasonable conditions," so tragically absent in south Russia, still prevailed in another part of the world.

8

Somewhere in Russia
July–August 1920 _____

*I doubt whether all history can furnish a finer example of brav-
ery, courage, and devotion than these men fighting day after day
against a ruthless enemy, practically without pay, without clothes,
without the simplest necessities of life, without any of the glamour
of battle, without encouragement of their countrymen, almost
without comrades. (September 1920)*

While Wrangel's army tried to consolidate its hold on the northern
Tauride, Koehler spent much of July and August sorting and translat-
ing the cache of documents he had lifted from Bolshevik headquarters
in Melitopol, interrupting this work for a brief visit to the front on 20
July.

The American mission became concerned when several incidents
seemed to indicate that Wrangel was sanctioning the return of a czar.
In one instance, a Sebastopol newspaper began circulating with the
motto "For the Faith, the Czar, and the Fatherland." On 14 July Mc-
Cully decided to see the general himself about this. He interviewed
Wrangel alone, advising him that the incidents could compromise the
neutral position of the American mission and "indicated a sentiment
about which I felt it necessary to inform the Department, and asked
him if he wished to make any statement in regard to them, or in regard
to his own position."

Wrangel's response, as usual, was brief. In reference to the newspaper, "he said it would be the first and last issue of that paper, and that
he would hold the censor responsible for permitting this stupidity."
The next day Wrangel issued a proclamation suspending the newspaper
and dismissing the censor.

When the general stated that he would accept any government freely
chosen by the Russian people, McCully asked if this included a freely
chosen *Bolshevik* government. "He said he thought it impossible that
the Russian nation, if given a free choice, would elect such a govern-

ment, but that if it did he would submit to it, but not if it were headed by the persons now in control. He said that he could accept a Soviet government of which General Brusilov might be the head."

McCully added his thought that "what has been accomplished has had to depend too much on Wrangel himself. He is fearless to the point of recklessness, and if anything should happen to him, it is doubtful if there is another leader who would be sufficiently strong to hold the movement together." And that "the determination of the Soviets to crush Wrangel is . . . unshaken. . . . If there is sufficient discontent and distress in the interior of Russia to prevent the Soviets from using their full strength, Wrangel will have a chance, but unless there is, the best he can hope for after making such fight as he may be able, is to retire into the Crimea and hold it as long as possible, which may be for another year."[1]

The tide began to turn against the Black Baron on the Polish front on 15 August 1920, when Polish forces under generals Sikorski and Pilsudski supported by the French under General Maxime Weygand defeated the Soviets at the gates of Warsaw. After this Battle of the Vistula, seventy thousand Soviet troops were taken prisoner while another one hundred thousand escaped into East Prussia. The following spring a treaty was finally signed that bound four million Ukrainians and Byelorussians under Polish rule.

It was a crushing defeat for the Reds, but in the subsequent peace they concentrated their forces on driving Wrangel from the Crimea. Without the diversion of a Polish invasion, Wrangel knew his situation was hopeless. Nevertheless, he gave the order to attack and, in the series of desperate lunges begun in June, won the approaches to the Crimea and advanced into the northern Tauride.

But his army was rapidly becoming outnumbered and outgunned. The White Army fought valiantly to hold the northern Tauride and the approaches to the Crimea, but the full weight of the Red Army was now concentrated upon them. Without the huge army and tons of material that Denikin had ineptly squandered the year before, not to mention the dozens of tanks, aeroplanes, and field guns that had been pushed off the docks of Novorossisk in March, Wrangel's patchwork band was forced gradually back into the Crimea.

But unlike Denikin, Wrangel had anticipated such a possibility and had laid in ships and coal for an evacuation he seemed to know would be inevitable. When the collapse came in the fall of 1920, he was ready for it.

The situation had again become desperate. On 27 August, Koehler again left for the front.

Sebastopol, Russia
September 4, 1920

Left Sebastopol August 27th, at exactly 6:00 P.M., a remarkable performance since this was the hour scheduled for departure—an ordinary mixed freight and passenger service. More remarkable is this exactitude caused no comment; it is no longer the exception. So I was somewhat prepared for the improved appearance of all railroad yards and stations—improvement noted in sanitary conditions and extending to a new coat of whitewash inside and out. This improved appearance was brought about by a few decided hints from General Wrangel accompanied by prompt falling of the official ax. The entire service has been speeded in spite of a great increase in traffic. It is working more smoothly now than when it had the assistance of a large British railroad mission. Great stacks of wood are piled alongside tracks at many places, and stores of coal are to be seen in all the big yards. All along the lines are guards, with special posts at bridges. . . .

At Djankoe station the following morning we passed our fourth sanitary train en route to the rear, cars so crowded the slightly wounded were on steps and platforms and even the roofs. . . .

At Melitopol, I called at the headquarters of General Kutepov, who now, as Commander of First Army, has the same small staff he had as Commander of First Corps. I was received very pleasantly, as I had come to know the officers of the staff intimately during my previous stay with General Kutepov, and they explained . . . that the present movement was critical and the outcome far from certain. Pressure from much greater forces of Reds had increased steadily and it was simply a question of whether Russian troops already suffering from frightfully severe casualties could stand the strain of further attacks. The fact they were greatly outnumbered by Reds made difficult maneuvers and long marches necessary, and troops were very much worn. Even General Kutepov himself with all his indomitable energy plainly showed from overwork; he had not had more than an hour's sleep in seven days. He explained that although strictly military considerations might demand a withdrawal from the present extensive front on account of the heavy cost in casualties in holding so long a line against superior numbers, he felt that political conditions and loyalty to the inhabitants of the occupied territory who had aided the Russian forces (and many of whose

12. General A. P. Kutepov. (Photo courtesy of Baron Petr Vrangel Collection, Hoover Institution Archives.)

younger men were now in the army), demanded the Tauride be held at almost any cost. He stated it had cost more in casualties to hold a line than to advance even against heavy odds, and . . . if he retired at this time he could advance again at a favorable time, at half the cost of holding the present line. Nothing short of absolute necessity could force him to retire and leave those who had befriended the Russian armies to persecution of the Reds. . . .

I was particularly interested in present conditions in Melitopol as my first visit had taken place even before the Bolsheviks had entirely cleared the town, so I had been able to get an idea of conditions in the town under the Red regime. At that time not a single mill or factory was working or had been working since the previous year. No shops, save government depots, had been open for months. A week after the Bolshevik evacuation the only shop open was a hardware merchant timidly selling cherries. Streets were filthy and in parts of the town the stench was frightful even though the many dead horses on the streets had not had time to add their quota. Now I noted the streets had been swept, no refuse was about, and though the town could not be called clean according to any European standard, still there was no stench, and general improvement was marked. Each of thirty-odd flour mills in town was running full blast—even those that required anthracite managed to shuffle along on fuel made of soft coal and oil cakes (sunflower seed residue). Food, though considerably dearer than before, was plentiful and cheaper than in the Crimea, and hotels and restaurants, all closed before, were thriving. A local tannery, brickyard, and veneer factory had all restarted, and though feeble were actually turning out needed products. I talked to the mayor, whose wife, on the previous occasion when Bolsheviks had reentered the town while I was talking to her husband, had fallen on me and torn the pages from my notebook for fear that the Bolsheviks would get it and her husband implicated. This same lady was now all smiles and informed me if only the Bolsheviks would be kept out everything would be all right, for her husband expected to get his brewery going within five days. The mayor explained that although some of the articles now in the shops had been sent up from the Crimea, the greater part had been buried during the Bolshevik occupation and were brought out as soon as the shopkeepers felt secure. Later visits to the shops found some better stocked than those of Sebastopol, with articles . . . considerably less than factory price.

I talked with town officials, shopkeepers, people in the library (an inheritance of Bolshevik loot), and people before bulletin boards. All had the same dread of a return of the Bolsheviks. Many who had remained in Melitopol during the Bolshevik occupation would be forced to flee the town if it were retaken by the Reds, since the town is full of Jews who undoubtedly would give evidence against them. Those who aided or participated in present town government, those who brought out stores secreted during Bolshevik occupation, in fact any who showed sympathy for the south Russian cause, all would have to flee. They had no doubt the fate that awaited them should they again fall under the power of the Bolsheviks. Many families had their effects in carts ready to trek to the Crimea if news from the front became threatening.

From Melitopol we went to Feodorovka, where as usual I made inquiries concerning what was being done towards carrying out the new Land Law. . . .

I found the amount of work actually done towards putting the Land Law into effect was in inverse ratio to the distance to the front. A cynic might with justice attribute this to lack of sincerity of the government, in that they were giving away lands of which their control was problematical at best, while at the same time were taking no measures in the case of lands really held by them. After a determined search, I was unable actually to put my finger on any land that had been allotted. . . .

We proceeded to headquarters of General Pisarev, Commander of First Corps. He reviewed the military situation and seemed confident of success of his encircling movement, begun some two days before with the object of breaking through in rear of the advancing Red column and then surrounding it. Present tactics, both Bolshevik and Russian, represent nothing so much as a giant game of cross-tag: each side attempts to cut in behind the other, then to outflank the other's flanking column, then again to outflank this outflanking flanking column— and so on. . . .

Of particular interest was the visit of General Volodian, one of Makhno's atamans, who commands the largest detachment of Makhno's troops.*

---

* Nestor Ivanovich Makhno (1889–1934) was another of the many "characters" produced by the Russian Civil War. At the age of nineteen in 1907, Makhno was sentenced to hang for revolutionary activities, but his sentence was commuted to an indefinite stay in prison. He was, however, unable to adjust to a life in confinement, and during his nine years of imprisonment he was repeatedly placed in irons or in solitary confinement. Released after the Revolution, Makhno became a utopian anarchist and skilled guerrilla leader whose tactics included rapid movement of troops and weaponry through the use of machine guns mounted on peasant carts. When cornered, his men simply buried their weapons and dispersed as individual peasants back to their fields. Makhno could reconstitute his force, though, with remarkable swiftness. Neither the Reds nor the Whites managed to capture and execute him. In fact, representatives of both sides were sent to Makhno to make truces. All were caught and promptly executed. Trotsky twice sentenced Makhno to death, failing to carry out the decree both times. In complete disagreement with what "Volodian" told Koehler, MERSH indicates that "Makhno, who personally condemned discrimination of any sort, strove to bridle the anti-Semitic feeling of his peasant followers, meting out severe punishment for anti-Jewish actions or declarations. The pogromist label that his enemies tried to pin on him was totally without foundation" (Paul Avrich, cited in MERSH, 21: 18). As for "General Volodian," Koehler is probably

Purpose of this visit was a request for money, ammunition, and instructions for cooperation against the Reds. He was given money and ammunition—though not in large amounts—and a request he attack the rear of the Bolshevik column then pressing Pisarev's front, to worry Red communications, and if possible, take Nikopol, the point at which the Reds repeatedly attempted to cross the Dnieper. Volodian agreed and departed pleased with the success of his mission. General Pisarev stated he was not leaning too heavily on this assistance but had definite information Makhno's forces had already harried the Reds considerably. As a matter of fact, capture of Nikopol by Makhno's troops has just been announced. Volodian is a former Russian general and well known for bravery. He appeared at Pisarev's headquarters in a very gay and picturesque uniform (his own design) and wearing three St. George's Crosses, two Czar Medals, and 72 wound stripes. The Czar Medals were worn reverse forward, i.e., with the czar's head turned inward, and wound stripes stretched from his wrist to his shoulder. However, the Russians said they represented actual wounds, for Volodian has been in every war or skirmish Russia has had for thirty years. Volodian said Makhno had only 3,000 troops a fortnight ago but could get 30,000 within a fortnight anytime he wanted. He expected to begin active operations with a force of some 20,000 by the middle of September. He said Makhno divided all prisoners into three classes: Communists, Jews, and mobilized men. The first two classes he hanged promptly—the last he allowed to go free. He said he took nothing whatever from the Russian peasants but stripped everything from the rich and from German and other colonists. As for aims, they were simply to get land for peasants and then not be interfered with—much emphasis on the latter. . . .

From Melitopol we returned to Djankoe and en route inspected in detail the Sivash and Taganash defenses, which we found well planned, well executed, and ready. Many barbettes and gun shields from men-of-war have been effectively used as machine-gun emplacements and have added to the strength of the position. Robbing ships to make land defenses is an art in which Russians are masters par excellence! In this case at least the result has been worth the effort, for an army the temper

referring to one N. Voronovich. Brinkley writes that Makhno's "Greens" took "organized form in November 1919 with the election of a 'Committee of Liberation' [with] a military staff headed by N. Voronovich" (Brinkley, pp. 225–27). Contacted by the British, Voronovich later tried to meet independently with Denikin to coordinate military actions. Voronovich is also mentioned in Kenez, pp. 241–44, but Koehler's is the first English language account of Voronovich's cooperation with Wrangel.

of present Russian forces makes these defenses impregnable against even greatly superior numbers.

En route to Djankoe we spent the night as usual in a straw stack close to the railroad, and were twice awakened by distant machine-gun fire, which we learned later had been directed against Bolshevik advance patrols. This incident had greater significance than simply showing the high-water mark of Bolshevik penetration, for it was unaccompanied by panic or even excitement, so confident were all that General Kutepov's encircling movement would force the Reds to retire before they reached the railroad, no matter how close they might get—certainly a far different affair than the automatic retirement of the Denikin armies six months ago whenever Red cavalry rode along parallel to the railroad and forty versts away. . . .

Whenever I arrived on the fighting line, I found the division commander and his chief of staff in the front line or ahead of it, instead of in their classic post two miles in the rear. I noted a general of artillery with a rifle wound in his leg and a saber cut in his head, certainly a most unorthodox proceeding, but here the artillery is immediately behind the infantry if not on the line with it. Wounded Bolshevik prisoners were evidently getting the same treatment as the Russian soldiers. . . .

Heavy artillery fire going on since the early morning indicated that an action of more than usual intensity was going on [near Tchaplinka]. Upon arrival at the first artillery post, the corps commander simply saluted his officers instead of shaking hands with everyone in sight and on leaving he again saluted instead of shaking hands with at least thirty people, the invariable practice on such occasions. The general noticed my surprise at this unorthodox procedure, for he explained it was the result of a new order just promulgated to save the hours lost by interminable shaking hands with everybody in sight. The matter is a detail . . . but it shows the distinct tendency towards speeding the whole machine even though certain good old customs must go. The general was on his stomach in a haystack, comfortably but energetically directing fire. Joining a line of skirmishes moving into position, we gained the first line in minutes, for here as elsewhere artillery was placed almost immediately behind the infantry. Bolsheviks occupied a line of shallow entrenchments effectively camouflaged behind small heaps of cut grain, so they could not be distinguished from sheaves lying in the fields all about us. Heavy machine-gun as well as artillery fire was kept up by both sides, the Russians having a preponderance in the former and the Bolsheviks in the latter. At this time a reinforcement of machine guns was rushed up to the Russian line and quickly got into action. Machine guns are mounted on small, very sturdy steel trucks about a foot high, which in turn are carried on the back seat of an old-fashioned country "surrey," or cart, from which they can readily be operated, although it is the work of only some seconds to lift off this truck and gun and haul it into place by hand, in case the terrain is too difficult for the larger vehicles. At first sight this seems an awkward and extravagant equipment for a machine gun, but it has proved its value in this partisan war, and is used by all forces. Its development is credited to the Reds—Makhno first used it on a large scale—and the Volunteer Army entirely adopted it.

Under cover of machine-gun fire, the entire Russian line now took up the advance, moving in echelon at good speed. . . . We now gained a slight eminence from which we had an excellent view of the entire movement, including the retreat of the Reds. . . . [The Whites] were outnumbered about 3 to 1, but in actual battle the Red superiority in numbers really had comparatively little consequence on this front; they had encountered some single regiments that were worth more than other entire divisions. However, in maneuvering and the possibility of exerting a general pressure all along the line, numbers were, of course, very valuable. The general said that regiments composed entirely of Communists invariably fought well, as did also the Latvians and certain international regiments made up mostly of Magyars. . . .

Among the prisoners I talked to . . . [was one who] had formerly been an electrical worker in a large factory in Moscow. . . . [He explained] a great hatred was growing against Jews and commissars. I asked him why, if there was this hatred, the people didn't rise. He answered that they did rise, and repeatedly, that especially in summer there were many risings, but such risings were always local and sporadic, since lack of communication prevented them having any wide support. On one occasion there had even been a great number of local risings in a small area, yet even these were without effect, because although simultaneous, they were not in touch with each other and the usual result was simply that the men took to the woods. Consequently, the woods were all full of [Makhno's] "Greens" in summer, but in winter they were all forced to return to the towns for food and shelter, so the Communists were able to make short work of them. Moreover, if a man had a family this restrained him from any open action, for his family was invariably punished for whatever he did.

Another prisoner who had been an instructor in the Bolshevik army, said the system of instruction was thorough in some respects but entirely lacking in others. All recruits were first instructed in what they were fighting for, in wrongs poor people had suffered for generations under the old regime, and the fundamental reason for those wrongs. Great pains were taken to show that suffering caused by the present regime was not inherent in that system but due to the difficulty of righting in a few months accumulated wrongs of generations. Soldiers were told while they were fighting at the front their families and property would be cared for, their fields would be plowed and sowed for them [and] grain gathered, and all else necessary would be done by the labor battalions. Moreover, grain gathered from these fields would belong to their families, who were to be provided facilities for exchanging it for manufactured goods. Of course, soldiers have found out this is not true except in the case of the Communist regiments, which contain few peasant farmers. However, there is nothing they can do about it except that the men who are without families deserted at the first opportunity. But men who had families could do nothing because desertion on their part would mean simply that even the little that remained to their families would be taken away. These are men who allow themselves to be made prisoners so readily—who call out to opposing troops they will not shoot if only they are saved from their own cavalry. For the Red cavalry is the big stick that drives the infantry into the fight. . . .

In spite of efforts of Communists in deriding the church and exposing its shams (for unfortunately Russian priesthood was not above imposing on the credulity of peasants) the peasants refused to oust the clergy, and though many churches shut down for a time, all are again functioning. In some places, Communists tried to use church buildings for other purposes, but they were not able to put this through, as people quiescent under all other outrages stood firm on this; if churches were to be closed, synagogues also should go. Though Communists took church property and also that of the clergy, and insulted the priests, the peasants actively resented insults to the church itself. The Communists realized they were on dangerous ground and finally gave up active open measures against the church. A number of peasants in a village near Tchaplinka gave me an account of a commissar who rode into a churchyard on his horse but was promptly pulled off by the angry peasants and after further rough handling was thrown over the fence. No action was ever taken against the peasants for this. . . .

I could find no traces of schools functioning during the Red regime in the Tauride, either in large cities or in villages. Reds told villagers the old schools taught false doctrines, so the system would be rebuilt from ground up. Accordingly, schools had been closed, books destroyed, and buildings used for other purposes, such as council room for the "Tchresvechaika." No new schools were started. I was told by a prisoner that Bolsheviks started an elementary school in Kharkov, but as the first subjects taught were communism and other Bolshevik doctrines, only Communists sent their children and the school soon broke up for want of pupils.

I would invariably ask the prisoner or peasant to whom I was speaking what good had been accomplished by the Bolsheviks or during their regime. The more frequent answer was a flat-footed "None whatever," but some answered that in the beginning there was more personal freedom, and a few said that the Bolsheviks had actually put through a reform in regard to prohibition and prostitution. They said that there was literally no drunkenness in Soviet Russia, or even any drinking, and that the most stringent measures were taken against prostitution. Diseased prostitutes were summarily shot, and those not diseased were sent at once to women labor battalions. The most intelligent of the prisoners with whom I talked said the only real contribution of the Bolsheviks was the theory that the man who did not work should not eat, but the theory was not carried out, for thousands of Jews and Communists did no work but lived on the fat of the land. This same man, in answer to my question as to why people did not rise against these intolerable conditions, said that of course the very stringent and thorough repressive measures of the Bolsheviks was one reason, and the lack of organization was another, but the first reason they did not join the south Russians' government was because they knew nothing about it; the commissars took great pains to destroy handbills dropped by Russian aeroplanes, and inasmuch as handbills were printed no one would believe them anyhow save for the fact that commissars made such efforts to prevent them being circulated.

In most villages of the Tauride . . . the Land Council had already been elected. . . . However, in true Russian fashion, these so-called Land Councils began [with] the time-wasting process of gathering statistics. . . .

[White] control over this southwestern district was exceedingly doubtful. . . . [For example], a certain Taran, the leader of some 200 bandits or "Greens," amalgamated his force with about an equal number of Bolshevik deserters, and had suddenly fallen upon the town of Skadovsk, which was held by a land force of some 500 Russian sailors under Commander Rikov. However, Rikov offered no resistance to this attack and promptly embarked his force on board an auxilliary cruiser . . . and proceeded to . . . [sail away]. When reports of the affair reached General Vitkovsky,* he sent preemptory orders to Rikov to return to Skadovsk and recapture it, as the force there was no greater than his own. Rikov protested but . . . recaptured the town without much difficulty. Rikov was then relieved from his command, but I am not sure that his tactics were much of a departure from the best Russian naval traditions!

Initiative on the part of the naval forces is not to be expected, a fact regretted since it is doubtful Kakhovka can be taken without active help from the navy. And Kakhovka must be taken, or it will remain a dangerous threat to the entire Tauride. Its location at the narrowest point of the Dnieper and on the low lands of the right bank make it an ideal bridgehead for the Bolsheviks. . . . The only answer is to cross the river and attack from the rear, which demands first that enemy cavalry be disposed of, and second that the navy force the defenses at the mouth of the Dnieper and disembark a landing force. Neither General Vitkovsky nor General Kutepov seemed in the least staggered by it and spoke confidently of carrying it out. . . . Kutepov had been up against worse and still had found the answer. . . . When I discussed the danger of a cavalry raid from Kakhovka to Perekop, General Kutepov said he still had a few men to bar the way.† . . . I doubt whether all history can furnish a finer example of bravery, courage, and devotion than these men fighting day after day against a ruthless enemy, practically without pay, without clothes, without the simplest necessities of life, without any of the glamour of battle, without encouragement of their countrymen, almost without comrades, for they have been thinned out painfully. And nothing to show for their efforts except along the roadside and in the fields are many new graves with crude wooden crosses with names marked in blue pencil. . . .

The Cossacks are fighting to get back to their stanitzi†† in the Don and the Kuban—nor do they see much beyond that. They do not loot now but resent being deprived of (as they look at it) a well-earned privilege. . . . Russia means nothing to them. . . . They . . . fight

---

* General Vitkovsky is briefly mentioned in Luckett (pp. 372–73) as the leader of the attack on Kakhovka on 13 October 1920, during the great trans-Dniepr operation.

† In fact, this is precisely the route the Bolsheviks took when they overran the Whites a month and a half later. See Luckett, pp. 372–77.

†† "Stanitzi" were Cossack villages.

any . . . power or regime or idea that interferes with their old privileges.

One morning at breakfast in a farmyard near Fedorovka I complimented my muzhik host on the excellent quality of his grain, stacked up all around us, and asked him the price of wheat. "Who could tell?" he answered. He went on to explain that Bolsheviks took it for nothing, Wrangel's forces offered sheaves of paper money for it—if that was standard, he added critically, it evidently must be worth something. Yet Bolsheviks came a long way for it, and Whites were extraordinarily anxious to get it, so it must have value for everyone except the man who had grown it. His account as to what he had suffered under the Bolshevik regime was a long one. But summed up, it amounted in three years to the loss of some 45 poods [36 English pounds] of grain, sundry chicken and eggs, and the forced sale of a horse. . . . He complained of his inability to buy manufactured goods. However, he had lived well and had even had tea, sugar, and tobacco, in spite of almost prohibitive prices. And though I found many peasants who suffered grievously, this case was far from unusual. Not so in the case of townspeople—they have all suffered. In not a single case did I find anyone who had gotten off as easily as so many of the peasants. The more I learned directly of conditions in Red Russia . . . the more evident it becomes that it is townspeople who suffered most from the Bolsheviks and conditions brought about by the Red regime. They gladly welcomed the Russian troops and quickly allied themselves with the new Wrangel regime. Peasants, although they suffered a certain loss from seizure of grain and horses, and although bitter against mobilization, nevertheless in general never suffered hunger or the many requisitions of clothing, linen, household effects, and about everything else of value townspeople had to endure; nor have they seen at close hand the conduct and methods of the commissars. Millions of peasants suffered little except for shortage of manufactured articles; and those who had grain and cattle taken from them shrewdly reckoned in many cases these losses amounted to less than their usual taxes. Freedom from the hundred and one restrictions of the old regime did much to make up for the many disadvantages of the Soviet regime. In these years the man who produces from the soil is king—even in Red Russia. So the answer to the often-asked question as to why the peasants do not rise and put an end to this Red terror becomes plain when one talks to enough of them: it is simply that in the mass they've suffered little compared to townspeople, no matter how much certain individuals have suffered. Add to this that they see comparatively little of evils of the system—many have never seen a commissar except at rare intervals—and then, too, the extraordinary difficulties of organization against a regime with so widespread a system of espionage and such prompt and efficacious methods of repression—all this in addition to the fundamental difficulties of organization in a country of great distances, with no press, no freedom of speech nor of communication—it becomes almost obvious only the most intense suffering would produce a spontaneous outbreak, would cause an uprising among the peasantry sufficiently serious to threaten the Soviets. Far more likely would be a rising of townspeople—they have suffered most, have been closest in contact with the evils of bolshevism, their propinquity, experience in organization, the presence of former leaders—all make the task of organization much simpler than with the peasants. Nor does the concentration of Soviet power in the cities weigh too heavily against chances of an uprising, for in towns there is also a concentration of disillusioned workmen kept in order only by soldiery and the control of bread lines. But the spirit of the townspeople is broken—their brains and wills are as weak and starved from lack of food as are their bodies—sufferings have left them exhausted. Once these townspeople get sufficient food inside them to restore stamina, and when the interior weakness of bolshevism gives them an opportunity, they must restore commerce and industry; yet the latter would also restore the towns—and strengthened, people would no longer submit to the tyranny they have suffered for years. So even in its success bolshevism contains the elements of its downfall.

The millworker in Alimovka expressed the idea of thousands when he said that formerly the Russians had a czar, a fool, to rule them, [and] taxes were very bad, but bread was five kopeks a pound and plentiful, and a man could get all the shirts and shoes and sugar and tea and tobacco he wanted. Now Russia was ruled by very clever men, [and] there were no taxes at all, but bread was 500 rubles a pound and scarce, and neither shirts nor shoes nor sugar nor tea nor tobacco were to be had.[2]

Hugo W. Koehler

It is likely that Koehler joined in on the fighting during this visit to the front, for on 27 August Kutepov awarded him the Order of St. Vladimir, 4th Class, with swords and bow. Among Koehler's papers are several telegrams in Russian congratulating him on the award.

13. Order of St. Vladimir, awarded to Hugo Koehler by Gen. Kutepov, August 1920.
(Photo courtesy of the Division of Numismatics, Smithsonian Institution.)

"I heartily congratulate you on your being awarded with the Order of St. Vladimir, 4th Class, with swords and bow."

General Kutepov

"With the feeling of sincere pleasure I learn that you have been awarded, sir, with the Order of St. Vladimir, 4th Class, with swords and bow and congratulate you with this high award, which commemorates the day of your visit to the fighting line of my corps."

General Vitkovsky

"Allow me, sir, to congratulate you with all my soul on your receiving the Order of St. Vladimir with swords and bow, which is one of the highest awards for a soldier's bravery."

Colonel Korchakovsky
(Senior Adjutant of 2nd Corps H.Q.)[3]

Koehler's St. Vladimir and also his Order of St. Anne were likely the last imperial decorations awarded to a foreigner or, for that matter, given the circumstances, to a Russian.

The strict neutrality of the American mission, so scrupulously adhered to by Admiral McCully, was evidently less than a pressing concern for the Commander.

9

Somewhere in Russia

September–October 1920 _____

In answer to my question what good the Reds had accomplished, she said they made theaters free and had open-air movies almost every night in summer. (October 1920)

_____

Barely two weeks passed before Koehler returned to the front. The weather, as had the fortunes of the Whites, turned bitter. Their Crimean bastion, the last small piece of White Russian resistance to Bolshevik rule, was about to vanish.

It was during this last visit to the front that Koehler witnessed the final desperate strike of Wrangel's army, the crossing to the right bank of the Dnieper. History would mark this operation as the last forward thrust against the Bolsheviks on Russian soil until the arrival of the Wehrmacht in 1941.

Alexandorovsk, Russia
14 October 1920

Departing from Sebastopol about a month ago, I commented with considerable emphasis that my train had left at the time scheduled; but upon my arrival at Melitopol on this occasion I was without words, for the train *arrived* on time. I traveled from Novo Alexksievka to Melitopol in a third-class coach, outwardly the same as other third-class coaches and as frightfully overcrowded, but on the inside enormously different, for it had been cleaned—really cleaned, under seats and overhead; at frequent intervals the provodnik swept down and carefully gathered watermelon rinds and sunflower seeds from under benches.

The stationmaster at Novo Alexksievka had served at his post with equal calm during the imperial regime and all other regimes, including three Bolshevik occupations, which had swept back and forth across this little junction. All places on this next train for Melitopol were taken and the stationmaster was no longer allowed to sell more tickets than were places available on the train. However, when the train arrived two passengers alighted, so I was allowed to purchase two tickets. The tickets I received were evidently remnants of the imperial regime for the cost stamped on them was 1 ruble 94 kopeks. I paid 1,940 rubles for each, or rather, 2,000 rubles, for these days no one bothers to make change for a mere 60 rubles. Upon entering the car there was a scramble for the upper (third-tier) bunks, which I could not understand, for smoke from a hundred cigarettes and wood samovars collected there, since windows were hermetically sealed. I soon learned the reason for the scramble upwards, for only there could one safely stretch out—in all other bunks one's projecting feet were jostled continuously by too many neighbors in the aisle. Besides, a general of artillery pointed out to me, the upper tier alone had that small ledge so handy for one's bread and herring. On noting the provodnik several times filled the washroom tank, I decided this could not be a real performance—it must be I chanced upon a provodnik made in heaven and trained in Pullman service. Accordingly, I moved into the next car, but conditions there were quite the same, so finally I was forced to believe this new scheme was the rule and not the exception. This may seem an overimportance to give to details, but this is not mere detail—it has this real significance: government actually controls the railroads, has put organization and system into its work, and an important if unspectacular step [has been] taken toward bringing order out of chaos.

Upon arrival at Melitopol I saw General Kutepov, who explained the operation that resulted in the capture of Alexandrovsk and an immense amount of military and other stores, armored trains, 14 steamboats, some 2,000 horses, and more prisoners. Most important was capture of more than 1,000 serviceable railroad cars and 33 "hot" locomotives, i.e., ready to run. A most brilliant operation, but most significant it has keenly whetted the army's appetite for more operations on this same large scale. The region in advance of the new line has been cleared of Red troops beyond any possibility of further attacks for at least a month, so the army will be able to turn its attention to the thorn in the flesh at Kakhovka. General Kutepov said his reports indicated no Bolshevik forces of appreciable strength anywhere between Alexandrovsk and Ekaterinoslav or Kharkov, and he could probably take either town without great effort.

To do so would extend his lines dangerously for the size of his present force, so he decided to make haste more slowly. He expected to hold Mariuopol (captured that afternoon 25 September) only two days, as he destroyed the Bolshevik naval base there and captured or destroyed all but 500 of the forces operating from there; the safer plan would be to retire to a safe line and strike again when all was ready. Reports from Mariuopol mentioned frightful atrocities the day before Russian troops entered, and two days later three friends who had been there confirmed these accounts in detail. General Kutepov also hoped by this retreat to draw Red forces north of Mariuopol after him and capture them by a flanking movement. His plans worked well, for on 12 October 1920, 4,000 Red troops were surrounded and captured in this region. The policy of short advances after preparation, rather than overrunning in a single advance, was shown when the entire Alexandorovsk operation cost less than 50 killed and 300 wounded. I have entire confidence in anything General Kutepov says, but I took great pains, by means of hospital figures and statements of regimental and division commanders, to verify this estimate of casualties. I found the total number of patients admitted to hospitals of the entire First Army during the period of this operation was 307, of whom 19 died. [The number of] men who died in the field was estimated as not more than 25 during the same period.

Between Melitopol and Alexandorovsk were none of the herds of cattle so conspicuous in the southern Tauride, and approaching Alexandorovsk was not a single haystack—all had been taken by the Reds. Much less winter wheat had been sown there than in the Crimea and southern Tauride, and such plowing as had been done was shallow—worse than usual in Russia, where the plowing is proverbially shallow. I asked a peasant whose plowing was little more than a scratching of the surface, why he didn't plow deep enough to grow four or five ears of corn on a stalk, as in America, instead of only a single ear per stalk as here on this very fertile soil. He answered he had heard of two ears on a single stalk, but four or five ears was impossible. He added that as Bolsheviks had taken all but one of his horses, he couldn't plow all his land in any case, and it was easier to plow a lot of land badly than to plow a little well. There were not enough horses in the district to plow half the land next season even if every horse did more than any horse had ever done before. This peasant previously cultivated 29 desiatins* but planted only 11 desiatins this last year. Some of his best fields had produced nothing but thistles for two years, and except for more thistles would produce nothing next year. He was in rags, and so was his family. In general, children and women of the Tauride all had much poorer clothing than peasants of the Crimea. Alexandorovsk was a discouraging-looking city despite large buildings and well laid out bou-

---

* A *desiatin* (or *desyatina*) is a unit of land measurement, equal to 2.7 acres.

levards, for streets were filthy and rows upon rows of shops on main streets were boarded. A normal population of about 50,000 has an additional 90,000–100,000 refugees from north Russia who fled from the Bolsheviks but could get no further south and had to remain here during the Bolshevik occupations. They give the same account of Bolshevik outrages, ceaseless requisitions, oppressions by countless Jew officials and commissars, of women being prisoners in their own houses for a month at a time, the general horror of the Bolshevik regime. Atrocities committed by Bolsheviks were less during the second occupation than the first, but oppressions and tyranny of Jew officials became progressively worse as occupation continued. I stayed at the house of a formerly prosperous owner of a large local agricultural implement works. He recounted how the Reds took all finished machinery from the factory saying that it belonged to the workmen, then ordered the factory to continue work, but under conditions that were impossible. Factories promptly closed down; none had started again. Workmen took up bartering in foodstuffs and old clothing, or were forced into the army. The town was governed by a council of five appointed from Moscow, there being no local participation in the government—not even by the local Bolsheviks. Besides two Tchresvechaika bureaus—one for city, another for district—there were bureaus of all sorts with many officials and clerks. Public buildings and schools were occupied as offices, and former shops, restaurants, and the two hotels were likewise crowded with officials. The greater part of these officials were Jews. As the local jail had been burned by Bolsheviks when they first came to town, cellars of these office buildings were used as prisons, full of people who failed to report in obedience to the published work list.

All men between 18 and 50, and women between 18 and 40, were required to work for the government, without pay, whenever called. . . . My host lived on a so-called bourgeois street, i.e., the best residential street, so although he was not in robust health he was frequently called to clean streets, and twice to haul lumber, while his wife cleaned the stairs of Bolshevik office buildings and washed clothes for commissars. On the other hand, I saw people in the poorer quarter of the town who had never been called to do any work.

Two weeks prior to entry of the Russian army, my host and 129 other house owners had been given 15 days to vacate their houses and . . . find lodgings in one of the villages nearby. They were forbidden to take any furniture, bedding, or any articles other than clothing. Their houses had been selected only because they were the best houses in town not owned by Jews. Owners were in despair, for not only did this order mean loss of practically all their belongings, but meant they would be without shelter for the winter; there would be no work on the land in winter and peasants would receive them only when they could be useful in the fields. While we were talking, a woman in frightful rags suddenly entered through an open window and, seizing bread and a glass of tea on the table, threw them out the window and started screaming. She was quite mad, and my host explained there had been a large local insane asylum but all the inmates had been turned out shortly after the Bolsheviks arrived and now wandered the streets in pitiable condition.

Our chauffeur was a native of Alexandrovsk, and his mother and sister, whom he had not seen in more than two years, were still living there, having been unable to leave during Bolshevik occupation. They repeated the same stories of shootings of many so-called White para-sites and counterrevolutionaries, and all the hundred and one oppres-sions we had already heard so many times. The chauffeur's sister, a very capable-looking young woman of about 23, said she had rarely left the house during the Bolshevik regime, and then only in rags, for if one had good clothes one would be stopped in the street and told to hand them over then and there. It often happened that men and other commissars or officials took things from people, but there was no way of telling whether they were taken by a real commissar or not, and people were too afraid to dispute the point, for many had been imprisoned for failing to obey a commissar. As she and her mother lived in the work-men's quarter of the town, they had never been forced to work, al-though they had lost many things by forced requisition. During sum-mer they worked in the fields and earned grain they thought would carry them through winter. However, returning to town with this grain, they had been arrested as "speculators" and the grain taken from them, because the peasant who gave it to them was afraid to come to town and testify before the Tchresvechaika that they had worked for it. On one occasion her uncle had gone with her to get some of this grain. Arriving at the village, a man sitting near the well remarked that bread was dear now, whereupon her uncle said something to the effect that things were frightful indeed, for bread used to be 4 kopeks a pound and plentiful, and now it was 200 rubles a pound and scarce—which remark resulted in her uncle being hauled before the Tchresvechaika as a "white sympathizer." In answer to my question what good the Reds had accomplished, she said they made theaters free and had open-air movies almost every night in summer. The only trouble with these was if one wore good clothes, some commissar would take them away, and no one dared resist. One could also travel on railroads without tickets, but if one carried any parcels, one was arrested as a speculator and the parcels were taken away. Bolsheviks also established two playgrounds, but for children of workmen only. They were going to open schools and soup kitchens for young children, but this had never been done, as all schools, except three conducted by the synagogue, had closed. During our talk these women became more and more nervous, so I finally asked if anything were wrong, whereupon the mother said if Bolsheviks came back to Alexandorovsk, she and her daughter were lost, for spies would tell the Reds our motorcar had been in front of this house for a long time. I assured her I felt very sure the Reds were not coming back, but inasmuch as Reds were bombarding the town from across the river all this time, and explosions sounded very near, I left with apologies.

A member of the town council, elected during the short period of the Denikin regime, verified my previous information concerning conditions in Alexandorovsk and added many details. He was bitter against the persecution of priests and church, which he said were not so much the result of Bolshevik doctrine as due to the fact that in the Bolshevik regimes Jews were in control. He recounted many incidents of old priests forced to sweep streets, while no Jew, young or old, has done any forced work. I asked several rich Jews, who stated they had been robbed by Bolsheviks, whether any of them, or their families, had ever been forced to work. They answered they had been told to work but had not turned up at the appointed time, and no action had been taken against them. Although all churches were closed, outcry by women was too great, and large churches were soon opened again, although small churches and chapels not readily kept under surveillance were closed permanently. For a time no priest could perform any ceremonies, such as weddings, christenings, or bethrothals, without a permit in each case from the Soviet Council—for which a large fee was charged; this too had soon been abandoned. People had been arrested for using the word *Zhid*, meaning Jew—as Jews wished to be called *Ievrae* (Israelites). Bread was sold at 6 rubles a pound to Communists and 200 rubles a pound to others. Large numbers of cattle had been shipped to Moscow, but the price in the town was prohibitive for rich as well as poor, though it was sold at low prices in Communist stores. During the last two weeks, sale of meat was prohibited altogether.

In Alexandorovsk is a large railroad repair shop, often mentioned in Bolshevik wireless communiques, so I was interested in visiting with a view to establishing the accuracy of the communiques. I met some of the workmen and the master mechanic, an intelligent man, who worked in these shops ever since his apprenticeship in 1889. When Bolsheviks first came, they decided to do away with the master mechanic and shop foreman and turned the works over to a Council of Workmen. As little was accomplished under this regime, a new council was elected, then another and another, until dozens of councils had succeeded each other in rapid succession. It was then decided there would have to be someone in control, but all the workmen wanted to be chiefs, no one would take orders, and nothing was accomplished, although workmen were given high pay and great privileges, such as being allowed to purchase food and clothing at Communist stores. When Makhno took Alexandorovsk from the Reds, all work stopped, as Makhno didn't care a straw what became of the factories. Makhno was in Alexandorovsk five weeks, was followed for a short time by Denikin's army, and then the Bolsheviks came again. Previous to Makhno's entry, in accordance with orders from Moscow, factory owners were given a voice in management and were to receive a small share of profits in return for services in management. Things went better for a week or two, but after that the workmen's council refused to carry out plans of the owner's council, and things were as bad as before.

During the last occupation of the Bolsheviks there was a marked change in attitude toward the master mechanic and foreman. In normal times the master mechanic received nearly twice the pay of the most skilled workmen, but when the Bolsheviks took charge they gave him only 25 rubles per month more than the ordinary workmen. Now, pay of the master mechanic and foreman was greatly increased, every attempt was made to attach them to the Bolshevik regime, and workmen were ordered to follow them until new chiefs could be developed from among workmen. However, workmen received the same pay and privileges if they worked or not, so little was accomplished and the factory dwindled to about 150 men at the end of August of this year. In the last five months, odd jobs have been done and work was going on on a large number of locomotives, but only two had been completed. During normal times this factory had employed about 720 men and completely overhauled and repaired from 100 to 110 locomotives per annum. During the Bolshevik regime the same number were employed—at times more—but never were more than two locomotives repaired in any month, and work was not thorough. The master mechanic said occasionally Moscow and Kharkov papers came to town, and he used to read in *Pravda* that the Alexandorovsk shops had repaired 141 or 174, etc., locomotives in the proceeding month, but not more than two locomotives had ever been repaired in any one month.

The master mechanic said the great bulk of workmen were sick unto death of bolshevism, for though under the Red regime they could loaf and still draw pay, not one was as well off as formerly. However, there were some workmen, from five to ten percent, who still preferred bolshevism and always would, simply because they could not exist under any other system, since they were fundamentally opposed to real work. He was certain a secret ballot would result in an overwhelming vote for a return of the factory to the owners. That did not mean the men would ever go back to prerevolutionary conditions, for they would not—their eyes opened these last years, if no other good had come to them. But they had no faith in bolshevism any longer and would turn to any regime that offered peace and order. As for General Wrangel, he doubted whether up to the arrival of Russian troops any feeling favorable to General Wrangel had greater depth than a welcome relief from bolshevism, for the workmen knew nothing about his regime. He did not think the incident of the 33 locomotives reported out of order to the Bolsheviks but turned over to General Wrangel in working order indicated any real enthusiasm for General Wrangel, as the purpose of reporting to the Bolsheviks that these locomotives were out of order was simply to prevent their use to transport more grain out of the district. The same reasoning . . . helped in destruction of bridges and in impeding transport. It was not any idea of aiding General Wrangel's forces.

There were many accounts of a meeting of workmen held on June 11, 1920, under Soviet auspices, at which all were to be privileged to speak their minds whatever their beliefs. At first all were too frightened to speak out frankly, and Communists held the floor, but finally one man said what he actually thought, and in a few minutes the whole assembly was proclaiming against the Red regime. Nothing was done at this time, but it happened later that all the vehement speakers were arrested on some charge or other and tried before the Tchresvechaika; no more such meetings were held. On August 29, 1920, Trotsky came to Alexandrovsk and addressed a meeting of Communists and workmen. It was said he usually speaks very well but on this occasion spoke very badly, said nothing other than to revile enemies of bolshevism. The following day a large crowd of people gathered near his train and called on him to speak, but he would not appear, sending out word there were too many "White parasites" in the crowd who wished him no good. A bomb was thrown at him the same day, but he was not injured, although faces of two of his suite were torn. He again visited Alexandrovsk four days later, but his coming was kept secret. . . .

I talked to a peasant who two months ago had been appointed a member of the local Soviet Council and had been forced to serve as no one would accept either this post or that of village starosta—there having been eight starostas in as many months.* His principle duties had been to collect grain and cattle for the Bolsheviks. Reds took all the hay and grain in sight, saying they knew the peasants had hidden the greater part of their crops and so could look out for themselves. Reds also took all cattle except one cow for every three families. The result was many peasants had not thrashed this year's grain, having left it in the fields or stowed it inside straw stacks. . . .

On my return to Melitopol I met General Voloshinov,† a keen and energetic young cossack I had known in the Kuban. Asked where he had been all this time I had not seen him, he replied he arrived that morning from Novorossisk, via Rostov, Moscow, and Warsaw. . . .

When Novorossisk was captured by Bolsheviks he fought his way through to Tuapse with some 1,200 of his men. They were harassed the entire distance by Greens, and twice attacked by Reds, but held their own as long as ammunition lasted. Continual attacks by Greens made it difficult to get food, and his force gradually evaporated, most going over to the Greens when they got too hungry. After five days of continuous travel, most of it on foot, his wife on the only horse left, he could get no farther, so made his way to a peasant's house, where he fell down in a heap. He was awakened very shortly, for the peasants called in the Greens. The Greens turned him over to the Bolsheviks at Ekaterinodar where he was immediately imprisoned—his wife also being imprisoned, but separately. Bolsheviks shot no officers at Ekaterinodar during the first six days of occupation, but after the Tchresvechaika began to function there were daily executions of officers. About 400 officers were shot in the six weeks General Voloshinov was held in Ekaterinodar. He himself appeared before the Tchresvechaika and was tried with a group of officers, half of whom were sentenced to central Russia as prisoners, the other half sent to the Donetz coal mines to work as miners. He did not know how the selection was made. He was destined for the mines but, upon volunteering for service against the Poles, was sent to Moscow. He said many officers worked as miners in the Donetz Basin. If any officer escaped, five officers were immediately taken out and shot. . . .

---

* A *starosta* was elected to manage local administrative matters and to serve as a judge.

† Koehler is probably referring to General N. D. Vsevolodov, who had deserted the Reds in June 1919, "driving across the front with his family" (Evan Mawdsley, *The Russian Civil War* [Boston, 1987], p. 170). See also Kenez, p. 37

He had been in Rostov in June when Dumenko,* one of the most famous of the Cossack leaders in the Red Army and a corps commander in Budenny's Cavalry,† was tried by the Tchresvechaika on these charges: (1) engaging in anti-Semitic propaganda, (2) oppression of Jews, (3) shooting a Jewish commissar of his corps. When Dumenko was brought before the Tchresvechaika he asked where he was, who was questioning him, and by what right. The chief of the Tchresvechaika answered he was in a court of justice, his judge was questioning him, and by right of the will of the people. Dumenko replied by asking whether Jews then dealt out justice and, tearing off his Bolshevik decoration, threw it in the face of his questioner. At the same time, Dumenko's Cossacks sent word that if he were shot, they too would do some shooting. But the Bolsheviks were too quick. They transferred the corps to a distant post and then entirely disbanded it, most of the men being sent to the mines. Dumenko was shot.

In June, General Voloshinov left Rostov for Moscow. . . . En route, all passports and papers were minutely examined by large detachments of officials, who also confiscated all parcels, of whatever kind, carried by passengers. On the previous train, a large detachment of sailors proceeding to Moscow refused further to have their papers and belongings examined by these civil officials, and a pitched battle broke out in which some 30 were killed. General Voloshinov's impression of Moscow was everything in Moscow was locked up, not only shops and factories (except the few making ammunition and supplies for the army or busy on railroad repairs), but also hundreds of houses whose shutters were closed because of broken windows. Everyone was living on government ration supplemented by such as one could beg, borrow, or steal—all seemed dull and listless. Workmen understood their condition perfectly—realized they had no freedom and were worse off than before—but they knew too what happened to those who previously made attempts to strike for themselves, and that paralyzed them.

---

* Boris Mokeevich Dumenko (1888–1920), was a Don Cossack who had been a sergeant major in the czarist armies. After the Revolution he rose to the command of the combined cavalry division of the Red Army. His assistant at this post was S. M. Budennyi. Dumenko was accused of treason and subsequently executed. Dumenko's reputation has since been rehabilitated by the Soviets, and a street in Novocherkassk has been named in his honor.

† A former sergeant who became a marshal in the Red Army, S. M. Budennyi was one of the most famous of the Red cavalry commanders in this last European war in which cavalry was to play a major role. It was Budennyi who defeated Shkuro's Wolves at Voronezh on 24 October 1919, thereby sealing the fate of Denikin's army.

Moscow printers told the British labor delegates they had not come to a free country, yet had not dared to say anything further.

The great numbers of former Russian officers now in Red service were held there by dread of what would be done to their families if they left, but there were also many who believed bolshevism could not successfully be fought from the outside, and the only sound thing was to try to control it from within. . . . When one was inside Red Russia one readily understood why these men entered the Red service. Concerning published statements signed by Brusilov and other former Russian officers of high rank, he knew many signatories had never seen the statements supposedly signed by them—in certain cases, the Bolsheviks simply wrote whatever they wished and subscribed whatever names they wished. He had heard much talk outside of Russia that former Russian officers were getting control of the Red Army and the time would not be long before they broke away from the central government. All such talk was utter rot and the invention of people who knew nothing of the interior workings of bolshevism; Bolsheviks had made many mistakes, but whoever thought Trotsky was fool enough to be blind to such an obvious contingency was making a still greater mistake. A cataclysm could come, but it would be simply because frightful conditions had become unbearable, and not because of clever plans of former Russian officers or officials. One factor that would hasten the downfall of bolshevism was its fundamental weakness: it was controlled almost entirely by Jews, and bitterness against the Jews was becoming so intense among all classes of the population it was developing into an actual binding force. Voloshinov had been in Poland when various units had come over to the Poles from the Reds, but in every case he knew about, it had been the action of the men and not due to any suggestion of their officers. In fact, in most cases they preceded the operation by doing away with their officers. Labor armies mobilized by the Reds had existed as such for only a short time. As they had been organized on entirely military lines they were readily converted into military units— this done as soon as the need for troops became pressing during the Polish offensive.

While in Moscow, Voloshinov tried to see Trotsky but could not get within miles of him or of any other high official. . . . There had been numerous attempts at assassination, and all high Soviet officials are more than wary. It is impossible to get into the Kremlin, where all high officials have offices and many living quarters also. Three separate passes, each with numerous signatures, numbers, and countersignatures, are necessary, and one must have definite business in order to get any one of these passes—let alone all three. Trotsky is keeping clear of public meetings; when he does appear it is invariably without previous announcement. Trotsky's prestige for a time eclipsed that of Lenin but of late has been falling rapidly.

After five days in Moscow, General Voloshinov was sent to the Polish front. . . . He was anxious to get into a Cossack regiment, but this is exactly what the Reds avoid, their plan being to put Communist officers in Cossack regiments and Cossack officers in workmen's regiments—for workmen and Cossacks have little sympathy for each other, and danger of collusion between the two is avoided. Consequently, when during the Polish retreat he escaped, he was unable to bring any of his men with him. In the same way, four Cossack regiments that went over to the Poles at about the same time came without their officers. . . . .

After further conversations with my Melitopol friends—the miller, the foreman of the tannery that started up again after two years of idleness, the apothecary (the only one I've seen in Russia who is not a Jew), my former landlady, the mayor and his none-too-gentle wife, the peasant women in the market, the tailor who is now doing a thriving business in the rooms formerly occupied by the Tchrezvechaika, and the hardware merchant who already exhausted his huge stock of rusty hinges buried for nearly two years: one and all were full of enthusiasm after many months of idleness—I hurried on to Nijni Saragosa, the headquarters of General Dratsenko,* commander of the new Second Russian Army. He explained his army was having a brief rest and doing its best to entice the Bolsheviks into an advance from Kahovka, but the Reds had become cautious during the last two months since they had been outflanked so frequently, and nothing would induce them to come out from behind barbed wire and trenches, no matter how tempting the bait. They are busy fortifying Kahovka, although they already have three complete lines of trenches and entanglements in addition to two outer lines of entanglements and six supporting blockhouses—all this in addition to heavy artillery on the heights of Berislav, across the river. However, General Vitkovsky, who commands Second Corps, twice penetrated all five lines and the town itself but had to retire on account of exposed flanks and heavy artillery fire from the Berislav batteries.

---

* General D. P. Dratsenko is mentioned briefly in Luckett, chiefly for his failure to follow up with his infantry General Babiev's cavalry successes during the trans-Dniepr operation, thereby causing the retreat of the entire Second Russian Army (Luckett, p. 372). See also Brinkley, pp. 160 and 234, and Kenez, pp. 207, 299, 303, and 304.

Nevertheless, he intends to make the attempt again, but with assistance of tanks and aeroplanes. To draw away the large reserves of Red troops now at Kahovka, First Army has planned an advance from Alexandrovsk into the rear of Nikopol, and as soon as Reds have withdrawn from Nikopol, all Second Army except Vitkovsky's corps will cross at Nikopol and advance towards Berislav, while Vitkovsky's 34th Division will attempt a crossing at the French monastery 25 versts below Kahovka, and 13th Division . . . will storm Kahovka. . . . If this plan succeeds, the Russians will probably shift the whole First Army to the southeastern flank and attempt an advance into the Donetz. My own opinion is that no feint in the north or from Nikopol will make the Reds budge one inch from Kahovka—nothing but a threat of being cut off from the rear will cause any shift of troops from that position. However, if Second Army can put forth any such effort as First Army, there is no reason why an attack from the rear should not be successfully made. Then will come the advance into the Donetz, which if successful would mean the military power of bolshevism had come to a definite end—and the Donetz will be their last stand. For this reason, the purely Communist troops are being stationed there—they can trust no others.

I was interested in meeting the new generals of Second Army, as they are practically the only higher officers in the Russian forces I do not know. They were all pleasant and agreeable and, like General Dratsenko, friendly toward America and bitter toward England—bitterness pronounced throughout the army—men and officers. General Dratsenko was not a forceful man—distinctly the opposite. . . . His comments on important questions were superficial and based on little information. The most outstanding personality was General Skalon, recently returned from Poland, who commands newly created Third Corps.

I was prejudiced against General Skalon because his staff officers hailed from the Corps des Pages—an institution well known in Petrograd society but not distinguished by the brain-work of its graduates.* General Dratsenko's staff is composed of men who in the last six months have more experience as refugees in Constantinople and Serbia than in battle line—and battle-line experience is first requisite in these

---

* "General Skalon" is absent from English language accounts of the Civil War. The "Corps des Pages" in Petrograd was a Russian institution where, from 1731 to 1918, military officers, mostly nobleman, were trained.

times. General Maslovsky, chief of staff,* was youngest of this group of generals who on the whole were older than those of older units. . . . General Maslovsky is good-looking but seemed otherwise in no way distinguished. . . . General Wigran, who commands Second Cavalry Brigade, made a favorable impression with his quiet, forceful manner.† I found him particularly "sympathique," for he frowned on his neighbor, a general who twice quoted Russian proverbs as oracles concerning what to do in the present difficult situation. Apparently there is a pleasant old Russian proverb that perfectly though superficially fits all the needs of lazy thinkers—and sometimes makes them more dangerous than the most radical Red. On the whole Second Army is not of the same calibre as First Army, however—officers of First Army were selected by the hardest kind of test in the hardest kind of fighting. . . .

At headquarters of First Cavalry Division, I saw a series of cavalry and artillery evolutions by Second Brigade. . . . The brigade commander, General Agoieff,†† an Ossitine Cossack, is a dashing figure with the head of a Greek god, eyes continually full of laughter. . . . He is the Cossack chieftain of imagination. I had seen the *lava,*††† the famous Cossack attack, before, but never with the dash and spirit of Agoieff. Forming his bodyguard and transport train into the "enemy," he sent them in one direction and his own force disappeared in a cloud of dust in the opposite direction. Thirty minutes later we noted, from our position on the top of an old Tartar burial mound, a mass of cavalry approaching in solid formation. This mass soon spread into a long, thin line, which came on at a gallop. In the meantime, the enemy came and in a brilliant charge pierced the advancing line, which then split into two parts that retreated to the flanks, apparently in considerable disorder. At this point, the reserve hidden behind the advancing line suddenly came into sight, but on seeing the advancing enemy it too wheel-

---

* General E. V. Maslovskii is briefly mentioned in Kenez as chief of staff in January 1920 for General Erdeli, commander of the Caucasian Army (Kenez, p. 209).

† "General Wigran" is absent from English language accounts of the Civil War.

†† By "General Agoieff" Koehler possibly means P. M. Agaev, a popular Don cossack politician. The Ossitine Cossacks Kenez describes as an Iranian tribe, "engaged in agriculture and . . . reasonably well off. They had the highest level of education [of the Cossacks] and a sizeable intelligentsia." The area of the Caucasus where they lived Kenez describes as "an ethnographic museum," in its diversity of Cossack tribes (Kenez, pp. 123–24).

††† "Lava" is a Cossack term for an enveloping or flanking action.

ed and beat a hasty retreat with the enemy in hot pursuit. As the enemy pressed forward, the second reserve suddenly swept down and engaged the enemy in front, while the retreating first reserve, which had made a rather wide turn, now attacked on the enemy's flank while the two parts of the first line, which had retreated in apparent disorder, now came plunging in from the opposite flank and the rear, thus attacking the enemy from all sides at once. The result was a melee of men and horses, sabres and lances, banners and streamers, a whirlwind of dust. If battle is half as dangerous as this maneuver appears, one wonders how there can be any enemies of Cossacks left.

Two incidents pleasantly mark this day of inspection of Cavalry Corps. Upon conclusion of maneuvers of General Wigran's brigade, all troops started back across the plain as if to return to camp. When a half mile distant, they turned, and the whole brigade, cavalry, artillery, machine-gun detachments, all dashed up to our hillock and, led by the general, gave a rousing cheer for America. On the end of the cheer came another not led by anyone, but an inspiring cheer it was—"America, America." It was later explained this was a tribute to the American Secretary of State's note concerning Russian affairs,* a complete translation of which I had brought with me and given to General Kutepov, who published it to the army. Its general terms were already known through brief extracts and comments in the Crimean papers, but the

---

* This note, which is every bit as long as Koehler describes it, says among other things that the United States "strongly recoils [from the idea of] recognition of the Bolshevist regime," and goes on to say that: "The United States maintains unimpaired its faith in the Russian people, in their high character and their future. . . . The distressing character of Russia's transition has many historical parallels, and the United States is confident that restored, free and united Russia will again take a leading place in the world, joining with other free nations in upholding peace and orderly justice. Until that time shall arrive the United States feels that friendship and honor require that Russia's interests must be generously protected and . . . [we have] so instructed [our] representative in Southern Russia, Rear Admiral Newton A. McCully. . . .

"In the view of this Government, there cannot be any common ground upon which it can stand with a Power whose conception of international relations are so intensely alien to its own, so utterly repugnant to its moral sense. There can be no mutual confidence or trust, no respect even, if pledges are to be given and agreements made with a cynical repudiation of their obligations already in the mind of one of the parties. We cannot recognize, hold official relations with, or give friendly reception to the agents of a government which is determined and bound to conspire against our institutions; whose diplomats will be the agitators of dangerous revolt; whose spokesmen say that they sign agreements with no intention of keeping them" (Bainbridge Colby, Secretary of State, to the ambassador of Italy, 10 August 1920, cited in Stanley S. Jados, *Documents on Russian-American Relations* [Washington, D.C., 1965], pp. 47–48).

full text is much more effective, especially to Russians; for Russians take their notes, as everything else, long! Strangely, this note made more of an impression in the interior and at the front than at Sebastopol, for everywhere during the journey people have spoken about it in appreciative terms. It took a long time for the note to penetrate beyond Sebastopol, for when I was at the front a month ago very little was being said about it compared to all that I heard on this occasion; one of my distinct impressions of the last three weeks is the great amount of favorable comment concerning this note and the work of the American Red Cross. . . .

There is another pleasant incident that marks this day. As soon as dust raised by the *lava* had settled, the Cossacks all gathered in a great circle and started their songs and dances. Apparently the man who had the best time was a lithe young Astrakhan who danced with three large razor-edged knives in his teeth, and then came up to us with blood still dripping from his mouth but evidently very pleased with himself and entirely happy. . . . As we started off in our motor, the entire division, which was drawn up in a single line whose left flank rested on the road on which we were to pass, wheeled to the left and then came up to the road at full gallop. The maneuver was so planned and timed as to make it appear that in another ten seconds we would be in the midst of plunging horses, but each oncoming group reached the road just behind us as we passed along—the general, saber in hand, riding alongside us at full gallop. This heaving line of horsemen swept magnificently on into the horizon, lowering lances in salute as in succession they came pouring over the road just behind us; it was like a great wave pounding in from seaward and curling as it passes over a shallow; and, to save the figure, even the roar of breakers [was heard] as cries of "America, America," came from a thousand throats.

We proceeded to Tchaplinka with some difficulty, for with no sun it was far from easy to keep direction, for the shifting roads of the steppe bear little relation to those on the map. The best way to travel here is to set one's course across the steppe just as one does at sea, and then hold that course. I save much time and more worry by the simple expedient of never asking directions, and instead, I take the bearing of my destination from the map and then by sun and star I navigate across the steppe. On this occasion we changed course at the sight of haystacks in the distance, as it would be a great treat to spend the night in hay instead of straw. On approaching the stacks we were not a little surprised to see some half a dozen American bison come charging out, but when these were followed by a llama, several zebras, a gnu, a yak, some twenty different kinds of antelopes, and various other queer animals I had never seen before, we began to rub our eyes. I then remembered having heard that a very rich German colonist, a Mr. Falz Fein,* had an enormous estate in this district and had the greatest collection of animals in Russia and one of the greatest in the world. The odd assembly we saw was simply the result of bolshevism applied to a zoological garden, as the Bolsheviks had first stolen everything they could lay their hands on and had amused themselves by turning all the animals loose, saying that freedom was the order of the day in Russia. To me the most interesting of these more than a hundred different animals was the orochs, a great shaggy beast I could hardly distinguish from American bison. That the species is practically extinct, being much rarer than American bison, inspired Bolsheviks with the idea of a rare feast; so having inquired which was the rarest of the birds, and also the rarest of the smaller animals, they ordered prepared for themselves a dinner of black swan, a rare species of gazelle, and an orochs. The gazelle was good, said the cook who had prepared it and later gave me an account of the affair, but black swan was very, very tough, and the orochs, being over 27 years old, was worse; and the cook was frightened. Fortunately, the Bolsheviks got very drunk, so the cook used gazelle for all three courses, the first dish being decorated with black swan wings, the second with gazelle horns, and the third with the huge orochs head. These were evidently a jolly lot of Bolsheviks—quite the best I've ever heard of.

We passed the night at this estate, which had formerly been the most scientifically managed in Russia but was now a total wreck. A great mass of scrap iron indicated what had once been the latest American agricultural machinery, and all else was in the same condition, though the present government has now taken charge and is bringing in some semblance of order, having collected many of the animals [and] gathered such crops as had not been totally ruined, and is generally preparing the land for working with disabled soldiers. On these large estates everything thievable has been stolen, everything destroyable ruined, owners and managers fled or killed. . . .

At Tchaplinka an old friend, General Vitkovsky, Commander of Second Corps, explained the situation on his front and plans for the offensive against Kahovka the following week in conjunction with the advance of First Army at Alexandrovsk and a crossing of the Dnieper by

---

* "Falz Fein" is probably W. Falz-Fein, who authored the general natural history work: *Askania Nova das Tierparadies ein Buch des Gedentens und der Gedanten* (Berlin, 1930).

Third Corps at Nikopol. Simultaneous with frontal attack on Kahovka, Vitkovsky planned a crossing a short distance below Kahovka by means of a "perpetual ferry," as he called it. This consists of a large barge, anchored with considerable scope of light chain at the downstream end of an island in the middle of the river, at this point narrow and with a strong current. Point of attachment of the chain to the barge is so arranged that it may be shifted from side to side at the same time a large rudder is shifted, and current sweeping against the rudder propels the barge across the stream. This crossing is to be entrusted to a newly formed Guard Regiment of officers of the former Imperial Guard Regiments and a few mobilized peasants and large numbers of Bolshevik prisoners. When I first saw this regiment six weeks ago, it consisted of a handful of officers, sixty ragged prisoners recently captured, and eleven mobilized peasants. In the meantime, it developed into a full regiment of sixteen companies, each company officered by personnel of one of the sixteen former Imperial Guard Regiments—the plan being to expand companies into regiments as men and equipment become available, for already there are sufficient trained officers. I saw the regiment at drill and exercise in skirmish formation, and performance was good. Although the sight of colonels carrying rifles is no longer as common as it was early in the year, in this regiment there are many swanky young guard captains in the ranks. But they take it with good grace; revolution has accomplished something useful for them, at least as regards their point of view. Rifles of one of these companies found about every type of military firearm used in the last ten years, but the great majority were soviet manufacture. The latter were extraordinarily poor. Not only were they badly matched and fitted, but springs were weak and the entire mechanism was of crudest possible workmanship. But all were plentifully stamped with scythe and hammer. One detachment had so many captured Bolshevik rifles they used the poorest ones to make rafters for straw-covered dugouts in which the army is living now. These semidugouts consist simply of a hole in the ground about ten feet square and five feet deep, with bunks cut into side walls and in the center a table, which consists of an annular trench about one foot wide, two feet deep, and perhaps four feet in outer diameter—a trench for the feet, its outer edge the chair and inner circle the table. The stove is simply a hole cut into the wall with a small opening outside, which provides draft necessary for a straw fire. The roof is invariably a thick straw covering laid on reeds or wattles, for there is practically no wood in this country. This straw, which is found everywhere and in huge quantities, is a blessing, for being poorly threshed it provides food for horses, as well as fuel and building material, and in many cases suffices as a blanket. . . .

I met an officer of Ukrainian origin I had previously known in the Russian Intelligence Service, who for the last five months has been operating in the Ukraine in command of an insurgent detachment busy cutting Bolshevik communications and transport. I joined up with his band, and crossing the Dnieper swamps proceeded inland to the north-eastward of Nikopol to get firsthand information concerning these insurgent bands. . . . My guide and sponsor on this occasion was the ataman Vilkorski,* who had come in for supplies and whom General Kutepov had given 25,000,000 rubles in Bolshevik money, 10,000,000 rubles in Russian money, some machine guns, and medical supplies. He already had a large amount of rifles, ammunition, and other material previously captured from the Bolsheviks. After a trek across swamps— crossing the Dnieper in a small barge for all the world like a Missouri River flatboat—I arrived at a small village above Nikopol, where we spent the day concealed in a peasant's hut and then at night proceeded on. Our only introduction to this peasant was that we needed to be hidden from the Bolsheviks, and he even let us have horses without further guarantee than our saying we would send them back. At Teoulik were awaiting ten other atamans of the Union of Atamans, to which my friend belonged, who were waiting for their share of supplies. Inciden-tally, they were more interested in machine guns and medicaments that he brought, particularly the latter, than in the money. They all wore simple peasant costume and carried revolvers and long daggers but neither swords nor rifles. . . .

I asked what was the source of Makhno's popularity and his power, for certainly it must require some definite idea to hold together a force of 40,000 men. His popularity, they said, came from the fact when his bands were operating all over the Ukraine he had made them divide their loot among the peasants. He would loot a sugar factory and promptly distribute all the sugar among the assembled muzhiks. This process he repeated at practically every factory he came across, likewise with everything else he chanced upon that had not already been looted by the Reds. His power, they said, flowed from his sense of what the people wanted. He would then shout for whatever they wanted, and so of course they were for him. I commented that this appeared not an altogether bad plan in a civil war, but this was too simple an idea for them to grasp. . . .

---

* "Ataman Vilkorski" is missing from English language accounts of the Civil War. An *ataman* was a cossack chieftain.

They wanted the Ukraine to be a state in the Russian government, with status of a state as in the United States, except the Ukraine wanted its own flag and army like states of the German Federation. . . .

I had brought along a copy of a Sebastopol paper that contained the address made by Markotoun, senior member of the Ukrainian Paris delegation, in Sebastopol to confer with General Wrangel concerning the Ukraine.* They all laughed uproariously when they read this address, which made a considerable impression elsewhere, and said it was very fine stuff, but who on earth was Markotoun and how could he or anyone else in Paris speak for the Ukraine. The idea of Markotoun in Paris kept them amused the whole day, and as long as I was with them, I heard all manner of sallies about the "Paris Delegation of the Ukraine." When I left they said it was difficult to have definite information concerning what was really happening in the Ukraine, much less what was going to happen, but there was one definite outstanding fact, that no one in Paris or at a banquet in Sebastopol would have anything to do in settling the Ukraine question. . . .

The crossing of the Dnieper on October eighth and the advance into the Ukraine was one of the most interesting operations I saw, as it perfectly illustrated General Kutepov's methods. On the previous day I had seen the capture of Chertitsa Island . . . former stronghold from which the old Zaporogian Cossacks directed raids against rich towns from Constantinople to Poland. . . .

The Bolsheviks . . . had excellent information concerning the time and place of crossing, for they concentrated all artillery at the appointed place. General Kutepov considered it likely they would have this information; moreover this was the only good ford along this stretch of the Dnieper. Nevertheless all day long regiment after regiment, infantry, cavalry, and artillery, arrived and was massed near the crossing place. However, as soon as darkness set in, came the order to move, and with much sweating and swearing the entire army, with exception of two batteries of artillery and a machine-gun company, got under way, part going upstream but the greater part going downstream, where the river was wider and deeper. At daybreak, as soon as the opposite shore could be made out, artillery began a brisk fire, followed by all the noise the single machine-gun company could produce. Twenty minutes later, at three of the most difficult places to get across—on account of width and depth of the river—the army began its crossing, Red artillery meanwhile pouring in an overwhelming fire on the ford

---

* "Markotoun" receives a brief mention as a Ukrainian "federalist leader" in Kenez (p. 303) and in Brinkley (p. 268).

being so carefully avoided. Result was [one] division across at a cost of eleven men wounded, and [an] entire cavalry corps and [another] division crossed with no casualties whatever. Within forty minutes . . . some nine hundred Bolshevik prisoners were busy hauling White Russian artillery across the river. I talked with many prisoners within a few minutes of capture, and expressions of relief at being clear of Bolsheviks were sincere. . . . They were a ragged lot, many of them having only one boot—others none at all. I kept on with General Babiev's* cavalry and by nightfall . . . counted over 3,000 prisoners. Russian casualties amounted to eleven killed, fifty-nine wounded—which pleased General Kutepov as much as having accomplished his entire objective twenty-eight hours ahead of highest hopes. And not a man in the army but understood why he had marched all night [and] had waded through icy water at the widest part of the river. Gain in morale was worth more than all prisoners, machine guns, and artillery captured. At the same time these casualties indicate morale in the Red Army, for with any fight in them they could have entirely prevented this crossing, since they had great advantage in position and numbers, and could have made the attempt too costly for a second one to be undertaken.

Invariably the first comment of newly captured Bolshevik prisoners was surprise at the fine clothing all men in the Russian service had [and] the excellent food they received. I never considered the Russian army well clothed—far from it—but compared to Bolshevik troops the Russians are magnificently clad. This in itself has a great effect on morale, for to the muzhiks who compose the great mass of both armies, clothing and food are matters of no little importance. . . .

If the Russian army can survive this next offensive, [Wrangel's] government may be considered as definitely established—not again will Bolsheviks have the same opportunity to overwhelm it—for all reports confirm bolshevism past its zenith, and this government has been steadily forging ahead. There is every chance that the army will hold out; its morale is high. . . . Not . . . hardships it has known nor greater hardships in sight—a winter without shelter other than dugouts and straw shacks or fuel other than straw—have been able to keep down high spirits in the army or spoil its good humor. . . .

The morale of this army sounds like an oration at a regimental dinner. "Councils of war never fight" is an old military tradition, for

---

* General Babiev is described as the leader of one of Wrangel's cavalry units (Kenez, p. 303). It was Babiev's cavalry that outflanked the Red garrison at Kahovka, only to have this success wasted by Dratsenko's timidity (Luckett, pp. 371–72).

the task of a council of war is to let the general down easy—to point out [that] strategic reasons demand a retreat at once. But in this army, even a council of war fights; out of every session has come a decision for an advance—the more desperate the situation the more certain the decision for an offensive. And this last council of war—it, too, will fight.[1]

Hugo W. Koehler

10

Sebastopol
November 1920

Even the fact that for some years now the Bolsheviks have daily become stronger as Russia itself has become weaker has failed to make it clear in the minds of those who do not really know the Russians that ruination has strengthened the Bolsheviks, and that famine will keep up the process (June 1922)

Wrangel launched the great trans-Dnieper operation in part because he knew that Budennyi's cavalry would soon arrive from the Polish front. Once Budennyi appeared, the full weight of the Red Army would press upon the Whites.

As observed by Koehler, the operation came within an ace of success. After the capture of three thousand Reds on 11 October, Babiev's cavalry outflanked the thorn of Kahovka while Wrangel's First Army north of Melitopol cut elements of the Soviet Sixth and Thirteenth armies to pieces.

Then, disaster. Due to faulty intelligence from an aerial reconnaissance, Wrangel ordered a frontal assault by General Vitkovsky on Kahovka. The city was in fact heavily defended and ready for him, and Vitkovsky's tanks were destroyed. Then, as Babiev's Cossacks were about to surround the city, Babiev himself was killed by an artillery shell. His demoralized Cossacks began to retreat, causing Dratsenko to order a general retreat. The rout was on. As Luckett wrote:

> As light faded on 13 October the pontoon bridge was dismantled, and on 14 October the forces still remaining over the Dnieper crossed by boat. The expedition had begun well and shown every sign of achieving its objective. The dispositions were sound and the strategy was faultless, but the death of Babiev, the air force's mistake over Kahovka, and the incompetence of Dratcenko—who, however good he may have been as a defensive general, was quite unable to comprehend manoeuvre in attack—had turned it into a disaster.

Wrangel's last offensive, the last action in which he would be able to take the initiative, had failed.[1]

From that moment on, the Whites were in steady retreat. Koehler returned to Sebastopol on 17 October. By then the predicted Red counteroffensive had done its work: the back of Wrangel's patchwork army was broken in the Tauride. Thousands of beaten and demoralized Whites retreated toward the thin necks that separated the northern Tauride from the Crimea. Luckett movingly described the incredible scene:

> On 28 October the first Red attacks were delivered in shattering force. It was the coldest October in twenty-five years, and the scantily clad White soldiers lay shivering on the steppes awaiting the enemy's dawn assaults. Units of the Second National Army under Kutepov . . . bore the brunt of the fighting, and they were soon in retreat. Their shirts stuffed with straw and moss, their limbs bereft of feeling by frostbite, they marched painfully back through the Taurida. The morning of the 29th found the steppes enveloped in a thick fog, limiting visibility to a few yards; the temperature was fourteen degrees below zero. Red cavalry loomed out of the mist, subjected to an almost spectral magnification in the shadowly refracted light, and cut down the numbed defenceless infantrymen. The latter, out of visible contact with their officers, and often entirely unaware of their whereabouts, soon lost what vestiges of morale they still retained.[2]

There was nothing more for the American mission to do but watch the game played out. A week later Koehler was in Yalta with McCully, who wrote in his diary: "Summer is definitely over, although Koehler still goes in swimming."[3]

Koehler's testimony is eloquent concerning Wrangel's ability to re-organize and hearten the army, but it was too late. Everything was lacking but spirit—the Crimea simply could not support an army in addition to its civilian population, already greatly swollen with refugees fleeing the Bolsheviks. Once again, these ragged refugees jammed the Black Sea ports.

Wrangel later described the last days:

> It was evident that after the Armistice and the conclusion of the peace with the Poles the Bolsheviks would direct their forces against the Crimea, and the White Army could not struggle against such odds. What happened was that the Soviet Government concentrated on the front occupied by my troops more than five hundred thou-

sand men with all their Cavalry. Exhausted by long months of inces-
sant fighting, and weakened by all sorts of privations, the White
Army was overwhelmed. To save the remnant of the troops and the
people who had put themselves under their protection, I gave the
order in October 1920 for retreat. The troops fell back by forced
marches on the seaports and embarked according to a plan previously arranged. The civil population, those who served in the rear,
the sick and the wounded, women and children, were the first to be
put on board. The evacuation took place in perfect order. I inspected personally on the Cruiser *Kornilov* the harbours used, and I
was able to assure myself that all who wished to quit Russian soil
found it possible to do so.[4]

At the time of the Wrangel debacle on the Dneiper, Rear Admiral
Jackson R. Tate was "a lowly reserve ensign" attached to the USS *Borie
215* off Sebastopol. He recalled how he wrote himself a set of orders "to
escort the Princess Olga Sargieff Rostigieff, Admiral McCully's secretary, out of the Crimea." This, however, was not to be.

Hugo Koehler tore up the orders and said HE was escorting the
princess and I was assigned to escort out three of the children on the
[destroyer] USS *Overton*. There were over three thousand people
aboard, mostly standing on deck. The children were not at all popular with the C.O. of the destroyer. They—and most of the refugees—had "cooties," the nickname at that time for body lice. . . .
I saw little of Koehler. He was a very dapper and dashing individual and quite a lady's man. He spoke excellent Russian and was
very highly thought of by Admiral McCully.[5]

With nothing more to be done, Koehler sailed for Corotany and
Constantinople on 1 November 1920, and made a yachting trip to
Egypt. On 14 November 1920, Sebastopol was evacuated. General
Wrangel waited on the dock until everyone who wanted to leave Russia
had done so. He then embarked himself, sailing into exile. White Russians who did not leave with him soon wished they had. It is estimated
that between the November evacuation and the end of 1921, the Reds
executed between 50,000 and 150,000 Russian citizens in the Crimea.[6]

Constantinople, Dated Nov. 16, 1920.
Secretary of State, Washington, D.C.
581, From McCully. 91, November 14, 10 P.M.

Without any fighting or disorder Sebastopol was quietly evacuated
at 3 P.M. today and Reds have not yet entered city. About 20,000

Russian troops embarked in Russian vessels for destination unknown. General Wrangel was last to leave and now on cruiser *Kornilov*. About 4,000 refugees evacuated by French, 1,000 by British, and 1,200 on our naval vessels and American steamer *Farraby;* all undergoing great privation and entirely without means. American Red Cross under Major Ryden did extraordinarily fine work. So far no place designated for landing refugees but French admiral states that a place will be designated. All Americans are evacuated from Crimea. Unless otherwise directed I shall proceed to Constantinople.[7]

— ❧ —

With the evacuation of the Crimea by the Whites, the special mission was over.

Koehler's south Russia dispatches are notable for many reasons, not least for their exposition on the Semitic aspects of the Russian conflict. The anti-Semitism of the modern Soviet state is such a long-accepted fact that the Jewish contribution to the Revolution has been all but forgotten. Even those scholars of the Holocaust who attempt to lump Soviet Jewry into a general scheme of universal persecution come up short when dealing with post-1917 Russia. Almost grudgingly, they admit that Soviet laws "against antisemitism [were] enforced until the late thirties," as Yehuda Bauer has written.

Yiddish-speaking schools were at first supported, as was Yiddish literature, which in the twenties experienced a renaissance, but in the thirties the trend was reversed. Slowly, Yiddish schools were emptied of any specifically Jewish content, although Soviet propaganda was taught in the Yiddish language. As Yiddish education increasingly became a dead end, parents began to prefer Russian schools and the number of Yiddish schools declined. Required to conform to the paean of Stalinist adulation, Yiddish literature began to wither. Slowly and thoroughly, the Jewish national and cultural existence was being eliminated.[8]

Koehler had predicted this with uncanny accuracy in 1921, as well as anticipating the rise of Stalin. "All Russia is on the lookout for this dictator," he wrote in 1920, "and every new leader that crops up is examined in the light of his aptitude for the job."

European opinion has already outlined the specifications for this dictator in general accord with Tolstoy's famous prophecy of "The Man from the North." In the interior of Russia, too, they have defined him and very definitely, but along broad and simple lines: he must be strong enough to seize power and hold it while he gives peace and order to his people. And he must think clearly enough and pronounce himself simply to be understood by the millions.[9]

— ❧ —

The Commander's dispatches are also remarkable when considered from the corner of the Allies. The victors of the First World War—the early supporters of the anti-Bolsheviks—withdrew their support from the White Army and cut their losses soon after the fall of Denikin in February of 1920. From Koehler's letters and dispatches, however, it would seem that, given timely if even minimal Allied support, an effective anti-Bolshevik government could have been sustained in the Crimea and into the northern Tauride well into the 1920s and perhaps permanently. Wrangel barely missed making it happen even without the support and materiel of the Allies.

Even into October 1920, less than a month before the final withdrawal of the Whites from Sebastopol, Koehler was encouraged by the successes and prospects for the Whites under Wrangel. But bad intelligence and the timidity of Dratcenko are only two of the reasons the Whites failed to successfully cross the Dnieper. In their 1978 work, *Philip Mironov and the Russian Civil War*, Soviet historians Serge Starikov and Roy Medvedev provide another piece of the answer.

A popular Don Cossack cavalry leader, Philip Mironov, sentenced to death by Trotsky in 1919, was granted a last-minute reprieve by Lenin himself. After the commutation of his sentence, Mironov was permitted to perform work for the Communist party in the Don region. After the defeat of Denikin, Mironov appealed to the former's Cossacks to join the Red Army, and through the power of his personality many did.

In the spring of 1920, it was Lenin's greatest fear that Poland would invade and link with Wrangel's army, which still held out in the Crimea, and launch a new drive on Moscow. Poland did attack in April 1920.

As Koehler described, Wrangel advanced from the Crimea into the northern Tauride in June. By late summer, the combined Polish and White Russian offensives had the Soviet government reeling. The looming threat of prolonged civil war haunted Lenin, for internal Soviet Russia was a chaos of food shortages, poor communications, and general unrest. As Starikov and Medvedev wrote: "In this critical time it was decided to use Mironov in a military capacity once again," as commander of the Second [Red] Cossack Cavalry Army.

Mironov assumed command of the Second, which was being held in reserve, in the beginning of September, and successfully recruited volunteer Cossacks from the Don eager to fight for him. Starting with

2,760 "sabers" (cavalry troops), 130 machine guns, and 19 field pieces, within three weeks Mironov had tripled his striking power.

Wrangel renewed his offensive northward and westward at the same time, attempting to link with Polish forces and cut off Soviet access to the Ukraine. By the first of October Wrangel was at the Dnieper. Too late, Mironov hurriedly tried to fortify the right bank of the river. Kutepov, also at the Dnieper, carried out his brilliant crossing on October 8 with a shock force of three infantry and three cavalry divisions.

The only thing standing between Wrangel and the complete destruction of the Red Sixth Army was Mironov's Second Cavalry. The battle between Mironov's cavalry and Kutepov's shock troops was joined on the right bank of the Dnieper between October 11 and 14, and Kutepov managed to take Nikopol before Mironov learned that another corps under Pisarev was also threatening him on the right bank. Here Mironov decided he would make his great stand.

He later wrote:

> The day of October 14 should figure as a red-letter day in the history of the 2nd Cavalry Army and in that of the revolutionary struggle. . . .
> The time had come for rapidity, purposefulness, and decisiveness. It was sheer hell, what with the thunder of the artillery and the clatter of machine guns and rifles. . . .
> The commander turned to the commanding officer of the 2nd Cavalry Division, who was nearby. "Comrade Rozhkov," he said, "throw in one of your reserve brigades to strengthen the army's left flank. But in order to make an impression, and reduce losses from gunfire, move it out in a *lava* formation, squadron after squadron, over a distance of 200 to 300 paces."
> Before the eyes of those looking on, there now flashed an unforgettable *tableau vivant*. Over a distance of 200 to 300 paces, eight squadrons went at full gallop toward where merciless death was reaping a bountiful harvest. From behind the heights where they had been concealed up to that time, living targets presented themselves to the enemy every five minutes. It seemed they would never stop coming. The enemy tried to stop this flow of Red cavalry with artillery fire. But no sooner had he fired one volley at his target than a new target would appear. Hence his furious artillery fire was nervous and virtually ineffective. . . . And the first squadrons were coming closer and closer to the living defenders of the trenches, who were beginning to lose confidence under the influence of this scene

they were witnessing. . . . While continuing to observe the picturesque battle, the commander dictated a report to southern front
headquarters. The report's conclusion was laconic: "We have hopes
of throwing the enemy back to the left bank of the Dnieper. The
battle is continuing." Fighting continued all along the front. But so
long as we had not taken Grushevka, where the enemy's infantry was
dug in with a large number of machine guns, it could not be thought
that the enemy's cavalry would abandon the village of Marinskoye. . . . One more effort, one more bit of pressure. . . . The enemy abandoned Marinskoye, because Grushevka had been taken.

Such was one of the military events ["pages"] of the Russian
Revolution—an event that took place on October 14 in the bot-
tomlands of the Dnieper; an event anxiously awaited by the worker-
peasant regime; an event being monitored, with equal tenseness, by
Kharkov, Kiev, Moscow, the Kremlin, and Lenin.[10]

Wrangel's advance across the Dnieper was smashed. After a forced
retreat to the left bank, the Whites regrouped to find that the Markov
and Kornilov divisions, General Babiev and his cavalry, Barbovich's
corps, the Sixth and Seventh Infantry divisions, had been crushed and
left behind on the right bank of the river. The battle sealed the fate of
the White resistance in south Russia, sealed, in fact, the fate of all of
Russia for the next seventy years.

Wrangel was just as succinct:

> I was awakened in the middle of the night. General Dratsenko re-
> ported that, having encountered strong enemy forces on the right
> bank of the Dnieper, having suffered heavy losses, and not wanting
> to subject the army to destruction, he had been compelled to order a
> withdrawal back to the left bank. . . . The entire operation was
> doomed.[11]

This battle, not Denikin's farcical and unnecessary withdrawal and
defeat at Novorossisk in the spring of 1920, was the crucial struggle that
ended resistance to Soviet rule following Russia's Communist revolution. And it was this battle that forced the U.S. special mission from
Russia. It would be many years before Americans returned to Russian
soil.

As many as twenty-five million deaths have been attributed to the
Russian Civil War.[12] Following the great evacuation of November
1920, White Russians were scattered to the ends of the earth.

Of those whom Lieutenant Commander Hugo W. Koehler met or

tracked during his year in Russia, all experienced ignominious fates. The Soviets hunted down and destroyed the remnants of "Father" Nestor Makhno's band of peasant anarchists in 1921. Makhno himself escaped to Rumania and then Poland. To the surprise of everyone, he died in his bed in Paris in 1935, an enigma long since forgotten.

Shkuro also escaped, and during the interwar years established himself as a popular horse rider who performed daredevil feats in a European circus. When the Nazis invaded Russia in 1941, Shkuro volunteered to train cadres of exiled Cossacks who then fought alongside the Germans in south Russia. "His duties consisted of visiting Cossack camps, where he did what he pleased. He would be found among Cossack groups drinking vodka and delivering a repertoire of bawdy jokes that appeared to be almost limitless."[13] After the war Shkuro was caught by the British and turned over to the Soviets, who executed him in 1947.

General Denikin also died in 1947, though in the markedly more peaceful surroundings of Ann Arbor, Michigan. Denikin had lived out the war in France, where, unsuccessfully, the Nazis tried to persuade him to deliver anti-Communist radio broadcasts. In one of his last diary entries Denikin noted wryly: "The ignominious Finnish campaign and the defeat of the Red Army on the Germans' way to Moscow, took place under the sign of *International Communism*; the German armies were defeated under the slogan *Defend our Homeland!*"[14]

Even in exile, Wrangel's aim was to hold his army together so that it might one day rise to fight again. He died in April 1928, a victim of the strain of such an endeavor, along with his ceaseless efforts to provide for the thousands of Russian refugees.

General Kutepov succeeded Wrangel as head of the Russian military exiles organization. On the morning of 26 January 1930, he was kidnapped off the streets of Paris. Later that day, several people were seen carrying "a long package wrapped in sacking down the sea-cliffs near Villers-sur-Mer. On the beach they loaded it onto a motor launch, which set out for a [Soviet] cargo-ship hove-to off the coast."[15] Only after thirty-five years did the Soviet secret police admit to the kidnapping and execution of Koehler's "sworn brother."[16]

There is yet another strange postscript to the year in south Russia. Returning to the United States aboard the *Aquitania*, Koehler met Mrs. Clare Sheridan, an English sculptor. She had gone to Moscow to do portrait busts of the Bolshevik leaders. The British Foreign Office had agitated against Mrs. Sheridan's Russian journey, to the point of threatening to forbid her to leave England. Sheridan was on her way to

America to give lectures on her Russian adventures. On her first day in New York, Koehler took care of her young son while she faced a barrage of reporters, well-wishers, and agents.

The first twist to this story comes in a letter Koehler sent from Poland in 1922, in which he mentioned a similar international incident that reminded him of "the famous case of Mrs. Sheridan, at whom the Foreign Office thundered so loudly when she announced that she was going to Russia. The Foreign Office even went to the length of refusing her a passport and putting all manner of difficulties in her way. And yet, be it known (although this, of course, is very closely guarded) that Mrs. S. went to Russia as an agent for the British Intelligence Service!"[17]

The second twist came many years later, when Koehler's grandson was going through an old unused trunk and found the canceled passport, its cover torn off, of Mrs. Clare Consuelo Sheridan.[18]

In 1922, looking back on his experiences in Russia, Koehler wrote to his mother from Poland: "There is much discussion and very real interest [here] in the effect of the American relief work in Russia." With penetrating clarity of insight he continued:

> The most prominently accepted idea is that the tremendous scale of the American relief, which is today feeding ten million people and is expected shortly to feed eleven million, means nothing other than that America has in large part saved the Bolsheviks from the most terrible of the economic consequences of their program. . . . I must admit that there is an enormous volume of opinion that supports these points of view, for these supplies release other supplies they can make use of, and to that extent I think our famine relief is useful to the Red authorities. But the Bolsheviks will not stand or fall because we send in famine relief—the question is much greater than that. I think the reason people usually get on the wrong track is that they start out with the thesis that if the famine becomes bad enough the Bolshevik authorities will be destroyed. But I know of no theory that is so widely accepted that is so absolutely and entirely wrong. The Bolsheviks will remain in the saddle just as safely even if the famine gets twice as bad, or three times, or four times, or any number of times! In such event, all that will happen is that Russia instead of having 120 million will before long have 110 million, and then 100 million, and then perhaps 85 million; but in any case the millions that remain will be ruled by the Bolsheviks. Even the fact that for some years now the Bolsheviks have daily become stronger as Russia itself has become weaker has failed to make clear in the minds of those who do not really know the Russians that ruination

has strengthened the Bolsheviks, and that the famine will keep up the process. . . . To sum up months of study on the subject, I would say that perhaps the most important truth we must now realize about Russia is that Bolshevik control becomes more absolute as the misery of the people increases, and that the famine, far from shaking their power, has only made it more absolute.

Another factor that is to be considered is the intensity of the terror felt all along the great line of the Russian frontier, and felt, too, a great deal further west. The peasants say that the seriousness of the famine that has already begun in Russia will before long become so terrible that the final result will be a migration of the famished hordes towards the west. Not only do the professors and students tell you of the migrations in history when the hordes of the east poured westward, for such stories are a part of the crude history that almost every peasant knows. There are many who explain that the Russians are after all a great nomad race, that deep in their very soul is bred the idea of avoiding starvation, not by thrift and saving in the years of prosperity, but by moving on from the colony that is barren to the land that has plenty. The fundamental reason that communism has obtained such a wide hold on the Russians, say these people, is that the Russians are a nomadic race and as such have no deeply ingrained idea of private property. And even the peasant who has neither theories nor theorems has the dread that the hungry from the steppes will descend like a flight of locust and eat him out of his ground. The danger is not immediate, I think, but it does exist. When the hordes of the hungry come to their borders they will be shot down at the frontier if they come simply as hordes. But if the hordes come as the Red Army, still well fed but with the dread of hunger at their backs, then that is another question![19]

On 30 November 1920, McCully sailed from Constantinople with seven Russian children he had adopted. A special dispensation was given to the bachelor admiral to allow him to bring his children home to America, where he raised them as his own.

11

Poland and the Baltic States
1921–1922

I took a look into this freight car, typical of the whole train. It was the usual type of small boxcar, and in it were 47 people of all sizes and ages, all in rags and all filthy, sitting, sprawling, huddled on top of innumerable ragged bundles. (November 1921)

Koehler had been back in Washington but a few months—where he continued to write of his experiences in Russia—when the Secretary of the Navy asked the State Department if Koehler would be acceptable as naval attaché in Warsaw. Replied State: "[We] do not consider it necessary to make inquiries of the Polish Government as to Commander Koehler's acceptability, and accordingly designate him Naval Attaché to the American Legation in Warsaw."[1] As with so much of the Commander's career, this action swept aside the usual protocol.

Koehler's job, as he saw it, would be to spend a year "combing Europe from one end to the other with no purpose more definite than to see what's really happening, on the theory that that might give us some idea of what's going to happen."[2] His new diplomatic passport described him as "35 years of age, 5 feet 8 inches tall, high forehead, hazel eyes, straight nose, medium mouth, round chin, brown-gray hair, ruddy complexion, and oval face." The passport, signed by Secretary of State Charles E. Hughes, is itself a chronicle of where Koehler went to "see what's really happening." It bulges with over sixty visas, stamped in little over a year.[3]

Poland was newly independent in 1921, after 126 years of political oblivion. From 1795 to 1918, administrative control over the territory of Poland was variously exerted by Russia, Prussia, and Austria-Hungary. Only the collapse of Poland's neighboring nations in 1917–1918 allowed Poland the space to reassert its own national character.

However, everyone seemed to have different ideas as to just what "Poland" was. As Koehler discovered on his journeys throughout Poland and the Baltic states, the new territory of Poland that was created

14. Hugo Koehler in *World's Work Magazine,* which published Koehler's account of the mission to South Russia, in 1921. (Photo courtesy of Clarkson N. Potter.)

at Versailles in 1919 included in large measure parts of the old Russian Empire, entities called the Congress Kingdom and the Eastern Kresy. These areas were populated predominantly by White Russians, Lithuanians, Poles, and Ukrainians, along with small concentrations of Jews. The area of the new Polish state that was taken from Germany included the agricultural regions of Pomerania and Posnania, plus the industrial area of Upper Silesia. From Austria-Hungary came the areas of Galicia and Austrian Silesia.

These various areas had different legal systems, customs, and even different languages, and there was no unified transport system. Taxes were assessed differently in different areas, and education, where it was available, was of various and sometimes dubious quality. Not until 1920 was a single currency, the Polish mark, introduced. Any attempt to forge a unified country out of this geographical conglomerate was complicated still further by the ruin of six years of warfare that had laid waste to cities and farmlands alike. The degree of destruction of the countryside alone was formidable: bridges, 55 percent; railway stations, 63 percent; locomotives, 48 percent; buildings, 18 percent—all destroyed.

Throughout his journeys through Poland, eastern Germany, and the Baltic states in 1921–1922, what Koehler found was a twisted pathway to the future of Europe, tantamount to a carnival corridor lined with distorted mirrors. And the Commander was among the very few with the prescience to recognize the distortions for what they in fact were: the stark reality of a world once again falling into the abyss.

American Legation
Warsaw, Poland
Office of the Naval Attaché
3 November 1921

Motored to Warsaw from Danzig . . . [though] the direct road does not follow the line of the Polish corridor, and we passed in and out of Germany and Poland so often that we soon lost count of the number of frontier stations. . . .

I had heard much about the thousands of Poles being repatriated from Russia, so almost immediately after my arrival I headed for Baranowicze, a great concentration camp just inside the Polish border, where from one thousand to three thousand refugees have been flocking in daily. En route I stopped at Brest-Litovsk, which is battle scarred enough to look the part it played in the war as the tide rolled back and forth. The most interesting thing there was the scrawl on the wall of the room where the Bolshevik treaty with Germany was signed. "Neither Peace nor War," it reads, and is signed "Leon Trotsky, December 1917, Brest"—certainly not a bad estimate of the situation, especially so, considering the date.

We motored on from Brest-Litovsk to the frontier, past miles of trenches and dugouts, those of the Germans, built of concrete and steel and evidently intended for an army of a hundred thousand to keep back a million. . . . All this region is desolate as a burned forest, for in accordance with age-old Russian strategy the armies laid waste the countryside as they retreated, and with a thoroughness worthy of a better cause. In all this great belt stretching from north to south and a hundred kilometers wide, there is hardly a house intact. Wonderfully thorough they were, these poor Russians, in destroying their own houses and fields.

As we entered Baranowicze a long trail of freight cars came crawling in. As the train stopped, an old man thrust his head out of one of the cars and called to me, "Where are we?" I answered "Baranowicze." "What country is this?" called another. "Poland," I answered. "What kind of government is this? Is there a king? Who is the king? What will they do to us? Is there any food?" came the shouts in a jabbering of Russian and Polish and German. Then one of the A.R.A. [American Relief Association] men came up and told them that they would get food at a kitchen a short distance up the road. "When? When? When?" And after they had tasted the cocoa and beans, "Where does it come from?" "From America," I answered. "America? Where is America?" "A place where there is much food," answered one of his more erudite companions.

I took a look into this freight car, typical of the whole train. It was the usual type of small boxcar, and in it were 47 people of all sizes and ages, all in rags and all filthy, sitting, sprawling, huddled on top of innumerable ragged bundles. The questions asked were principally whether they would really get warm food. Children with swollen stomachs, young men with wrinkled, yellow faces, and women crying silently. No sound, just tears. They came from all parts of Russia. Some of them had been en route for months in the same car, other had trekked across the steppes and had finally been thrust into freight cars when their horses died and they could drag their carts no further. They had all been caught in the great Russian drag of 1915 and had been taken to central Russia; concerning what had happened in the world in the last six years they had no idea. All they knew were local conditions in the villages where they had lived and how difficult it was to get food during the journey back. . . .

Arriving at the border, we found a long line of prairie schooners coming in. "Is this Poland? Are we out of Russia? God be praised!" came again and again in the same jabbering Russian, Polish, and German. It happened that in this crowd were German colonists from Russia. Though they had been in Russia for many generations, they had never mixed with the Russians but kept close together in their little farm colonies along the Volga. When the war came, the Russians would have nothing to do with them, nor would the Germans, since they had been Russian citizens for generations. Arriving at the border they were more bewildered than ever, for now they had no place at all to go; before they had at least the great desire of getting out of Russia and the general direction of the border for which to set their course. I talked to one peasant who was under twenty-seven although he looked over forty—and small wonder, for he had tramped over five thousand versts and during the last stretch had dragged the cart himself, as the Bolsheviks had taken away his horse. I examined the cart he had brought all this distance and with so tremendous an effort: an old bed, bits of sacking, an assortment of battered pots and pans, an old sheepskin, part of a wolfskin, rags, nine potatoes, a handful of radishes, some pieces of tallow—nothing else. The complete inventory would not net a dollar; he explained that he had had a cow, but the Bolsheviks had taken it away from him at the border. Yet he was much better off than thousands, for having been out in the open air he was in comparatively good health although drawn and wasted, whereas the others who had come back by train were feeble and diseased and bleeding from bites. The children, of course, were the most tragic sights. They are young only when they smile.[4]

21 February 1922
[A postscript to his mother.]

Some days ago, while I was peacefully working away in my study, without thought of harm or strife, I was suddenly pounced upon by about a dozen women who had just had a committee meeting in the house not very far from where I live. They had been discussing the position of women in Poland, and they were trying to find out some way in which they could help these women of aristocracy that lead a life just about as free and independent as slaves in a Turkish harem, for there are many conventions that are remarkably like those in the average harem and still others that are not nearly as sensible as the Turkish. One of these women of the committee mentioned something that I had said on the subject, and then another one suggested that on their way home they stop by my house to see if I was in. So suddenly appeared the dozen, all demanding tea. I was not a little startled by a point-blank question about what I thought about women in general—what they could do in life, and what they ought to aim at. But, as you know, it is a subject to which I have given much thought, so I was not so embarrassed as I perhaps ought to have been. So a most interesting discussion followed, for these women were very much in earnest, although they were groping around rather blindly. As they were going, one of them turned to me and asked simply, "You love your mother very much, don't you?" I was not a little surprised, of course, at the direct question, but nodded yes. She may have detected the note of surprise in my voice, for she continued on: "She is an exceptional woman, is she not?" I answered yes, whereupon she added that she had known it because it always is that men who have a high opinion of women have had exceptional mothers.[5]

15 June 1922

I celebrated Easter by going to the famous Zakopane district, one of the most delightful places in all the lovely Tatra mountains, formerly Austrian and Hungarian and now Czecho-Slovakian and Polish, but where one can still get along quite well by speaking only German. There one appreciates the quality of the air and the sunshine without heat, just brightness. The forests are lovely not only for magnificence of trees and the charm of the blend of the many greens, where birches fringe the pine forests and patches of beech and ash have worked their way into the dense fir, but more because the great forests manage somehow to give one their own quietness. The breadth of the mountain's horizons give broader views—small thoughts and cramped ideas fall away simply because the mind is focused for wider views. And so I wandered about in the sunshine I had not seen for many murky months in Poland, and talked to great numbers of peasants, men and women and children, on subjects varying from crops and native songs to land tenure and nationality.

The simple wooden peasant houses of mortised joints and chinks stuffed tight with braided straw have charm, because they do not take away from the magnificent simplicity of the mountain scenery. For the need of shelter from winter winds has decreed that the house be built in the curves and hollows of the mountains—they dare not stick out where the wind will catch them in full sweep; and the low walls of stone or unpainted wood, and the roofs thatched with straw and sod, soon blend with their surroundings. One day a smiling peasant woman with soft, brown eyes, glowing with pride in the new house she herself was finishing while her father was struggling in his terraced fields on the other side of the mountain, took me in to see the splendor of the many cakes she was baking for feast days that were to begin the next morning. I noticed a child's top in a corner with a cord all ready for spinning, so I asked where were the children. She knew little German and less Russian, and my Polish is of the feeblest, so with few words and mostly with signs and a dumb sort of acting she began to unfold the story of her dead children and her man lost in the war. But somehow she could not control herself, and she would give up the slow method of signs and motions, and a torrent of words would pour forth. Though I missed her words, I could not help feeling her sadness even through her useless unclear sounds, and she told me of the loneliness of life on the mountain with no children. And in some strange manner she managed to tell me about her sister who had too many children and would sometimes lend her a child; and then she would bake cakes and be happy until her sister wanted the child back. She was very rich, she explained, and showed me all the hay in the loft, the rows upon rows of dried mushrooms and strips of dried mutton, her scarfs that had come down from many generations, the tablecloth of real linen, and the gaily embroidered trousers of the man she had lost . . . and ended by taking me out to the lean-to cow barn where were calves and chickens and more hay stacked high on the rafters. She was very rich, she repeated, and could have many children, but her man was lost in the war, and it was very sad on the mountain, though there was always sun in her window and her house was so built that even in winter the snowdrifts would pass over and leaver her little garden clear. As in many other peasant cottages hereabout, I noticed that the many images of saints painted on wood and also copper and silver, had silver and gilt ornamentation that made them resemble the Russian icons much more closely than they do Catholic pictures. I continued on my way across tiny fields bordered as in our own New England with stones gathered from the fields, but sharp, flat stones. . . Then down into delightful little villages surrounded by blossoming trees, which made them look for all the world as if they had been embroidered into a green and white background, the green of the dense pine thickets and white of snowcapped mountains sparkling in morning sun. Sometimes the green would be paler where new growth had pushed up through the snow, and sometimes the snow would have a blue light and often even violet, for the snow changes color as does the sea, changing with the color of the sky and the different angle of the light. . . .

The next day was a holiday, which meant, of course, a great thronging to the church. . . .

The church was so crowded that many could not find room even to kneel and so remained standing for the full two hours of the service, for of course there were no chairs. And because the small church could not hold all, nearly half the churchyard was filled with the kneeling figures of the devout. After the service the congregation split into little groups, the young girls giggling, the old women gossiping, the young men lounging about, the old men sitting quietly in the sun and smoking a terrible-looking black weed in queer-shaped little copper pipes. . . .

As is always the case, it was easy to tell the mountaineers from the lowlanders, though there was little difference in costume. Mountaineers are a superior race the world over, I think. They hold their heads high, they have a bold air and a free one, they feel themselves men; for continuously they must battle with the elemental forces, and they win. I think they have a considerable similarity to sailor-men who too bear the marks of their struggle with the elemental forces. They too have the look of wide spaces in their eyes; and so have the men that rove the steppes. They have wide natures, too—natures that will not fit into the canons of city streets. . . . I talked at great length with these moun-taineers, for I wanted their opinion about their new country. Many of them had a most indefinite idea of what Poland really is, and yet Poland has a distinct meaning for them, for they felt that Poland meant free-dom. But freedom as they saw it, or rather, felt it, had no especial political significance; it meant simply an absence of irksome re-strictions. I asked them about what they would do if the Russians came back. They answered that they would still hold their mountains no matter who came. Altogether they strongly confirmed the opinion that is growing firmer the more I see and hear of the great national aspira-tions of various groups so ably expressed by foreign lawyers hired for the purpose. For I find that in the mass these magnificent aspirations are either inspired by alien interests or they are the ideas of professors and students, which by violent and frequent repetition come finally to be accepted by the masses as their own ideals and aims. The only real evidence of a national feeling I can find among the great masses in Poland, as well as in Russia, is the attachment of the peasant to his soil and to the manner of living to which he is accustomed. Language means something, of course, and religion, too, but less, for the idea of religious difference is largely stimulated by the clergy. The great factor in these cruder ideas of nationality seems to be simply an attachment to the soil and contentment with customs that usually have an intimate relation to the soil. . . .

I wandered about Germany for some weeks . . . always stopping at some small hotel for the night, usually spending the early afternoon and evening in wandering about and talking to all manner of people. Often I would see a group of German peasant women with their babies, and smilingly I would ask them if they were raising these fine babies for "Canonenfutter" (cannon fodder). The invariable answer was an indig-nant "No." Yet on talking to them further there would just as invariably be comments to the effect that these boys would someday have to fight just as their fathers fought—because the French would not let them live otherwise. "*Frankreich muss noch weinen*" "The French will be made to weep yet") I heard over and over again. . . . But the most remarkable thing of all was that when I said to the hundreds of Germans of all classes to whom I talked that after all it had been a blessing for Germany that Germany had lost the war, since the overbearing attitude of the military of a victorious Germany would have been quite insupportable, not a single German would disagree. Apparently the memory of the swank of the military is too strong to be forgotten in a single generation. . . .

It happened that for a part of the journey a French officer was with me, and all this evidence of prosperity was a bitter pill for him to swallow, as he thought of devastated northern France. Over and over again he muttered that there would be another war, and it was clearly written on his face that the sight of all these sturdy Germans working so hard, going so earnestly about their business, filled him with dread. On Sundays we would pass hundreds of men and often women, too, with knapsacks on their backs, trudging along, usually to some distant height from which they could have a view onto a convenient beer-garden, always plodding along steadily. The sight of all this energy, this trampling along the dusty roads on Sunday after a week of the hardest kind of work, really struck terror to the soul of my French friend; for although he spoke German well enough not to be taken for a Frenchman, I doubt whether on the whole road he met a single German who did not damn France and all Frenchmen. Small chance indeed that a Frenchman feeling as he did would agree to a reduction in the French army! So again and again comes up this principle that to understand a people one must know not only the facts of the case but what they consider to be the facts, for no power on earth could have persuaded that Frenchman that it would not be ruinous to France to reduce her army. The tragedy is not only that the French do not realize that by keeping an army beyond their means they are weakening themselves, but the fear and terror that they all feel makes it impossible for them even to understand it until that terror is removed. . . .

But all the smiling fields, and all the beautiful villages, and all the sturdy Germans working so industriously, all the busy factories at Dusseldorf and Essen and the Ruhr—and in fact almost every little village has a factory of some sort—all these many evidences of prosperity could not take from the dread that Germany has a hard time ahead of her, and the sort of hard time that is full of danger for the rest of Europe as well. Some time ago I made an analysis regarding the present cheap production in Germany, and all the work I've done since has confirmed that this cheap production has been on an unsound basis— that Germany was selling below the cost of actual production, and that though the crash might be postponed for some later time because of the great advantage of full employment, still it could not be kept off for long, and when it would come it would come all the harder because of the weakened financial condition of Germany. . . .

To pull through, Germany will need statesmanship wiser than the greed of manufacturers that has been the directing force since the armistice. As it is, the German people seem blighted with the curse of false leaders, for the interests now at the helm, though more greedy than the old, are less farsighted; and again the German people suffer for their lack of ability in choosing leaders. . . .

Elsewhere, the people I met on these journeys asked me whether Poland had any possibility of continuing its existence for long. My invariable answer was yes, and that not only was there a possibility, but that there was also some probability even if not a large one, which seemed to astound them very much; and one and all they began to explain to me the utter impossibility of Poland's future. They usually ended the discussion by saying that it was an axiom that if there were any real reason for the existence of Poland, there would have been a Poland long before this. . . . They concluded with the statement that independence is a thing that a nation, like a man, has to win for itself. Neither can receive it as gift, not even on a silver platter. And over and over again one hears it stated that if there had been any real vitality in the idea of Polish nationality, the Poles would long ago have thrown off the yoke of the oppressors they hated so bitterly. But however sound these statements may be in themselves, I do not find that they quite fit the Polish situation. It is all very well to say that a country should itself throw off the yoke if it aspires to nationhood, but when all is said and done, once Poland was partitioned, it was really impossible for Poland to rise until at least one of the oppressors had fallen. It is true that a country must itself achieve its independence, since the fundamental character of independence is that it cannot be received as a gift.

It is equally true that no country has any vitality if it is simply the by-product of the foreign policy of another country. Nor is it difficult to multiply historical examples to illustrate these cardinal principles. It is a fact, too, that Poland has not achieved its independence; yet that means nothing more than that Poland's independence is still to be achieved. Poland has been reborn and has a fine start in life, but whether or not Poland will ever arrive at manhood depends entirely on the Poles. There is no royal road to knowledge, we were told as children, nor is there any royal road to manhood or statehood. . . . Very pertinently do I remember the feeling in General Wrangel's army when the Poles were advancing to Kiev. Although Wrangel's men were fighting for existence against the Bolsheviks, in the hardest and bitterest kind of fight, still there was a time, at the height of the Polish advance, when the feeling in Wrangel's army was such that they would almost have made common cause with the Bolsheviks rather than see the Poles advance into Russia. And when the Bolsheviks finally threw back the Poles, although the Wrangel army knew that would mean that the Bolsheviks could now concentrate their entire strength against them, and practically that the days of the Wrangel army were numbered, nevertheless a silent cheer went up from the moribund. That cheer did not come from above or outside, or from propaganda or the speeches of demagogues, but simply from a feeling in the left side of the breast of every Russian in the army. Luckily for Poland, the Poles were thrown back from Kiev, but the feeling in the Russians that they would have Russia for the Russians, is a thing with which the Poles will have to reckon one day. No Pole can quite understand this. His love for his country makes him blind in this respect. But the certainty that there will someday be a reckoning on these scores remains nevertheless.

Some few Poles understand that those too far extended borders are a great danger, but still they say that those borders are their "due" and, for one reason or another, are "absolutely essential." They do not seem to realize that what they call their "due" may most likely be their un-doing, and what they call "absolutely essential," although highly desir-able, perhaps, from one point of view, is fraught with too many dangers from other points of view to make it anything but a liability. And the Danzig corridor, that artificial product of overambitious amateur pol-iticians and well-meaning idealists, made possible only by their fear and hatred of the Germans—they "must" have it, say the Poles; it too is their "due," they explain. That all historical precedent indicates the unsoundness of any such artificiality means nothing in the scale as against these ambitions and aspirations.[6]

13 July 1922

In the forest regions there are many Jews in the little villages that here consist usually of a single row of houses around a square instead of the single, very broad street of the Russian style. I heard many com-plaints against the Jews: that they did no real work, no farming, no cutting of wood, yet they became rich on the labors of the peasants. "If they do not farm and do not cut wood, then what do the Jews do?" I asked a peasant. "Oh, they buy stolen logs and trade stolen horses and sell vodka," was the answer. "You wicked anti-Semitic propagandist!" I reproached him; but his only reply was that just nine days before, his brother's horse had been stolen and found at a Jew's house seventeen versts away, and that certainly everybody knew that the Jews bought the stolen logs and cattle as well as the horses. "But the peasants must steal the logs first in order to sell them to the Jews," I answered. "Yes," he admitted, "but if the Jews did not buy, the peasants would not steal." I told him the parable about the pot and the kettle, but he was not impressed. . . .

The peasants are a weird lot, at once docile and savage, good-hearted and cruel, with wild eyes and soft voices. In general they live in tiny, crowded, dirty hovels, whose only furnishings are a few crude chairs and benches and a rough bed where any number of persons may sleep. The ornaments very seldom go beyond the soiled tissue-paper flowers and frills of gay colors, and numerous oleographs of holy pictures or of a dog or horse, or here and there a photograph made by some peripatetic photographer. . . .

The more I wander about these regions, the more I marvel at all the precise little maps I used to see at the peace conference in Paris, where little red, green, and blue dots showed so definitely whether the population was Polish or White Russian. I have often wondered where these geographers got their data, for most of these people, whose race, nationality, and origin are so precisely charted on the maps, have themselves precious little idea of where or to whom they really belong. . . . "What are you, a Russian or a Pole?" I would ask. "Oh, I am a man from here," was the usual answer. "What language do you speak?" "Our language," he answered. . . . The safest way to differentiate between Poles and Russians in these regions of mixed proportion is along the lines of Greek Orthodox and Catholic religion, about which there never is the slightest doubt. . . .

Not long after crossing the Lithuanian frontier, we passed what appeared to be a small army post, so I stopped there, spoke to the soldiers and a passing officer, asked the direction to the next stop, and this being given, proceeded on. We continued on our way for about an hour and a half, when suddenly we came upon a line of soldiers drawn up across the road with rifles and charge-bayonets, and all gesticulating wildly. An officer then approached and informed me that I would have to return at once to the frontier in order to have my passport stamped, as I had evaded the frontier guard. I explained that I had seen no frontier guard, although I had been on the lookout for one, and also stated that I had telegraphed some ten days previously to his government concerning my arrival at this hour on this date and by this route. He insisted that I return to the frontier. Inasmuch as the frontier post he described was some hour and half back, and over very bad roads, I refused point-blank to go back but added that I would be glad to go to any station in the direction of Kovno, my destination. He called general headquarters by telephone; but always the same answer about returning to the frontier would be hurled at me.

Finally I took up the telephone myself and talked to various regimental commanders, divisional commanders, and goodness knows what, all of whom repeated that the frontier was closed inasmuch as Poland and Lithuania were at war, and that I could therefore not have passed the frontier. In reply I suggested that the mere fact that I was in the middle of Lithuania ought to be sufficient evidence that I had crossed the frontier, and that the frontier was very evidently not closed inasmuch as I had come over the main road at the time designated and had not been stopped, nor had I been able to find a frontier post in spite of the fact that I had been looking out for one. After more lengthy powwows, I was finally informed that if I would not go willingly I would be forced to return to the frontier. I replied that I would not go willingly and that under the circumstances I considered that the same international law that applied to blockades also applied to a frontier; that is, that just as a blockade in order to be binding must be effective, so it was with a frontier.

After still further powwows, my new friends changed their tactics and begged and implored me to return to the frontier, saying that I would be held up there for only the single minute it would take to stamp my papers, and that I could then proceed immediately to Kovno. I answered that since this was Lithuania, the Lithuanians certainly had a perfect right to exclude me if they wished to do so, but inasmuch as they themselves said that they had no intention of excluding me, but only wished me to go all the way back to this indefinite post merely for the sake of a rubber stamp, a journey that would require altogether at least three hours travel over very bad roads, I regretted that I could not agree to their request. Of course, my own theory was that this was merely subterfuge on their part, and that the minute they got me back to the frontier they would push me across the border. And that, of course, was exactly what I did not want.

So I stuck to my ground, with the result that my suggestion that I should proceed on to divisional headquarters to see the divisional commander was finally agreed to. I had made this suggestion because the divisional headquarters were in the direction of Kovno and away from the frontier, for my estimate of the situation was that my strategic position would be much improved the nearer I got to Kovno and the farther away from the frontier.

As I started out for divisional headquarters, I was told that a soldier would have to go along in my car. I refused to have him in the car, saying if I were under arrest I could, of course, do nothing but comply with the order of my captors, but until I was under arrest I refused to have any stranger enter my car except by my own invitation, and that I most certainly did not invite anybody to enter. This caused further confusion, but after a council of war it was decided that instead of putting a man in my car a cavalryman would follow. So we started off, but at the last moment my escort was called back, given a handful of cartridges and showed how to put them in his gun. He looked a little bewildered, for apparently this was his first experience with real cartridges, although he had probably been toting a rifle for months.

Arriving at divisional headquarters, the first result was more discussions, telephoning, arguing, and beseeching. But the upshot of it all was that instead of proceeding to Kovno I was told I should have to wait where I was until the Lithuanian Foreign Office had authorized the visa of my passport and this in turn had been notified to the general staff so that the latter could inform the military authorities that I should be allowed to proceed. However, as this process promised to take a good many hours if not days and weeks, and as the discussion had already lasted some four and a half hours, I cast about for a happy idea. Up to this time my main plan had been not to go backward under any conditions, and to keep hold of my good humor during all the discussions. Now, therefore, I approached the general's adjutant and mentioned to him quite casually that inasmuch as I had been in Poland for a long time I knew the Polish side of the Polish-Lithuanian controversy very thoroughly, but I had never had a really thorough explanation of the Lithuanian side of the case. I added, parenthetically, that it might be very interesting on the journey to Kovno to hear an expose of the Lithuanian side of the story. The effect of this gentle hint was electric! The adjutant dashed off to his colonel, and within three minutes the answer came back that I could proceed at once to Kovno, and that, if I wished it, an officer would accompany me to show me the way. And so with much handshaking and many good wishes for a pleasant journey, we finally started off, and eventually even arrived at Kovno without further mishap other than that the bright young officer who accompanied us was so interested in his story that he mistook the way, although he had been over it only the previous morning.[7]

12 September 1922

The collapse of the German mark is the center of interest and the grave concern of every German in the land, from high to low. The latter discuss it principally as it affects the cost of living; the former view it not only as a barometer of general conditions in Germany but as an index of the health of all Europe. As a matter of fact, it looms quite as large in conversations outside of Germany as inside. . . .

Concerning general conditions in Germany, a typical example must serve. Although I knew present economic conditions must inevitably produce want, I was not prepared for the number of children I saw obviously suffering from malnutrition. And this at the time of the year when food is most plentiful and the added stress of shortage of fuel and clothing is not felt. Noticing a group of women working in the field I stopped to ask them their hours of work, wages, and general conditions. They were weeding sugarbeets—and backbreaking work it is. Their hours were from 6 A.M. to 7 P.M., with 20 minutes off for breakfast and 35 minutes for dinner. They received 69 marks per day. As marks on that day were 1,900 to the dollar, it meant that their wages were less than 4 cents a day. However, this is, of course, not a fair way to judge their pay, since these 69 marks in Germany have a purchasing value much greater than 4 cents would have in America. So at the next village I stopped to ask the price of food. Margarine was 140 marks a pound, butter 300 marks, meat 85 marks for the cheapest cut, bread 42 marks the loaf, and the other prices in proportion. In other words, for twelve hours of the hardest kind of work, these women received in wages less than half a pound of margarine, or less than a pound of meat, or a quarter of a pound of butter.[8]

12

At the Rainbow's End

1923–1941

After five years of exhaustive explorations from Queenstown to Crimea and from the Baltic to the Adriatic, Koehler in 1923 settled back into a more typical Navy career. He was First Lieutenant on the *Utah* for the first five months of 1923, then Aide and Flag Secretary to Vice Admiral H. A. Wiley, Commander of the Battleship Division of the Battle Fleet, until September 1925. Koehler's last cruise was with Wiley aboard the *West Virginia*, when the fleet coursed the South Pacific. As Koehler wrote at the time, "I often wonder what I am going to do when one of these days I come back to earth and start messing in my proper mess—I mean with officers of my own rank—for I have for so many years now been messing with one admiral or another that I almost look on people of my own age and grade as inexperienced young striplings."[1]

When the Commander did come back to earth, the truth was that he would do very little. He became restless and wanted back into the intelligence game. Anticipating the importance of the Soviet Union, he specifically wanted the billet as attaché to Moscow, a job that would not even be created until long after his retirement from the Navy. To complicate matters, he was also in love with Matilda Pell. She was the wife of Herbert Pell, a friend of FDR and future Minister to Hungary and Portugal, and she was the mother of future U.S. Senator Claiborne Pell.

It was Lord Gladstone who warned Koehler not to leave the Navy without a clear alternative, adding: "If you were in our Navy you would now be an Admiral."[2] Gladstone also extended to Koehler more than good advice, for he had circumspectly countenanced a long affair between Dolly, his much younger wife, and Hugo, who was then at his

15. Hugo Koehler with Herbert Gladstone in England, ca. 1930. (Photo courtesy of Hugh Gladstone Koehler.)

16. Hugo Koehler, riding to hounds, ca. 1930. (Photo courtesy of Hugh Gladstone Koehler.)

most dashing. They had met during Koehler's stay in London after the armistice. Over the years, in his letters to Koehler, Gladstone's salutations modulated in warmth from "My dear Commander" to "My dear Hugo" to "My dear Old Fellow" to "Dear Old Boy."[3]

No letters survive from 1926. Whatever he did write was likely personal and later destroyed by Matilda, who burned all his letters to her after Koehler died.

The Commander served on the staff of the Naval War College in Newport, Rhode Island, from April 1926 to October 1927. In April 1927 Koehler was invited to Annapolis to deliver a lecture on Russia at the Naval Academy. In Newport, he lectured on intelligence gathering techniques under the new scheme of instruction begun when Rear Admiral William V. Pratt became college president in 1925. Pratt had always admired Koehler for his "great mental ability," noting that the Commander was "different, a clash of wits and brains. To be with him was always mental refreshment for me." Among those receiving intelligence pointers from Koehler that year was one Raymond Spruance, who in fifteen short years would become Spruance of Midway.[4]

After Newport, Koehler felt certain he would be offered the assignment he had been working toward his entire life, the billet as naval attaché in Moscow, sure that once diplomatic relations with Moscow were restored the job was his. In his younger days he had burned to attain to it, but now his heart was elsewhere. He was in love with Matilda Pell and anticipating her pending divorce from Herbert Pell. Koehler and Matilda Pell became husband and wife on 2 June 1927.

It was in many ways an unfortunate coupling. The role of navy wife did not at all suit the aristocratic Matilda. "Can you see Matilda in Moscow?" Hugo asked friends at the time. They really could not. Almost more at home on Russian soil than on the decks of a man-of-war, Koehler made the supreme sacrifice and resigned from the Navy to live in Newport with the woman he loved.[5]

Notwithstanding Gladstone's warning, Koehler had no clear alternative to his Navy service. From his resignation as Commander in February 1929 until his death four days before the Nazi invasion of the Soviet Union in 1941, which Koehler, by then far from the action, predicted would never occur, his life was barely more than a long gradual decline.

Having been an able professional, he became an avid dilettante. He grew orchids, tried bananas and pineapples in a little greenhouse, and bought expensive antique furniture and gold snuff boxes. But the good times were short lived. The Austrian trust fund, which had enabled Koehler to indulge his eccentricities while collecting his meager Navy

17. Hugo Koehler with his two-week-old son Hugh Gladstone Koehler, Sept. 1929.
(Photo courtesy of Hugh Gladstone Koehler.)

pay, was terminated after the marriage to Matilda. Their son, Hugh Gladstone Koehler, was born on 3 September 1929. The Wall Street crash came less than two months later. Money suddenly became very short. Sneered one acquaintance, "They both thought the other had money, and were both fooled."[6]

They moved to England for the greater part of the year, where Koehler was able to live the British gentry life he so cherished.

In the summer of 1933, in one last global reach, Koehler went to the Soviet Union. This temporary assignment was presumably offered to him by British Intelligence, which did not want to risk another of its own agents being captured. Koehler took a great risk, not knowing how he, who had a price on his head in 1920, would be received. Dozens of famous anti-Bolsheviks had been lured back into the Soviet Union only to vanish, and British spy Sidney Reilly, induced to go back in 1925, was never heard from again. It is possible that Koehler went back in part to find out the fate of his friend General Kutepov.

The Commander, happy to be back in his natural element, made his usual thorough rounds. A friend remembered,

He saw lots of artists, and says the few who transferred to the new regime are doing great things. He spoke especially of the man who designed Lenin's tomb. . . . He heard one man addressing an intent crowd, without bombast or harangue, on the *philosophy* of money, not discussing any specific measures, but simply examining the theory and philosophy of exchange. The Soviets have barred our dancing as capitalistic, and are teaching folk dances; group after group will have one man and one woman and a harmonium, teaching them steps. Then they count seventeen, and the seventeenth person must step into the center of the group and perform likewise. Hugo happened to be the seventeenth, so he stepped up and danced with great vigor and enthusiasm. The crowd was delighted—it had been explained who he was—and demanded a capitalistic dance; so he asked for the tune "What to do with a drunken sailor," and again gave such a dance that the crowd swelled in numbers and cheered and sang— triumph! Two or three days later he was informed that Stalin wanted to see him; so he went, was enormously impressed, talked for hours, and went again two or three times. . . . Stalin says all the world is moving towards communism, although in different ways. Revolution was the way for Russia, with her low-grade peasant population; in Germany Hitler is going so far that by a violent revulsion the people will turn toward communism; England is imposing higher and higher taxes until the government will own everything and it will be a socialist state. And America, under Roosevelt, is moving toward communism sideways like a crab by making business run itself without profit, and by putting control in the hands of labor leaders.[7]

The Russian journey was Koehler's last intelligence mission. In 1934 Koehler moved his small family back to America, aware that Herbert Pell did not want his son Claiborne, then fifteen, raised as an English boy. After their return, Koehler made no more unexplained trips. Later when Herbert Pell toured a German battleship as Minister to Portugal he wrote to Koehler that he wished the Commander could have been there to explain it all to him.

Settling near Newport, Koehler bought Eastover, a beautiful water's edge farm on the Sakonnet River. There he planted raspberries, built a sea wall, made a rose garden for Matilda, and moved fern-leaf beeches. There young Hugh could have a dog and some chickens and a pony named Broadway Bill. When Koehler had the house rewired he ordered that extra-large cable be used and buried six inches deeper than usual. His intention was that it would last a hundred years for his son.

The Koehlers dined at the houses of friends, gave a few dinner parties in return, and watched tennis at the Casino. But Matilda was bored with Koehler's Navy friends, and her Newport crowd was unnerved by the mysterious Commander. One of the few exceptions was Reggie Lanier, on whose sloop *Istalena* Koehler was navigator. The two raced and cruised together and were firm friends.

Matilda's other friends were not as kind. In Newport Koehler was regarded as a liar and a braggart. One woman thought he looked like he was in disguise. Another thought he looked like a spy. Still another pronounced cheerily that "He was one of the few people to whose funeral I was glad to go."[8]

This attitude is to some extent understandable. Koehler had little time for pretensions, and felt that upper-class Newport was intellectually arid. He could give as good as he got and if necessary be every bit as rude as Matilda's insulated, aristocratic friends. During dinner one evening Koehler and an editor from the *Christian Science Monitor* were discussing what happens to men who are starving. Koehler expressed the view that soldiers would not obey an order to shoot at men who were rioting because of hunger. The *Monitor* editor answered that Lord Lothian, the leading Christian Scientist of England, thought the same thing. Koehler retorted that if Lothian held that opinion, then his, Koehler's, view of it must be wrong. An awkward silence ensued.[9]

The Commander was too alien, too exotic—not to mention too intellectual—for the Newport crowd. Tiger hunting in Mongolia in 1911 with a first cousin of the King of England and the Kaiser of Imperial Germany, disguised as an Armenian rug merchant in south Russia in 1920 during the Civil War, reporting after his 1919 Germany inspections to Winston Churchill, meeting in 1933 with Stalin—all this did not accord with his neighbors' Newport dinner-table conversation of horses and yachts. His stories seemed to them too fantastic to be believed.

And Koehler had eccentricities of his own, oddities that no doubt delighted men like Stalin and Shkuro, but that played to less enthusiasm in Newport. At one party at Eastover, Koehler bit the rung of the chair in two so Matilda could see that it was weak and therefore inferior. He also disgusted the Newporters by eating entire lamb chops, bone and all. He could easily have done the Greek waiter's trick of picking up a small dinner table in his teeth, and dancing with it, without spilling the wine from the brimming carafe.

18. Claiborne Pell and Hugo Koehler pose in Cossack outfits, ca. 1930. (Photo courtesy of Senator Claiborne Pell.)

Matilda, an artistic dilettante with little formal education, loved the sound of Hugo's musical voice, but it is unlikely that she understood what he was talking about. Her schooling ended in the eighth grade, when, as was often the case in such families, she was sent off to Italy for four years of art studies. She was not robust, however, and her health was a constant worry. She had persistent back trouble, which became the source of innumerable hospital stays and expense. Not having been informed before the marriage, Koehler was unaware that this condition was congenital, and so it was passed on to young Hugh. Yet, in one of life's perverse ironies, it was Koehler who died in 1941 in his early fifties of what was diagnosed as Bright's disease, a form of kidney failure, while Matilda lived on until 1972.[10]

Just as he was astute in reading others, Koehler was also clearly sensitive to the fact that he had not done all he was capable of doing. Before he died, he confided despairingly to a friend that he had "missed the boat," that he should have gone to Moscow and not settled for Newport. He thought it was partly because he could not have continued his naval career without "crucifying" Matilda, whose plain goodness and innocence disarmed the sophisticated womanizer in him. He simply could not bear to hurt her. And he thought it was also because he was not at all interested in himself, nor in advancing himself. "I made a terrible blunder. All the things I should have been but wasn't."[11]

On a winter cruise in 1924, Koehler wrote to his mother:

On a cruise across the Caribbean we ran into a tiny rain squall one afternoon just about sunset, or rather, about a quarter of an hour before sunset—and the sun was still brilliant though low on the horizon. We were heading nearly due east when we ran into the squall. Suddenly, the most brilliant rainbow I've ever seen appeared just ahead of us. It was so close I could really put out my hand and touch it. But instead of being an arch, in orthodox rainbow fashion, it was a complete circle—its lower edge just touching the water. On one side were two extra partial rainbows, and on the other, three. The bags of gold that lie at the rainbow's ends—where were they? For there were no ends![12]

.

Epilogue

Campeche, Mexico
March 1980 _____

Death, thou comest when I had thee least in mind.

Everyman

_____

Margaretta "Maggie" Potter, mentioned in the acknowledgments of this volume, deserves a special word, for indeed this work could not have happened but for her. Born, raised, and educated in Washington, D.C., daughter of a rear admiral, Margaretta became engaged to Koehler in the spring of 1921, just after Koehler returned from Russia and just before he became attaché to Poland, when she was 20 and he 34. Soon after arriving in Warsaw, however, Koehler broke the engagement, which left Margaretta with a broken heart, though in later years they again became friends and continued so until Koehler's death.

In the early 1980s, Senator Pell asked Margaretta to assemble materials for a biography of Koehler since she was the last alive to know him intimately. Beyond his Navy dispatches, there was not much to assemble. Still, in her mid-eighties, she struggled valiantly over microfilm readers, cursed missing files, and fought against age and failing eyesight to compile much of the material that appears herein. On 10 May 1985, three days after she completed this work, Margaretta passed away.

What follows are some of her recollections of Koehler, thoughts she recorded just before she died.[1]

As I look back, it is evident that, after Hugo's resignation from the Navy, I was his confidante; he would talk and I would listen. . . .

In his apartment in Washington, when I first knew him, there was a bookcase and its three or four shelves were filled, not with books, but with photographs of women. I do not think they were trophies; he genuinely liked and appreciated women and never denigrated ability in a female as many men of that period did. . . .

He said it was stupid for us in Washington to associate with only our friends, who think as we do. One should seek out the obscure midwestern congressman and find out what he thinks, what his motives are. Of course Hugo was right. . . .

I think I saw him truly. I saw him as he appeared to most people: worldly, flamboyant, out of scale with Matilda's New York and Newport milieu; but also I saw what was behind his protective exterior, a deeply loving man, full of compassion and insight, always ready to help someone else. . . .

He loved and appreciated children. When we were walking one long-ago day in Washington, we came upon a few small children playing on the sidewalk. To my surprise, Hugo stopped, leaned down to talk with them, laughed with them, while I marveled—at that time, before I had learned on my own offspring, I considered little children not only uninteresting but tiresome. In the first letter he wrote to me after his marriage, he told me about his stepson, Claiborne, "Whom I adore," and he certainly adored his own son later. . . .

During his last years, he concentrated his attention and his hopes more and more on his son Hugh. He adored the boy, but it frightened me, for Hugh's sake, how much Hugo demanded of him and what impossibly high standards he set for him—it was too great a weight of expectation for any boy to bear. I do not think it hurt Hugh, who was only eleven when his father died, but if Hugo had lived longer it might well have been very damaging. . . .

Before he died, he asked Claiborne and me to attend to his desk, in order to spare Matilda that sorrowful task. All we found was a drawer full of unpaid bills, the envelopes not even slit open—and a packet of sonnets I had written. . . .

Also before he died, 17 June 1941, . . . he was baptized. I gave to Matilda my High Renaissance gold crucifix for him to hold in his hands, and he has it with him in his grave in the churchyard of St. Colombas by the Sakonnet River.

Twenty years later my husband, Jack, died. Matilda lived until 27 July 1972, and I am the only one still alive who can remember.

It is a curious fact that in all this vast country, Hugo and my Jack should be lying in the same graveyard within twenty feet of each other. Hugo once said to me, "Margaretta, it's remarkable, if you are anywhere near on the scene somewhere, God always leads me to you," and I had confessed that sometimes I helped God a little. But this time I did

19. Hugo Koehler near the time of his death in 1941. (Photo courtesy of Clarkson N. Potter.)

not; I had nothing to do with Hugo and Matilda's purchase of a grave plot almost adjacent to that of the Potters.

Anyway, in death we shall be, all four of us, very near together. . . .

During our Washington interlude, he came to see me every afternoon or evening. As he walked up the little hill to our house on 22nd Street, he would announce his arrival with a whistled bird call, clear and limpid, in two sentences, so to speak, the first musical phrase like a question, the second like an answer. I asked him what bird he was imitating, and he told me, but, alas, I cannot remember. . . .

In March 1980, my sister and a friend and I went to Yucatan to look at Mayan ruins. In Campeche I had an eerie experience: during the night, in our ultramodern hotel, I heard a bird call—and it was unmistakably the bird call Hugo had imitated as he walked up 22nd Street to our house in Washington to announce his arrival, in 1921. In my sleep, without waking up wholly, I heard it several times . . . and when I awakened in the morning, the door of my room was slightly ajar. . . .

Notes

Prologue

1. "*Tchresvichaika* is an antiquated transliteration of a colloquial rendering with diminutive ending of the first word in the full name of [the Soviet secret police] the Cheka. The word in Russian means *extraordinary*. Ergo, the nickname Koehler heard was literally "the little extraordinary" (Prof. Gary Thurston to the author, 8 November 1988).
2. Hugo W. Koehler to Mathilda Koehler, 29 June 1920, cited in Margaretta Potter, *Memoir of Hugo* (unpublished), pp. 129–30 (hereafter cited as *Memoir*).
3. Hugo W. Koehler, service record, RG 45, Subject File, 1911–27, Desg. File T, 7024-167 Nav-327-MK, 5 July 1941, National Archives (hereafter cited as NA).
4. *Memoir*, p. 4.
5. Ibid., p. 4.
6. Ibid., pp. 4–5.
7. *Memoir*, p. 5; Margaretta Potter relates this quote from one of her many private conversations with Koehler between 1921 and 1941.
8. Ibid., pp. 5–6.
9. Ibid., p. 6.
10. Hugo W. Koehler to Mathilda Koehler, 14 September 1902, cited in *Memoir*, pp. 6–9. This was Koehler's second letter to his mother after he went east for school, datelined Adams House, No. 553, Washington Street, Boston.
11. *Memoir*, p. 9. Potter describes this simply as a story that "survived."
12. *Memoir* pp. 9–10. Potter: "He told me that during the summers he and his grandfather traveled in Europe, mainly in England and in Austria."
13. John Benbow to Matilda Pell, June 1941, cited in *Memoir*, p. 417.
14. *Memoir*, p. 10. Potter: "[At Harvard] he was enrolled in the following classes: rhetoric and English composition; English literature; introduction to German literature of the eighteenth and nineteenth centuries; an elementary course in French; modern European history; and elementary geology—an interesting combination that foreshadows his later interests."
15. *Memoir*, pp. 13–15. Potter describes this simply as "the wonderful letter," undated, written on "letter paper of 'The Republican Club of the City of New York, 54 and 56 West 40th Street.'" Hugo W. Koehler to Herbert Koehler (Hugo's brother), 2 August 1911, datelined Port Arthur, Russia, cited in *Memoir*, pp. 11–13.
16. *Memoir*, p. 15.
17. Ibid., pp. 15–16.
18. Ibid., pp. 16–17.

19. Ibid., p. 17; Potter: "Judging from four old letters that his mother, Mrs. Koehler, sent to Hugo in 1938, two from 'Tante Sophie' (one dated Lausanne, 1888, and the other Amherst, 1895) and two from his grandfather, all written in German, he was brought up to speak German as well as English." *Memoir*, p. 6.
20. Ibid., pp. 17–18.
21. Ibid., p. 18; Potter cites the source of this comment as Captain William Amsden, USNA, class of 1907. It should also be noted that Amsden thought Koehler was "the greatest liar in the Navy" (*Memoir*, p. 374).
22. Cited in *Memoir*, p. 20.
23. *Memoir*, pp. 20–26. Tantalizing explanations of Mayerling are offered in Countess Marie Larisch's reputedly unreliable book, *My Past* (London, 1913) about the secrets of the Hapsburgs. She recounts that after the incident, a child, supposedly Rudolph's son, was born in St. Louis to a Russian princess, who died in a hospital ward, and that the child was brought up in Missouri. But the matter didn't rest there, for in 1955, 248 documents pertaining to Mayerling and purportedly collected or written by Baron Krauss, chief of police in Vienna, found their way into the press in Austria, France, England, and Denmark. One Danish paper reported that "Crown Prince Rudolph had a child with Agloja Auersberg, the daughter of Duke Auersberg and that this child was adopted away." An outraged Auersberg was reported to have confronted the Emperor over the shame brought on his daughter and family. The Emperor decided the way to settle the matter was by a duel, in which each man was to draw a ball from a bag containing one white and one black ball, with the duelist drawing the latter being honor bound to kill himself. According to this account, the black ball was drawn by Rudolph. The major works on the subject shed little light on a possible child involved at Mayerling, but any of the legion of Rudolph's lovers could have produced a child. Rudolph did not meet Mary until 1888, and some accounts say that she was pregnant when she died, which eliminates her as a potential mother of Hugo. So far as any records go, the prefect of the Vatican archives once stated that no records relating to Rudolph had ever been deposited there; on the other hand, Count Eduard Taaffe, the man with whom the distraught Emperor was supposed to have forever deposited the Crown Prince's papers, later claimed: "You will never find these things. They have long been in the Vatican archives," in which case a Swiss bank account administered by the Vatican for a bastard son becomes a possibility. Important explanations of the event are contained in Fritz Judtmann, *Mayerling: The Facts Behind the Legend* (London, 1971), pp. 342–50; Carl Lonyay, *Rudolph: The Tragedy of Mayerling* (New York, 1949), pp. 118–39; and Richard Barkeley, *The Road to Mayerling: Life and Death of Crown Prince Rudolph of Austria* (London, 1958). Yet Potter also recorded: "[Hugo once] told me . . . 'I have forgotten it all long ago'" (*Memoir*, p. 26). Potter also added yet another twist to this story. "Hugo told me that [after he became naval attaché in Warsaw] he had had several conversations, or conferences, with the Papal Nuncio, Achille Ratti, who later became Pope Pius XI. . . . I feel more urgently [than ever] that they had to do with Hugo's possible future. Matilda [Koehler's wife] once said to me, 'I think it was a shame how they got his hopes up,' and I was too diffident to press her as to exactly what she meant by that. Now I suspect that . . . Ratti had some plan for Hugo." A restoration, perhaps? (*Memoir*, p. 319).
24. *Memoir*, p. 21.
25. Interview with Senator Claiborne Pell, Newport, R.I., 27 August 1988; also cited in *Memoir*, p. 21.

26. Interview with Senator Pell, 27 August 1988; also cited in *Memoir*, p. 24.
27. *Memoir*, pp. 25–26.
28. Ibid., p. 20.
29. Ibid., p. 26.
30. Telephone interview with senator Claiborne Pell, 25 January 1989; also, Jeffrey M. Dorwart, *The Office of Naval Intelligence: The Birth of America's First Intelligence Agency, 1865–1918* (Annapolis, 1979), pp. 106–12.
31. Dolly, Viscountess Gladstone, to Matilda Koehler, July 1941, cited in *Memoir*, p. 417.
32. *Memoir*, p. 77.
33. Conversations with Hugh Gladstone Koehler, 27 August 1988, Newport, R.I.
34. Hugo W. Koehler to Mathilda Koehler, 19 June 1920, datelined Enzeli, Persia, cited in *Memoir*, pp. 132–34.
35. Ibid., p. 134–35.
36. Hugo W. Koehler to Mathilda Koehler, 21 February 1922, datelined American Legation, Warsaw, cited in *Memoir*, p. 324a; Hugo W. Koehler to Mathilda Koehler, 19 June 1920, datelined Enzeli, Persia, cited in *Memoir*, p. 136.
37. Hugo W. Koehler to Lady Gladstone, 7 May 1920, cited in *Memoir*, p. 140.
38. Lt. Comdr. Hugo W. Koehler to Rear Adm. N. A. McCully, "Observations on Russian Front from 23 September to 13 October, 1920," Office of the Special Agent of the U.S. State Department for Russia, Alexandorovsk, Russia, 14 October 1920, cited in *Memoir*, p. 277.

1. The Right Spy

1. Rear Adm. Jackson R. Tate to Margaretta Potter, cited in *Memoir*, p. 307.
2. Interview with Rear Adm. Kemp Tolley, 29 August 1988, Monkton, Maryland; also cited in *Memoir*, pp. 307–8.
3. Lt. Hugo W. Koehler to the Secretary of the Navy, 26 November 1917, cited in *Memoir*, p. 67a. This note was written while Koehler was a lieutenant aboard the USS *South Carolina.*
4. *Memoir*, pp. 312–13.
5. Ibid., p. 31.
6. Hugo W. Koehler to Herbert Koehler, 2 August 1911, datelined Port Arthur, cited in *Memoir*, p. 28.
7. Ibid., p. 30.
8. Ibid., pp. 29–30.
9. Rear Adm. Kemp Tolley to the author, 14 November 1988; Hugo Koehler to Herbert Koehler, 2 August 1911, datelined Port Arthur, cited in *Memoir*, p. 29.
10. Log of the *Villalobos*, 11 October 1911, cited in *Memoir*, pp. 33–34.
11. Rear Adm. Kemp Tolley, U.S. Navy (ret.), *Yangtze Patrol: The U.S. Navy in China* (Annapolis, 1971), pp. 68–69.
12. Log of the *Villalobos*, cited in *Memoir*, pp. 35–36.
13. Ibid., p. 36.
14. *Yangtze Patrol*, p. 69.
15. Ibid., p. 70.
16. *Memoir*, p. 39. It was Kemp Tolley who told the author that tigers were extinct in Mongolia.

17. *Memoir*, p. 41.
18. Ibid., pp. 41–42.
19. Secretary of the Navy Josephus Daniels, 16 September 1914, cited in *Memoir*, p. 44.
20. *Memoir*, pp. 45–46.
21. Ibid., p. 49. Commander (later Admiral) Wiley, recalled of this incident: "I fell in with him first in China, at which time he was a young ensign. . . . He was then in command of a large ocean-going tug [*Piscataqua*] for general fleet work. That year Congress failed to pass an appropriation for the naval service prior to 1 July. That left a number of young officers with families somewhat hard pressed for funds temporarily. It was commonly understood at the time that Koehler went deep into his own pocket to relieve these young people. They were not particular friends of his. I know of no incident that could better illustrate the man's generous nature" (Wiley to Potter, cited in *Memoir*, p. 49).
22. *Memoir*, pp. 50–52; also U.S. Navy Department Court-Martial Order No. 7—1915, 15 February 1915, Navy Department Court-Martial Orders 1914–1915, vol. N1.14:915, RG 287, Box N87, NA, Washington, D.C.
23. Cited in *Memoir*, pp. 53–57; Secretary Daniels acknowledged "a communication regarding target practice and gunnery conditions in the German navy" and noted: "The Department is pleased to note the zeal on your part, which has resulted in the procuring of an interesting and valuable intelligence report" (Secretary of the Navy Josephus Daniels to Hugo W. Koehler, 3 February 1914, cited in *Memoir*, p. 53).
24. *Memoir*, pp. 61–65.
25. *Memoir*, p. 66.
26. Hugo W. Koehler to Herbert Koehler, n.d., cited in *Memoir*, p. 67a. Harold Stirling "Mike" Vanderbilt (1884–1970), great-grandson of Commodore Cornelius Vanderbilt, whose steamship lines and railroads built an American fortune, was a better sailor than Hugo let on. He won the America's Cup races three times and, on the side, invented contract bridge. In fact, Stone and Taylor wrote that "Mike Vanderbilt . . . who was to defend the America's Cup three times, must be ranked among the all-time top sailors. . . . He was an excellent helmsman, tactician, strategist, and judge of boats and weather. He had, practically from boyhood, always sailed big yachts" (Herbert L. Stone and William H. Taylor, *The America's Cup Races* (Princeton, 1958), pp. 196–97). Of course, a rich day-sailor, no matter what his skill, wouldn't have impressed a lieutenant commander in the U.S. Navy.
27. Cited in *Memoir*, pp. 68–69.
28. Thomas Robins to Margaretta Potter, cited in *Memoir*, p. 70.
29. Hugo W. Koehler to Mathilda Koehler, 28 January 1919, datelined London, England, cited in *Memoir*, p. 73a.
30. Thomas Robins to Margaretta Potter, cited in *Memoir*, p. 70.
31. Hugo W. Koehler to "Aunt Cora," undated, cited in *Memoir*, p. 67a.
32. Hugo W. Koehler to Mathilda Koehler, 28 January 1919, datelined London, England, cited in *Memoir*, p. 73a. "In an old unused trunk stored in an attic, Hugo's daughter-in-law found a roll of typewritten sheets of paper, so tightly rolled that it was difficult to smooth them out and read them, so no one had. It proved to be copies of two letters written by Hugo to his mother" (*Memoir*, p. 72).
33. Hugo W. Koehler, report of twenty-four hours aboard subchaser 271 cited in *Memoir*, p. 72. (This is likely the weekly report Koehler wrote for 26 October 1918). Hugo W. Koehler, report for the week ending 19 October 1918, cited in *Memoir*, pp. 75–76.

34. Vice Adm. Walter S. Delany, "Bayly's Navy" (Naval Historical Foundation, 1980), cited in *Memoir*, pp. 74–75.
35. Hugo W. Koehler to Mathilda Koehler, 28 January 1919, datelined London, England, cited in *Memoir*, p. 73a.
36. Hugo W. Koehler to "Aunt Cora," n.d., cited in *Memoir*, p. 67a. Interesting material relating to this period is contained in John Williams, *The Home Fronts: Britain, France and Germany, 1914–1918* (London, 1972), pp. 246–60.
37. Hugo W. Koehler to Mathilda Koehler, 28 January 1919, datelined London, England, cited in *Memoir*, p. 78a.
38. Hugo W. Koehler to Mathilda Koehler, 5 February 1919, datelined HMS *Comus*, At Sea: En Route Scapa Flow to Helgoland, cited in *Memoir*, p. 80a.

2. Germany and Versailles

1. Hugo W. Koehler to "Captain Leigh," 12–13 February 1919, datelined Wilhelmshaven, Germany, NA, cited in *Memoir*, p. 79a. A fascinating history of the High Seas Fleet can be found in Dan van der Vat, *The Grand Scuttle* (Annapolis, 1986) pp. 99–116.
2. William S. Sims to Hugo W. Koehler, 19 February 1919, cited in *Memoir*, p. 80a.
3. Hugo W. Koehler to Adm. William S. Sims, 24 February 1919, datelined USS *Chester*, Hamburg, Germany, cited in *Memoir*, p. 79a.
4. Hugo W. Koehler to Adm. William Sims, 16 June 1919, datelined HMS *Carysfort*, Copenhagen, cited in *Memoir*, p. 79a.
5. Hugo W. Koehler to Adm. H. A. Wiley, 4 July 1919, cited in *Memoir*, p. 82a.
6. This account of the German trip was given by Walter Dring to Margaretta Potter, *Memoir*, pp. 86–89.
7. *Memoir*, p. 83.
8. Hugo W. Koehler to Mathilda Koehler, 21 October 1919, datelined American Commission to Negotiate Peace, Office of Naval Advisor, Hotel de Crillon, Paris, France, cited in *Memoir*, pp. 95–101. This excerpt reads much in the manner of John Maynard Keynes's famous work, *The Economic Consequences of the Peace* (New York, 1920), pp. 28–55; the geographic nature of the 1919 peacemaking process is discussed in Charles Seymour, *Geography, Justice, and Politics at the Paris Conference of 1919* (New York, 1951), pp. 5, 9–10; other valuable material on the peace process as Hugo Koehler experienced it is contained in Winston S. Churchill, *The World Crisis—1919–1928, The Aftermath* (New York, 1929), pp. 140–63; Klaus Schwabe, *Woodrow Wilson, Revolutionary Germany, and Peacemaking, 1918–1919* (Chapel Hill, 1985), pp. 233–53; and Thomas A. Bailey, *Woodrow Wilson and the Lost Peace* (Chicago, 1963), pp. 170–73.
9. Hugo W. Koehler to Mathilda Koehler, 8 January 1920, datelined Embassy of the United States of America, Constantinople, Turkey, NA, cited in *Memoir*, p. 113a.
10. Rear Adm. Newton A. McCully to secretary of state, 7 January 1920, datelined Office of Special Agent of the U.S. State Department, for Russia, Constantinople, Turkey, cited in *Memoir*, p. 111.

3. Novorossisk, Russia

1. Charles J. Weeks, "A Samaritan in Russia: Vice Admiral Newton A. McCully's Humanitarian Efforts, 1914–1920," *Military Affairs*, vol. 52, no. 1 (January 1988): 12–17.

For a complete chronicle of McCully's career see C. J. Weeks, "The Life and Career of Vice Admiral Newton A. McCully, 1867–1951" (Georgia State University, 1975).
2. Newton A. McCully, *The McCully Report: The Russo-Japanese War, 1904–1905* (Annapolis, 1976).
3. Weeks, "A Samaritan in Russia," p. 13.
4. Ibid., p. 14.
5. Richard Luckett, *the White Generals; An Account of the White Movement and the Russian Civil War* (New York, 1971), p. 5 (hereafter cited as Luckett).
6. Robert Rhodes James ed., *Winston S. Churchill, His Complete Speeches, 1897–1963* (London, 1974), p. 2723.
7. Luckett, p. 245. For a discussion of the "Jewish question" in Russian history, and for a persuasive look at how the repression of Imperial Russia was responsible for driving many Jews into radical movements, see Hans Rogger, *Jewish Policies and Right-Wing Politics in Imperial Russia* (Berkeley and Los Angeles, 1986), pp. 1–24.
8. Department of State to Navy Department, 23 December 1919, cited in *Memoir*, p. 110.
9. Hugo W. Koehler to Mathilda Koehler, 8 January 1920, datelined Embassy of the United States of America, Constantinople, Turkey, cited in *Memoir*, p. 113a.
10. "Of fifteen Romanov grand dukes living in 1917, only eight survived the Revolution, and the fate of the leading Romanov women was proportionately the same. The most distinguished survivor was the Dowager Empress Marie, who in May, 1917, had left riot-torn Kiev for the royal estates in the Crimea. Here she was joined by . . . the tsar's . . . sister, the Grand Duchess Olga, and her new husband, Colonel Koulikovsky, a cavalry officer she had married during the war after deserting her first husband, the Prince of Oldenburg" (John D. Bergamini, *The Tragic Dynasty: A History of the Romanovs* [New York, 1969], p. 462, hereafter cited as *Tragic Dynasty*.) Olga died in 1960.
11. Koehler has this city confused with Novocherkassk; Ekaterinodar was actually the capital of the Kuban Cossacks.
12. Lt. Cmdr. Hugo W. Koehler, "The Real Revolution in Russia," *World's Work Magazine* (July 1921): 270–73.

4. Odessa, Russia

1. Newton A. McCully diary, 8 February 1920, McCully Mss, Library of Congress, Manuscripts Division (hereafter cited as McCully/LC). Cited in *Memoir*.
2. An unedited version of Koehler's report can be found in Charles J. Weeks, Jr., and Joseph O. Baylen, "The Aristocrat and the Bolshevik: Hugo Koehler and I. P. Uborevich, Odessa, 1920," *Indiana Social Studies Quarterly*, vol. 30, no. 1 (Spring 1977): 27–40 (hereafter cited as *Koehler and Uborevich*). "Koehler returned at 6 P.M., having had interview with Bolshevik General Uborevitch, and seen Mrs. [Eli] Keyser who was apparently unmolested, and having an assurance from Bolsehvik General that neither she nor other Americans would be molested" (McCully/LC, 10 February 1920, cited in *Memoir*).
3. "This decoration was the Order of the Red Banner, at that time the highest Soviet military award" (*Koehler and Uborevich*, p. 39).
4. "Jacob H. Rubin, a representative of the Union Bank of Milwaukee in Odessa, later admitted that he had been a member of the American Socialist Party for twenty years.

In 1921 he returned to the United States disenchanted with the Soviet regime . . . [see] Jacob H. Rubin, *I Live to Tell: The Russian Adventures of an American Socialist* (Indianapolis: Bobbs-Merrill, 1934)" (*Koehler and Uborevich*, pp. 39–40).

5. Koehler to McCully, 10 February 1920, datelined The Special Agent of the U.S. State Department, for Russia, Odessa, Russia. State Department DF 861.00/6649, NA.
6. "The Bombardment of Odessa," n.d., Planning Division 104–23, RG80, NA, cited in *Koehler and Uborevich*, p. 40.
7. Annette Keyser to Hon. Edwin C. Denby, 10 January 1924, datelined Philadelphia, Pa., cited in *Memoir*, p. 117a.
8. Edwin Denby to Hugo W. Koehler, 12 January 1924, cited in *Memoir*, pp. 117 and 117a.
9. Hugo W. Koehler to Mathilda Koehler, 19 June 1920, cited in *Memoir*, pp. 115–16.

5. Novorossisk, Russia

1. Cited in Luckett, p. 349.
2. Ibid., p. 352.
3. McCully to Secretary of State, 30 March 1920, datelined Theodosia, Russia, State Department DF 861.00/6857, NA.
4. Luckett, p. 353.
5. Hugo W. Koehler to Mathilda Koehler, 26–27 March 1920, cited in *Memoir*, pp. 120–27.
6. McCully to Secretary of State, 30 March 1920, datelined Theodosia, Russia, State Department DF 861.00/6857, NA.

6. Yalta, Russia

1. McCully/LC, 4 April 1920. Cited in *Memoir*.
2. Richard Luckett, *The White Generals, An Account of the White Movement and the Russian Civil War* (New York, 1971), p. 192
3. McCully to secretary of state, 29 April 1920, datelined Sevastopol, Russia, cited in *Memoir*, p. 128a.
4. Ibid.
5. Wrangel's Land Law may have been flawed insofar as the peasantry was concerned, but it had advantages elsewhere. It was introduced by a man whose conservative credentials were unquestioned by the wealthy landowners who were required to give up pieces of their estates. With the White cause nearly hopeless, landowners suddenly became liberals in their rush to share their land and save their own skins. Unfortunately, the Bolsheviks had locked up this issue with the peasantry two years earlier. The Red policy was easily understood—peasants were allowed to work as much land as they possibly could without hiring additional hands. (Peter Kenez, *Civil War in South Russia, 1919–1920: The Defeat of the Whites* [Berkeley, 1977], pp. 269, 279–89; hereafter cited as Kenez.)
6. McCully to Secretary of State, 15 July 1920, datelined Sevastopol, Russia, cited in *Memoir*, pp. 144–202.

7. Melitopol, Russia

1. McCully/LC, 20 May 1920, datelined Sebastopol, cited in *Memoir,* p. 128.

2. Ibid., 27 May 1920, datelined Yalta.

3. Ibid., 9 June 1920, datelined Yalta.

4. McCully to Secretary of State, 21 September 1920, datelined Sebastopol, Russia ("Transmitted herewith is a report by Lieutenant Commander Hugo W. Koehler, U.S. Navy, on a visit to the South Russian Front, June 9–20, 1920,") cited in *Memoir,* p. 128a.

5. Hugo W. Koehler to Mathilda Koehler, 29 June 1920, datelined Enzeli, Persia, cited in *Memoir,* pp. 129–37. Koehler not only received the Order of St. Anne from Wrangel for his foray into Melitopol, but also he was nominated by Admiral McCully for a Distinguished Service Medal for this same exploit. McCully's citation read: "During the capture of Melitopol by the Wrangel forces on June 10, 1920, he was in the advance guard [that] entered the town, immediately proceeded to the Bolshevik Headquarters, and began collection of their papers. While engaged in this work the town was recaptured by the Bolshevik troops and Lt. Comdr. Koehler for several hours was cut off from the troops which he accompanied. He managed to conceal himself and in addition saved the papers which he had secured and which were of much value" (McCully to Bureau of Navigation, 25 July 1923, cited in *Memoir,* p. 436). Koehler was turned down for the medal: presumably Washington had little desire to admit publicly that one of its agents had been inside Bolshevik Russia.

6. Hugo W. Koehler to Dolly Gladstone, 7 May 1920, cited in *Memoir,* p. 142.

7. McCully to Secretary of State, 15 July 1920, datelined Sebastopol, Russia, cited in *Memoir,* p. 202.

8. Somewhere in Russia

1. McCully to the Secretary of State, 31 July 1920, *Papers Relating to the Foreign Relations of the United States, 1920,* vol. 3, pp. 606–11.

2. Hugo W. Koehler to N. A. McCully, 4 September 1920, "Observations of Conditions on the Russian Front, 27 August to 4 September 1920," State Department DF, NA.

3. Cited in *Memoir,* pp. 437–38. The Order of St. Vladimir, established by Catherine II in 1782, was named for Grand Duke Vladimir, the first Christian ruler of Russia. The motto of the order inscribed in Russian appears on the reverse, "Utility, Honor, and Glory." See Col. Robert E. Wyllie, *Orders, Decorations and Insignia; Military and Civil* (New York, 1921), pp. 168–69. Koehler also had in his possession the Order of St. Stanislas, but under just what circumstances he acquired it remains a mystery.

9. Somewhere in Russia

1. Hugo W. Koehler to N. A. McCully, 14 October 1920, datelined Office of the Special Agent of the U.S. State Department for Russia, Alexandorovsk, Russia, "Observations on Russian Front from 23 September to 13 October 1920," cited in *Memoir,* pp. 244–300.

10. Sebastopol

1. Luckett, p. 373.

2. Ibid., pp. 374–75.

3. McCully/LC, 25 October 1920, cited in *Memoir*, p. 242.

4. General Baron Peter N. Wrangel, *Always With Honor* (New York, 1957), p. 336.

5. Rear Adm. Jackson R. Tate, cited in *Memoir*, p. 307.

6. John Dziak, *Chekisty: A History of the KGB* (Lexington, Mass., 1988), p. 174.

7. McCully to Bristol, 14 November 1920, cited in *Memoir*, p. 302.

8. Yehuda Bauer, *A History of the Holocaust* (New York, 1982), pp. 64–65.

9. Hugo W. Koehler, "The Towns, The Hope of Russian Deliverance," *World's Work Magazine*, October 1921: 626.

10. Medvedev, Roy, and Serge Starikov, *Philip Mironov and the Russian Civil War* (New York, 1978), pp. 203–4.

11. Ibid., p. 205.

12. Luckett, p. 385.

13. Joseph L. Wieczynski, ed., *The Modern Encyclopia of Russian and Soviet History* (Gulf Breeze, Fla., 1985), 35: 9.

14. Dmitry Lehovich, *White Against Red: The Life of General Anton Denikin* (New York, 1974), p. 466.

15. Luckett, p. 389.

16. Dziak, *Chekisty, p. 99.*

17. Hugo W. Koehler to Captain McNamee, 12 September 1922, datelined American Legation, Warsaw, cited in *Memoir*, p. 336a.

18. *Memoir*, p. 317.

19. Hugo W. Koehler to Mathilda Koehler, 15 June 1922, cited in *Memoir*, p. 324a. The U.S. relief efforts to which Koehler refers were two bills passed by Congress, the first, of 22 December 1921, provided for twenty million dollars in corn, seed grain, and preserved milk "for the relief of the distressed and starving people of Russia," and the second, approved on 20 January 1922, provided four million dollars for medicines, "medical, surgical, and hospital supplies, for the relief of the distressed and famine-stricken people of Russia." Both acts are cited in Stanley S. Jados, *Documents on Russian-American Relations* (Washington D.C., 1965), p. 56.

11. Poland and the Baltic States

1. Edwin Denby to Charles E. Hughes, 25 May 1921; Henry P. Fletcher to Edwin Denby, 9 June 1921, cited in *Memoir*, p. 319.

2. Hugo W. Koehler to Herbert Koehler, 14 September 1922, datelined American Legation, Warsaw, The Naval Attaché, cited in *Memoir*, p. 336a.

3. *Memoir*, pp. 321–22.

4. Hugo W. Koehler to Captain Galbraith, 3 November 1921, datelined American Legation, Warsaw, Poland, Office of the Naval Attaché, cited in *Memoir*, p. 320a.

5. Hugo W. Koehler to Mathilda Koehler, 21 February 1922, datelined American Legation, Warsaw, The Naval Attaché, cited in *Memoir*, p. 324a.

6. Hugo W. Koehler to Mathilda Koehler, 15 June 1922, cited in *Memoir*, p. 324a.

7. Hugo W. Koehler to Mathilda Koehler, 13 July 1922, datelined American Legation, Warsaw, The Naval Attaché, cited in *Memoir*, p. 336a.

8. Hugo W. Koehler to Captain McNamee, 12 September 1922, datelined American Legation, Warsaw, The Naval Attaché, cited in *Memoir*, p. 336a.

12. At the Rainbow's End

1. Hugo W. Koehler to Mathilda Koehler, 17 October 1925, cited in *Memoir*, p. 346.

2. Lord Gladstone to Hugo W. Koehler, 6 February 1925, cited in *Memoir*, p. 350.

3. Cited in *Memoir*. p. 351.

4. *Memoir*, p. 351; William V. Pratt to Matilda Koehler, n.d., cited in *Memoir*, p. 354; see also Hattendorf, John B., et al., *Sailors and Scholars: The Centennial History of the U.S. Naval War College* (Newport, R.I., 1984), pp. 130–31, 327.

5. *Memoir*, p. 358.

6. Ibid., pp. 356, 359–60.

7. Ibid., pp. 361–63.

8. Ibid., p. 373.

9. Ibid.

10. Ibid., p. 357.

11. Ibid., p. 365.

12. Hugo W. Koehler to Mathilda Koehler, 4 February 1924, datelined Culebra, Virgin Islands, cited in *Memoir*, p. 339.

Epilogue

1. Based on passages in *Memoir*, pp. 366–67, 388–89, 394–95, 397–98, 405.

Bibliography

Unpublished Papers, Diaries, and Archival Records

Potter, M. *Memoir of Hugo.* Unfinished partial collection of letters, dispatches, and personal reminiscenses of Cmdr. Hugo W. Koehler; includes material from Rear Admiral N. A. McCully Papers. Library of Congress, Washington, D.C. Access currently restricted. Unpublished. Special Collections, University Libraries, University of Rhode Island.

United States Department of the Navy Archives. RG 80. National Archives, Washington, D.C.

United States Department of State Archives. Decimal File. RG 59. Diplomatic Branch. National Archives, Washington, D.C.

Weeks, Charles J. "The Life and Career of Vice Admiral Newton A. McCully 1867–1951." Ph.D. diss., Georgia State University, 1975.

Published Documents

U.S. Department of State. *Papers Relating to the Foreign Relations of the United States, 1920.* Washington, D.C.: Government Printing Office, 1937.

———. *Foreign Relations of the United States, Diplomatic Papers, The Soviet Union, 1933–1939,* Vol. 1. Washington, D.C.: Government Printing Office, 1952.

Articles

Bushnell, John. "The Tsarist Officer Corps, 1881–1914: Customs, Duties, Inefficiency." *American Historical Review* 86 (October 1981).

Koehler, Lt. Comdr. Hugo W. "The Real Revolution in Russia." *World's Work Magazine,* July–August 1921.

———. "The Passive Peasant Wins in Russia." *World's Work Magazine,* September 1921.

———. "The Towns: The Hope of Russian Deliverance." *World's Work Magazine,* October 1921.

Weeks, Charles J. "A Samaritan in Russia: Vice Admiral Newton A. McCully's Humanitarian Efforts, 1914–1920." *Military Affairs,* vol. 52, no. 1 (January 1988).

Weeks, Charles J., and Joseph O. Baylen. "The Aristocrat and the Bolshevik: Hugo

Koehler and I. P. Uborevich, Odessa, 1920." *Indiana Social Studies Quarterly,* vol. 30, no. 1 (Spring 1977).

Books

Aten, Marion, and Arthur Orrmont. *Last Train over Rostov Bridge.* New York: Messner, 1961.

Bailey, Thomas A. *Woodrow Wilson and the Lost Peace.* Chicago: Quadrangle, 1963.

Barkeley, Richard. *The Road to Mayerling: Life and Death of Crown Prince Rudolph of Austria.* New York: St. Martin's Press, 1958.

Bauer, Yehuda. *A History of the Holocaust.* New York: Franklin Watts, 1982.

Benvenuti, Francesco. *The Bolsheviks and the Red Army, 1918–1922.* Cambridge: Cambridge University Press, 1988.

Bergamini, John D. *The Tragic Dynasty: A History of the Romanovs.* New York: G. P. Putnam's Sons, 1969.

Blayney, Michael Steward. *Democracy's Aristocrat: The Life of Herbert C. Pell.* Lanham, Md: University Press of America, 1986.

Bradley, John. *Allied Intervention in Russia.* New York: Basic Books, 1968.

Brinkley, George. *The Volunteer Army and the Allied Intervention in South Russia, 1917–1921.* Notre Dame, Ind.: University of Notre Dame Press, 1966.

Carr, Edward Hallet. *The Russian Revolution.* New York: Macmillan, 1979.

Churchill, Rt. Hon. Sir Winston. *The World Crisis—1919–1928: The Aftermath.* New York: Scribner's, 1929.

Denikin, Anton, *The White Army.* Gulf Breeze, Fla.: Academic International Press, 1973.

Dobson, Christopher, and John Miller. *The Day They Almost Bombed Moscow.* New York: Atheneum, 1986.

Dorwart, Jeffery M. *The Office of Naval Intelligence: The Birth of America's First Intelligence Agency, 1865–1918.* Annapolis, Md.: Naval Institute Press, 1979.

Dziak, John. *Chekisty: A History of the KGB.* Lexington, Mass.: Lexington Books, 1988.

Dziewanowski, M. K., ed. *The Russian Revolution.* New York: Crowell, 1970.

Falz-Fein, W. *Askania Nova das Tierparadies ein Buch des Gedentens und der Gedanten.* Berlin, 1930.

Fleming, Peter. *The Fate of Admiral Kolchak.* New York: Harcourt, Brace & World, 1963.

Footman, David. *Civil War in Russia.* London: Faber and Faber, 1961.

General Kutepov, A Collection of Articles [Sbornik Statey]. Paris: Publication of the Committee in Honor of General Kutepov under the presidency of General Miller, 1934.

Goldhurst, Richard. *The Midnight War.* New York: McGraw-Hill, 1978.

Gorky, ed. *History of the Civil War.* Gulf Breeze, Fla.: Academic International Press, 1974.

Halliday, Ernest, *The Ignorant Armies.* London: Weidenfeld and Nicolson, 1961.

Harris, John, ed. *Farewell to the Don: The Russian Revolution in the Journals of Brigadier H.N.H. Williamson.* New York: The John Day Company, 1971.

Hattendorf, John B., et al. *Sailors and Scholars: The Centennial History of the U.S. Naval War College.* Newport, R.I.: Naval War College Press, 1984.

Hoyt, Edwin P. *The Vanderbilts and Their Fortunes.* Garden City, N.Y.: Doubleday, 1962.

Hunczak, Taras, ed. *The Ukraine, 1917–1921: A Study in Revolution.* Cambridge, Mass.: Harvard University Press, 1977.

Jackson, Robert. *At War with the Bolsheviks.* London: Tom Stacey, Ltd., 1972.

Jados, Stanley S. *Documents on Russian-American Relations.* Washington, D.C.: Catholic University of America Press, 1965.

James, Robert Rhodes, ed. *Winston S. Churchill, His Complete Speeches, 1897–1963.* London: Chelsea House Publishers, 1974.

Judtmann, Fritz. *Mayerling: The Facts Behind the Legend.* London: George G. Harrop & Co., Ltd., 1971.

Kenez, Peter. *Civil War in South Russia, 1918.* Berkeley, Calif.: University of California Press, 1971.

————. *Civil War in South Russia, 1919–1920.* Berkeley, Calif.: University of California Press, 1977.

Kennan, George. *Soviet-American Relations, 1917–1920.* Princeton, N.J.: Princeton University Press, 1956, 1958.

Kettle, Michael. *The Allies and the Russian Collapse.* Minneapolis, Minn.: University of Minnesota Press, 1981.

Keynes, John Maynard. *The Economic Consequences of the Peace.* New York: Harcourt, Brace and Howe, 1920.

Larisch, Countess Marie. *My Past.* London, 1913.

Lehovich, Dimitry. *White Against Red: The Life of General Anton Denikin.* New York: W. W. Norton, 1974.

Lonyay, Carl. *Rudolph: The Tragedy of Mayerling.* New York: Scribner's, 1949.

Luckett, Richard. *The White Generals.* New York: Viking, 1971.

Maddox, Robert. *The Unknown War with Russia.* San Rafael, Calif.: Presidio Press, 1977.

Manchester, William. *The Last Lion, Winston Spencer Churchill, Visions of Glory, 1876–1932.* Boston: Little, Brown, 1983.

Manning, Roberta. *The Crisis of the Old Order in Russia.* Princeton, N.J.: Princeton University Press, 1982.

Marwick, Arthur. *The Deluge: British Society and the First World War.* Boston: Little, Brown, 1965.

Mawdsley, Evan. *The Russian Civil War.* Boston: Allen & Unwin, 1987.

McCully, Newton A. *The McCully Report: The Russo-Japanese War, 1904–1905.* Annapolis, Md.: Naval Institute Press, 1976.

Medvedev, Roy, and Serge Starikov. *Philip Mironov and the Russian Civil War.* New York, 1978.

Polonsky, Antony. *Politics in Independent Poland, 1921–1939.* Oxford: Clarendon Press, 1972.

Radkey, Oliver. *The Unknown Civil War: A Study of the Green Movement.* Stanford Calif.: Hoover Institute Press, 1976.

Raleigh, Donald J., ed. *A Russian Civil War Diary: Alexis Babine in Saratov, 1917–1922.* Durham, N.C.: Duke University Press, 1988.

Richards, Guy. *The Rescue of the Romanovs.* Old Greenwich, Conn.: Devin-Adair, 1975.

Rogger, Hans. *Jewish Policies and Right-Wing Politics in Imperial Russia.* Berkeley and Los Angeles, University of California Press, 1986.

Schwabe, Klaus. *Woodrow Wilson, Revolutionary Germany, and Peacemaking, 1918–1919.* Chapel Hill, N.C.: University of North Carolina Press, 1985.

Seymour, Charles, *Geography, Justice, and Politics at the Paris Conference of 1919.* New York: American Geographic Society, 1951.

Stewart, George. *The White Armies of Russia.* New York: Macmillan, 1933.

Stone, Herbert L., and William H. Taylor. *The America's Cup Races.* Princeton, N.J.: D. Van Nostrand Company, Inc. 1958.

Stone, Norman, *The Eastern Front, 1914–1917.* New York: Scribner's, 1975.

Strakhovsky, L. I. *American Opinion about Russia, 1917–1920.* Toronto: University of Toronto Press, 1961.

Svidine, Nicolas. *Cossack Gold.* Boston: Little, Brown, 1975.

Tolley, Kemp. *Yangtze Patrol: The U.S. Navy in China.* Annapolis, Md.: Naval Institute Press, 1971.

———. *Caviar and Commissars: The Experiences of a U.S. Naval Officer in Stalin's Russia.* Annapolis, Md.: Naval Institute Press, 1983.

van der Vat, Dan. *The Grand Scuttle.* Annapolis, Md.: Naval Institute Press, 1986.

Wheeler-Bennett, John W. *Brest-Litovsk: The Forgotten Peace, March, 1918.* London: Macmillan, 1956.

Wieczynski, Joseph L., ed. *Modern Encyclopedia of Russian and Soviet History.* Gulf Breeze, Fla.: Academic International Press, 1976–1989.

Wildman, Allan K. *The End of the Russian Imperial Army.* 2 vols. Princeton, N.J.: Princeton University Press, 1980, 1988.

Williams, John. *The Home Fronts: Britain, France and Germany, 1914–1918.* London: Constable, 1972.

Wrangel, Baron Peter. *Always with Honor.* New York: Robert Speller and Sons, 1957.

Wyllie, Robert E. *Orders, Decorations and Insignia; Military and Civil.* New York: G. P. Putnam's Sons, 1921.

Index